Nativism Reborn?

NATIVISM REBORN?

The Official
English Language Movement
and the American States

Raymond Tatalovich

THE UNIVERSITY PRESS OF KENTUCKY

Copyright © 1995 by The University Press of Kentucky

Scholarly publisher for the Commonwealth,
serving Bellarmine College, Berea College, Centre
College of Kentucky, Eastern Kentucky University,
The Filson Club, Georgetown College, Kentucky
Historical Society, Kentucky State University,
Morehead State University, Murray State University,
Northern Kentucky University, Transylvania University,
University of Kentucky, University of Louisville, and
Western Kentucky University.

Editorial and Sales Offices: Lexington, Kentucky 40508-4008

Library of Congress Cataloging-in-Publication Data

Tatalovich, Raymond.
   Nativism reborn? : the official English language movement and the
American states / Raymond Tatalovich.
      p.   cm.
   Includes bibliographical references and index.
   ISBN 0-8131-1918-9 (acid free)
   1. Language policy—United States.   2. English language—Political
aspects—United States.   3. English language—Social aspects—United
States.   4. English-only movement.   I. Title.
P119.32.U6T38   1995
306.4'4973—dc20   95-1354

To Anne,

my past, my present, my future

CONTENTS

TABLES

Acknowledgments

This research project, the most ambitious of my career, brought me into contact with scholars, librarians, and researchers across the nation. I met them during my on-site research trips, or when I made desperate phone calls to libraries seeking last-minute information, or as referrals by colleagues who wanted to support my scholarship. Here I want to express my appreciation in print to certain individuals who assisted this project in very tangible and important ways.

We at Loyola are so fortunate to have a library staff who go the extra mile to support researchers like myself, and I want to thank three reference librarians whom I called upon for help so many times I'm embarrassed to say: Daniel K. Blewett (Lake Shore Campus), Yolande M. Wershing (Water Tower Campus), and Sherman Lewis (Law School Library).

Loyola University Chicago was a major factor in my ability to produce a definitive work on this subject. Loyola granted me academic leave during the fall of 1989 to begin this project, three Small Research Grants to commission statistical analyses and to subsidize my research trips to North Carolina and South Carolina in 1990 and to California and Arizona in 1991, and a book subvention for The University Press of Kentucky. Special thanks goes to Thomas J. Bennett, director of Research Services, and his successor, Gerald W. McCulloh, and Edward I. Sidlow, director of Academic Affairs Administration.

My collaborator and colleague, John P. Frendreis, salvaged this project at critical stages by providing essential computer and statistical services, as did my graduate assistants over the course of this research project: Steven Doherty, Nick Latinga, and Brian Kurth. I am in their debt.

Some people I've never met offered their support. Stephen P. Mumme and Susan Kirkpatrick at Colorado State University kindly sent me their manuscript, "Fallacies in Setting the Agenda on Official English: The Foundations of Colorado's 1988 English Only Amendment." Jennifer Alstad forwarded me a copy of her honors thesis in political science at the University of Minnesota on "The English-Only Movement in the 1980s: A Power-Conflict Approach."

I began this project in 1989 and, along the way, made presentations to the Cidadel Symposium on Southern Politics (at the kind invitation of Robert Steed) and to annual meetings of the American Political Science Association and the Western Political Science Association. Portions of chapter 6 were published as "Voting on Official English Language Referenda in Five States: What Kind of Backlash?" in *Language Problems and Language Planning* (1995), and materials from chapter 8 appeared in "Who Sponsors Official English Language Legislation?: A Comparative Study of Fourteen States" in *Southeastern Political Review* 21 (fall 1993), 721–35. I wish to thank the editor of SPR, Roger Pajari of Georgia Southern University, and the editor of *LPLP*, Humphrey Tonkin, president of the University of Hartford, for permission to utilize these materials.

While the documents available in the states varied greatly, there was no variability in the professionalism and warmth of those persons who assisted a weary traveler on a tight schedule. To each of these individuals, who are professional staff at state libraries or archives or offices handling election statistics, I extend a heartfelt "thank you": in Alabama, Rickie Brunner, Sarah-Ann Warren, Vickie Balogh, and Hanna Bates; in Arizona, Dale Steele; in Arkansas, Kim Peabody, Jodi Dennis, Carol Robinson, and Jeffery B. Hampton; in Colorado, Karen Zoltenko; in California, Dan Mitchell; in Florida, Yvonne Richardson, Nan Currence, Mary Ann Cleveland, Lisa Close, Judy Young, and Nadine Tessel; in Georgia, Alaice James; in Illinois, Cody Wright and Martha Doyle; in Indiana, Jerry McLaughlin and Mariea Fox; in Kentucky, James M. Prichard, Peggy King, and Jane Minton; in Mississippi, Hank Holme, Anne Lipscomb, and Betty Robins; in Nebraska, Marie Wiechman, Reta Johnson, and Pat Loos; in North Carolina, Fran Carraway; in North Dakota, Sue Bickneil, Susan

Pahlmeye, and Audrey Sumner; in South Carolina, Susie Epps; in Tennessee, Genella Olker and Arthur Wagner; in Virginia, Bill Luebeke and Mary Dessypris; and John Peters of the Wisconsin Historical Society.

It was Lawrence J. McCaffrey, professor emeritus of history and a premier scholar of Irish studies, who permanently loaned me three classics on nativism and who recommended that I sign with the University Press of Kentucky. Thank you so much, Larry, because among all the faculty at Loyola, I've always considered you to be my intellectual godfather. I am proud to have published this volume through the University Press of Kentucky, which long has had a reputation for serious scholarship in state politics and policy. The Press gave me a contract based on preliminary findings and its commitment to this project was extraordinary. Extraordinary indeed are the persons who guided me to a successful conclusion.

How exceptionally fortunate I was to have two accomplished scholars review the first draft of this manuscript. The comments by professors Kenneth J. Meier of the University of Wisconsin-Milwaukee and Joseph Stewart Jr. of the University of Texas at Dallas immeasurably improved the final product and saved this novice at statistics some embarrassments. I hope I did justice to their suggestions.

There are others whom I recognize implicitly, because they are always there. I received my doctorate at the University of Chicago under a master, Theodore J. Lowi; he made a difference in my life. And Anne, my reason for being.

INTRODUCTION: LANGUAGE POLICY AS MORAL CONFLICT

This study addresses an issue that is not a salient matter of concern for most Americans, though it carries the potential, given the politics of the moment, to become a highly charged and emotional topic. In July 1992 Senator Robert C. Byrd (D-W.Va.) angrily suggested during floor debate on a Bush Administration proposal to aid the former Soviet republics and to make immigrants from other countries eligible for welfare that the United States should not continue accepting immigrants who speak no English. "I pick up the telephone and call the local garage," Byrd said. "I can't understand the person on the other side of the line. I'm not sure he can understand me. They're all over the place, and they don't speak English. We want more of this?" Later he apologized for the remark, saying, "I regret that in the heat of the moment I spoke unwisely."[1]

Whether or not Byrd meant that apology, one suspects that his reaction got a sympathetic hearing from people back home in West Virginia and elsewhere across the country. Others probably shared his sentiments though they were not in a position to express them on the floor of the U.S. Senate. When the opportunity does arise, whether in an opinion poll or in a referendum on a ballot, however, ordinary people rise to defend the English language against those who speak other tongues. Byrd's gut reaction is symptomatic of the debate over whether the United States should reflect a dominant English-speaking majoritarianism or encourage a multilingual culture. This emerging controversy over "English Only" versus "English Plus" seems analogous to other moral conflicts that have erupted in the United States and in other nations.

NON-ECONOMIC ISSUES

Generations of political scientists have known that foreign policy and domestic affairs involve different ingredients in the policy-making process. Recently analysts have begun to differentiate among the range of domestic problems that have prompted some kind of policy response by state and federal governments. Modern public policy analysis can be traced to a seminal article by Theodore J. Lowi, who categorized policies as distributive, regulatory, or redistributive based on their content.[2] Later he added a fourth category, constituent.[3] Lowi and those scholars who expanded upon his paradigm, like most policy analysts, were concerned about the vast and varied number of governmental programs that are the hallmark of the modern welfare state and the mixed public-private system of capitalism.[4] These programs involve economic transactions, not social behavior, and economic self-interest, not altruism.

The most impressive effort to apply Lowi to cross-cultural contexts was that of T. Alexander Smith. Smith was influenced by James Christoph's analysis of the controversy over the death penalty in Great Britain, and thus he modified the Lowi framework by adding an "emotive symbolism" category of issues. "Emotive symbolic policies, then," Smith wrote, "are types which generate emotional support for deeply held values, but unlike the other types . . . the values sought are essentially noneconomic. Rather, they are 'way of life' issues, and as a result they easily arouse the most intense political passions. This is hardly surprising when the conflict takes place over such issues as the death penalty, prayer in the public schools, abortion legislation, laws relating to homosexuality, and segregation in public schools and commercial establishments."[5] This new categorization has been validated by Donley Studlar's examination of British immigration policy toward nonwhites, Keith Richmond's study of daylight savings time in New South Wales, my early work on U.S. abortion politics, and the anthology edited by Joni Lovenduski and Joyce Outshoorn on the abortion controversy in Western Europe.[6]

One case study by Smith that illustrates the dynamics of "emotive symbolism" has special relevance, because invariably the argument over an official language for the United States generates analogies with the situation in Canada. Today there are foreboding signs that the fragile Canadian confederation may fly apart, though in 1964 such concerns were provoked by the "Great Flag Debate" about whether to retain the Union Jack, symbolizing the Anglo-Saxon majority, or to fashion a new flag that would not offend French Quebec. "The most salient tendency," Smith said, "has been strong resistance by ordinary English-speaking Canadians to French demands, a feeling that is particularly pronounced in the Maritimes and in the Prairie provinces." Anti-Quebec attitudes, Smith added, "derive from ethnic hostilities and not from a self-conscious concern about the quality of Canadian existence." The episode, then, "symbolized in a most dramatic manner the problem of Canadian identity."[7]

Emotive symbolism gives the individual an opportunity to express personal values in an emotional way. The flag issue polarized Canada along geographic, cultural, and political lines, though national identity can also be manifested by language loyalties. There is now a backlash by English-speaking Canadians against the French because Quebec separatists are demanding "special status" in the Canadian federation. In light of those developments, critics in the United States point to the sizable minority of Spanish speakers, who now constitute the majority in Miami and will grow to be a plurality in California early in the next century. Unlike previous groups, who arrived in the United States from European nations, these Spanish speakers emigrated from Mexico and Latin America. On whose terms will the "new" immigrants be accepted into American culture?[8] Will they join the economic mainstream of society, and do they pose a threat to the political regime? In other words, what "status" should the Hispanic minority enjoy relative to the Anglo majority in the United States?

Status Conflict

Sociologist Max Weber theorized that politics reflect group conflict based on social status and prestige as well as economic class. Groups with divergent lifestyles or social norms clash over whose values ought to be reflected in public policy, and such conflicts often erupt when new groups, whose members are viewed as "outsiders," come to a community and challenge those who had been dominant. Groups in decline may join extremist causes to defend their societal position.[9]

During the 1950s "mass society" theorists argued that people with psychological insecurities and without ties to established institutions were attracted to radical causes and charismatic leaders who offered them a sense of security against changes perceived as harmful to society.[10] At the same time historian Richard Hofstadter coined the term *status politics* to explain the rise of the Radical Right in the United States during that decade. Early research found that the supporters of anti-Communist senator Joseph McCarthy (R-Wis.) were either small-town, old-line Protestants whose status was falling or new immigrants who were eager to demonstrate their loyalty to America.[11] A theory of "status preservation" also has been used to explain the rise of various right-wing groups in American politics.[12]

The concept of status is used in sociological literature to explain why community conflict erupts over symbols representing dissimilar belief systems. Joseph Gusfield applied Weber's theory in his study of the Women's Christian Temperance Union. Alcohol use triggered a lifestyle conflict between the "old middle class" and the "new middle class," so Gusfield conceptualized the temperance movement as a moral crusade. A like approach guided a study of antipornography campaigns, whose authors concluded that "a primary function of the symbolic crusade is to provide those individuals whose life style is being threatened by social change with a way to reinforce that style."[13] Unlike the scholars of the 1950s, who viewed mass movements as erupting from widespread alienation and social breakdown, however, these scholars show how the disaffected can mobilize to defend values or a lifestyle that gives meaning to their existence.

Similarly, Ann Page and Donald Clelland studied a textbook controversy in Kanawha County, West Virginia, and found that "the protesters are adherents of a life style and world view which are under threat from . . . the educational system, the mass media, the churches—fundamentally from every socialization agency beyond their immediate control which impinges on their lives." Matthew C. Moen looked at the dispute over school prayer and determined that status politics had much to do with that issue: "People support prayer because they are religious, but even more so because they see in modern society a threat to their cherished values and their established way of life." And those who perceived that the Equal Rights Amendment posed a serious threat to the traditional women's roles as homemaker and mother were most likely to oppose it.[14]

But empirical research that applies status theory to explain the political behavior of individuals who presumably suffer from "status discrepancy" has shown results that are uneven at best.[15] Public opinion analysts have had more success in applying "symbolic politics" to determine how people evaluate political objects and minorities. Their studies indicate that objective self-interests or economic conditions seem to be less important in shaping popular attitudes than the intensity of feelings toward a group or political symbol.[16]

NATIVISM

The seminal work on nativism in the United States, *Strangers in the Land* by John Higham, traced the historical development of the phenomenon. It embodied, he wrote, anti-Catholicism, xenophobia, and a sense of the superiority of Anglo-Americans.[17] In a later essay, however, Higham applied status politics theory to argue that a certain coherence underlies outbursts against foreigners:

> In order to have a short-hand designation for such underlying stresses, we may call them status rivalries. By this I mean all of the activities—political, religious, economic, and associational—through which men of different ethnic backgrounds have competed for prestige and for favorable positions in community life. Status rivalries have not

arisen from irrational myths but rather from objective conditions; they have not usually reached the ideological expression; they have not risen and fallen in cyclical fashion. Instead, they are part of the slow processes of ethnic integration, and they have shaped profoundly the course of our social development.[18]

The very term *nativist,* Higham cautions us, "validates our sympathy with the out-group" by representing "primarily a one-way street, along which the native American moves aggressively against the outsider" and by portraying "minorities as victims rather than participants." To attribute group conflict to nativists means that "we need not ask too closely why the Irish were the shock troops of the anti-Chinese movement, how the American Protective Association could attract a following among Negroes, or why the Scots in America brought so much wrath upon themselves during the Revolution." In sum, when the term is stripped of its normative connotations, it becomes clear that nobody has a monopoly on nativist sentiments; old groups rally against new groups just as they were victimized by the earlier settlers of America. Thus, Higham lends credence to the view that "struggles for status underlie much that we attribute too easily to irrational prejudice, and I suspect that the question of status has touched the daily life of most Americans more intimately than any ideological warfare."[19]

Nativism is a form of collective behavior that Neil Smelser in his classic sociological study labels the "norm-oriented" movement. Its supporters "envision the restoration, protection, modification, or creation of social norms." In particular, "they may demand a rule, a law, a regulatory agency, designed to control the inadequate, ineffective, or irresponsible behavior of individuals." The term *norm-oriented* is also neutral—whereas the more commonly used phrase *social movement* implies change in a reformist direction—because a "norm-oriented" movement may draw political strength from the Left or the Right: "Many agitations commonly designated as 'social movements' or 'reform movements' are undertaken in the name of a norm-oriented belief—an agitation to establish harsh laws against sexual psychopaths (or to repeal such laws); a movement to integrate schools racially (or to keep them segregated); a movement for government subsidy of school buses (or against such a subsidy); a movement to restrict immigration (or the corresponding movement to relax quotas)."[20]

Smelser observed that "native Americanism has produced a number of distinct movements," represented by the Nativists of the 1830s, the Know-Nothings of the 1850s, the Loyalty League and the Ku Klux Klan of the post–Civil War era, the American Protection Association of the 1890s, the revived Klan following World War I, and the anti-Semites of the 1930s.[21] If the norms being undermined by the forces of social change are traditional ones, presumably those who rise to defend the status quo will be conservatives, not liberals. So many conservative movements arose during the 1980s that Clarence Y.H. Lo defined "right-wing movements" as "social movements whose stated goals are to maintain structures of order, status, honor, or traditional social differences or values. Right-wing movements sometimes directly advocate, and usually cause, the perpetuation or increase of economic or political inequalities. The right may be contrasted with the left, which seeks greater equality or political participation."[22]

Conflicting theories seek to explain what gives rise to the pattern of mobilization and countermobilization. Are such movements mass mobilizations or elite organizations? Are they irrational and myopic outbursts or rational acts toward a calculated end? Michael Rogin offered a counterthesis that McCarthyism was not so much a mass movement as an effort by local political leaders to exploit Red-baiting for electoral advantage. James Gibson offers support for Rogin's interpretation: he studied anti-Communist laws during the 1950s and concluded that there is "no evidence that political repression in the U.S. states stems from demands from ordinary citizens to curtail the rights and activities of unpopular political minorities."[23]

But certainly something has to trigger the popular backlash, whether the agitation is a mass movement or one generated by the elite. According to Smelser, a structural "strain" underlies all kinds of collective outbursts, including the "norm-oriented" movement, and he identifies four types of strain that may occur in society. First, "the appearance of new knowledge initiates a movement to apply this knowledge in order to eradicate a condition previously taken for granted"; for example, medical breakthroughs initiate a sense of urgency to supply cures for disease. Second, "the history of social movements abounds with agitations on the part of groups who experience a real or apparent loss of wealth, power, or prestige." Third, "any disharmony between normative standards and actual social conditions can provide the basis for a movement whose objective it is to modify the norms." This type of strain is most apt to occur "when either norms or social conditions undergo rapid change in a relatively short time." Fourth, "the rise of new values frequently creates bases for defining certain social conditions as 'evils'—social conditions which previously had passed less noticed."[24] Seemingly the first, fourth, and especially the third type of "strain" would encourage organization by those interests that favor changes in the status quo, whereas the second type of strain would provoke counterorganization by those defending the social order.

SOCIAL REGULATION

Case studies in the anthology I edited with Byron W. Daynes on social regulatory policies like abortion and school prayer point to three variables as primary indicators of moral conflicts.[25] First is a principled debate over noneconomic concerns and morality. A major consideration in this study is the assessment of the public debate over making English the official language of states and of the nation. Since language policy evokes feelings about love of country, citizenship, and community, one would not anticipate that much of the public debate would focus on purely economic issues. Issues of language loyalty are analogous to racial and ethnic conflict insofar as they focus on who you are more than on what you have, or your net worth.

Second, the courts invariably will become key policymakers. Social regulations are majoritarian, and existing opinion surveys and election results show that popular support for English Only laws reaches consensus levels. Since English has always been the dominant language of the United States, there has been no obvious need for state governments to police language usage. The contemporary effort to gain enactment of official English statutes is therefore a policy response to a perceived threat to the normative order. But this kind of social regulation will provoke counterarguments that it represents an infringement on personal liberty and individual rights. It does, of course, since the purpose of such regulation is to curb behavior contrary to what the majority considers vital for maintaining the social and moral order. The constitutionality of official English laws has yet to be adjudicated before the Supreme Court, but federal courts have ruled on laws enacted in California and Arizona.

Third, citizens will organize themselves into single-issue groups and ad hoc coalitions to fight the battle. The debate over English Only versus English Plus is not a national political conflict akin to the abortion controversy, though there are signs that it is developing along similar lines. Moral disputes do not activate established interest groups but mobilize citizens into new organizations that take absolutist positions and polarize the issue in nonnegotiable terms.

Thousands of interests in this country curry favor from government at some level, but most are organized to protect their economic self-interests. Exceptions are philanthropic organizations, religious lobbies, and, says Mancur Olson Jr., people committed to "lost causes."[26] Those defending traditional norms are likely to be more homogeneous and thus are likely to view the issue from one dominant perspective. Therefore they will be organized as a single-issue *lobby.* Those who advocate legal change are likely to be a more heterogeneous group concerned with differing aspects of the problem; they will come together as a *coalition.*[27]

The groups engaged in moral conflict represent a narrow band of noneconomic interests in the country. Mobilized interests are those directly affected by an issue, meaning that there are parameters to the scope of conflict that affect this category of policy disputes. Despite the hyperbole on both sides, moral conflicts do not envelop the whole society or the organizational life of the nation because most people have no personal stake in these kinds of issues. Those who do participate, however, bring a measure of intensity that is unusual in American politics.

U.S. ENGLISH

The organization U.S. English was established in 1983 as the primary single-issue group promoting official English language legislation. While U.S. English is best known for its advocacy of official English, two other groups were organized in 1986 to pursue similar objectives. English First was founded by Larry Pratt, former Virginia state representative and the president of Gun Owners of America. English First is affiliated with the Committee to Protect the Family. The American Ethnic Coalition, a group headed by Lou Zaeske of Bryan, Texas, failed to persuade the Texas legislature to enact an official English law in 1989 and has not yet attained that objective.[28]

U.S. English began with a small cadre of activists but is now a grass-roots movement with a reported membership of 450,000. Its beginnings are traced to Petoskey, Michigan, a small resort town on the shores of Lake Michigan, where Dr. John H. Tanton began an ophthalmology practice in the early 1960s. Tanton worked with the Planned Parenthood Federation and later with Zero Population Growth (ZPG), serving as its national president during 1975–77.

When Tanton failed to convince the ZPG board of directors to address the immigration issue (news accounts quote an anonymous source as saying, "They were uneasy about getting into ethnicity—they didn't want to be called racist"), he founded a group called Federation for American Immigration Reform (FAIR). Later, when Tanton came to believe that ethnic politicians had a stake in perpetuating language ghettos, he joined Senator S.I. Hayakawa (R-Calif.) to form U.S. English. Susan Weber, an executive director of ZPG, said that "there is a path" from organizations like ZPG and Planned Parenthood to concerns about immigration and language, though she said that Tanton, FAIR, and U.S. English "tend to focus on the United States and forget about the rest of the world, but, like it or not, the world population problem is going to come home to haunt us, in one form or another." Tanton agrees that overpopulation is a worldwide problem, but he adds: "I don't have any particular influence in Jakarta or New Delhi or Nairobi, but I can have some say in this country. I do think we have a responsibility to preserve these particular acres so there will be something left for those who come after us."[29]

A recent statement from U.S. English outlines the organization's mission and goals:

> A common language benefits a nation and all its people. In the United States, the language bond is more important than in most other nations because Americans are remarkably diverse in origin, race, lifestyle, ethnicity, religion, and culture. A common language bridges our differences and helps to promote:
>
>> Social, political, and economic advancement;
>> Equality of opportunity for all;
>> Full participation in the democratic process by in formed voters;
>> Economic efficiency and strength;
>> Shared values and national culture accessible to all.
>
> To achieve these aims, U.S. ENGLISH pursues two complementary goals: To make English the official language of the United States Government and to guarantee the right for all our people to learn English.[30]

S.I. Hayakawa (who died in 1992 at the age of eighty-five) was a semanticist, the author of the college text *Language in Action: A Guide to Accurate Thinking, Reading, and Writing,* and president of San Francisco State College from 1969 to 1973. His tough stance during those turbulent years of student unrest gained him the publicity that led to his successful election to the U.S. Senate, where he served from 1977 to 1983.[31] In 1981 Senator Hayakawa introduced Senate Joint Resolution 72 to declare English as the country's official language. It read:

> Section 1. The English language shall be the official language of the United States.
>
> Section 2. Neither the United States nor any State shall make or enforce any law which requires the use of any language other than English.
>
> Section 3. This article shall apply to laws, ordinances, regulations, orders, programs, and policies.

Section 4. No order or decree shall be issued by any court of the United States or of any State requiring that any proceedings, or matters to which this article applies, be in any language other than English.

Section 5. This article shall not prohibit educational instruction in a language other than English as required as a transitional method of making students who use a language other than English proficient in English.

Section 6. The Congress and the States shall have power to enforce this article by appropriate legislation.[32]

In 1984, hearings on Senate Joint Resolution 167, a version of the English Language Amendment (ELA), were held by the Subcommittee on the Constitution of the Senate Judiciary Committee.[33] The author of the resolution, Walter Huddleston (D-Ky.), a senator from 1973 to 1985, explained its purpose this way:

As a nation of immigrants, our great strength has been drawn from our ability to assimilate vast numbers of people from many different cultures and ethnic groups into a nation of people that can work together with cooperation and understanding. This process was often referred to as the melting pot and in the past it has been seen as an almost magical concept that helped to make the United States the greatest nation on earth. But for the last fifteen years, we have experienced a growing resistance to the acceptance of our historic language, an antagonistic questioning of the melting pot philosophy that has traditionally helped speed newcomers into the American mainstream.[34]

What had happened during the preceding fifteen years was the accelerated use of bilingualism in education, voting, and public documents. The senator had requested information from federal agencies and state governors on non-English forms and publications, and he told the Senate, "The non-English materials which I have received are in a stack that is about three feet high, and we are adding to it almost daily. I am told that if copies of all bilingual educational materials were sent, we could fill a large room." If such a profusion of materials reflected "large-scale legal and illegal immigration . . . there would not be cause for concern. However, what we are seeing is a decrease in the use of English and a widely accepted attitude that it is not necessary to learn English. . . . The United States is presently at a crucial juncture. We can either continue down the same path we have walked for the last two hundred years, using the melting pot philosophy to forge a strong and united nation, or we can take the new path that leads in the direction of another Tower of Babel."[35]

Following the successful 1986 California referendum that established English as the official language of that state, U.S. English prepared a memo for distribution that outlined "model language for an initiative to amend a state constitution to add official language provisions." Based on adverse experiences in California, where "the language was vigorously attacked," U.S. English proposed four improvements:

> –consistent use of the phrase "official language." Prop. 63 [the California referendum] also uses the phrase "common language," which, although accurate and clear in the context used, seems to confuse some readers. The California Attorney General believes that the two phrases are different, and that the distinction is legally-significant.
>
> –explicit coverage of state and local governments. Prop. 63 specifically discusses state officials but doesn't mention subdivisions of government. Although the California Attorney General agrees with us that California law includes lower governments as part of the "State of California," the law may be different in other states.
>
> –more explicit descriptions of which government actions may be taken in other languages, and when those actions may be taken. Prop. 63 only restricts the *Legislature* from making a law which diminishes English. The California Attorney General believes that this prohibition allows other branches of government to use non-English translations on English-language official documents.
>
> –more clear-cut exceptions to the official language rule, as in safeguarding public health and safety. This failure to delineate specific instances led to lengthy debates during the campaign about California law; such debates can be avoided in other states by listing exceptions.[36]

The "model initiative" comprised four sections. The first declares, "As the official language of this State, the English language is the language of the ballot, the public schools and all government functions and actions" and applies to "the legislative, executive and judicial branches," to "all political subdivisions, departments, agencies, organizations, and instrumentalities of this State, including local governments and municipalities," to "all statutes, ordinances, rules, orders, programs and policies," and to "all government officials and employees during the performance of government business." The second says that the "State and all political subdivisions of this State shall take all reasonable steps to preserve, protect and enhance the role of English" as the official language.[37] The third allows five exceptions:

> (i) to assist students who are not proficient in the English language, to the extent necessary to comply with federal law, by giving educational instruction in a language other than English to provide as rapid as possible a transition to English.
>
> (ii) to comply with other federal laws.
>
> (iii) to teach a student a foreign language as part of a required or voluntary educational curriculum.
>
> (iv) to protect public health and safety.
>
> (v) to protect the rights of criminal defendants or victims of crime.[38]

Finally, the fourth section provides for a private right of action: "A person who resides in or does business in this State shall have standing to bring suit to enforce this Article in a court of record of the State. The Legislature may enact reasonable limitations on the time and manner of bringing suit under this subsection."[39]

In 1988 testimony was received from members of Congress by the Subcommittee on Civil and Constitutional Rights of the House Judiciary Committee. Congressman Norman Shumway (R-Calif.), who served in the House from 1979 until 1991 and a year later became chairman of the board of U.S. English, told the committee: "English is the common language of the United States as a result of historical custom, not legal designation. That common language has been the 'glue' which has held us together, forging strength and unity from our rich, cultural diversity." Now, though, he asserted, the law must mandate an official language, because "without that missing measure of legal protection, I believe that the primacy of English is being threatened, and that we are moving toward the status of a bilingual society."[40]

The perceived threat came from the growing numbers of Spanish speakers, not from other ethnic groups. Three years earlier Hayakawa had charged that

> the ethnic chauvinism of the present Hispanic leadership is an unhealthy trend in present-day America. It threatens a division perhaps more ominous in the long run than the division between blacks and whites. Blacks and whites have problems enough with each other, to be sure, but they quarrel with each other in one language. . . . But the present politically ambitious "Hispanic Caucus" looks forward to a destiny for Spanish-speaking Americans separate from that of Anglo-, Italian-, Polish-, Greek-, Lebanese-, Chinese-, and Afro-Americans, and all the rest of us who rejoice in our ethnic diversity.
>
> It is not without significance that pressure against English language legislation does not come from any immigrant group other than the Hispanic: not from the Chinese or Koreans or Filipinos or Vietnamese; nor from immigrant Iranians, Turks, Greeks, East Indians, Ghanaians, Ethiopians, Italians, or Swedes. The only people who have any quarrel with the English language are the Hispanics—at least the Hispanic politicians and "bilingual" teachers and lobbying organizations. One wonders about the Hispanic rank and file. Are they all in agreement with their leadership? And what does it profit the Hispanic leadership if it gains power and fame, while 50 percent of the boys and girls of their communities, speaking little or no English, cannot make it through high school?[41]

As of 1990, fifteen versions of the ELA had been introduced by members of the House or Senate, but none had been cleared by a standing committee for a vote in either chamber. On January 5, 1993, Representative Bill Emerson (R-Mo.) introduced an omnibus bill entitled "Language for All Peoples Initiative."[42] And on

February 2 Representative Toby Roth (R-Wis.) was one of ten Republican co-sponsors of the Declaration of Official Language Act (House Resolution 739), which opened with the statement "America is no longer the melting pot; America is becoming more like a patch quilt." Roth's measure would amend Title IV of the U.S. Code to declare "English as the Official Language" and the "preferred language of communication" and would mandate that "communications by officers and employees of the Government of the U.S. with United States citizens shall be in English." In addition, House Resolution 739 would reform the naturalization requirements of section 165 to require the Immigration and Naturalization Service to establish an English language proficiency standard for all applicants for U.S. citizenship and to create a written and oral examination to test whether applicants had achieved that standard of English proficiency. Finally, Roth's legislation would repeal Title VII of the Elementary and Secondary Education Act of 1965, which covers bilingual education, and section 203 of the Voting Rights Act of 1965, which provides for bilingual ballots in areas with high concentrations of non-English speakers. "In the last election, people could vote in seven different languages in San Francisco alone," Roth told his colleagues; moreover, in the past "we had a wonderful bond called the English language," but today "in many parts of the country, English is not the primary language in schools, and in many parts of America, English is not the language of choice."[43]

EPIC

Meanwhile, opposition to official English has also mobilized. The English Plus Information Clearinghouse (EPIC), formed in October 1987 under the auspices of the National Immigration, Refugee, and Citizenship Forum and the Joint National Committee for Languages (JNCL) and headquartered in Washington, D.C., held its first general meeting on May 23, 1988. The National Immigration, Refugee, and Citizenship Forum includes more than one hundred national and community organizations committed to "democratic pluralism," while JNCL represents thirty-five national language associations dedicated to "the advancement of language study in the United States."[44] There were twenty-seven founding organizations of EPIC; at one point fifty-six groups endorsed its statement of purpose, but today there are forty-five official endorsers (see Appendix A).

Calling English Plus a coalition should not imply an all-encompassing organization. The member groups may share a common perspective, but they are hardly any more representative of American society than is U.S. English. While U.S. English seems to be driven by a normative goal to which its rank and file subscribe, EPIC is promoting an agenda based on more than principle. The American Civil Liberties Union and Jewish organizations are aligned for ideological reasons, but the mainstay of EPIC's constituency are groups that represent non-English speakers (Hispanics, Chinese, Puerto Ricans, Haitians), educators who directly benefit from bilingual instructional programs (the National Association for Bilingual Education and Teachers of English to Speakers of Other Languages), and local single-issue groups.

The EPIC philosophy is that "the core of the strength and vitality of the United States is the diversity of our people, and our constitutional commitment to equal protection under the law. Now, more than ever, our commitment to cultural and democratic pluralism is essential to enhance our competitiveness and position of international leadership. In an interdependent world, the diversity of our people provides a unique reservoir of understanding and talent." Thus, proponents of English Plus assert that the national interest can best be served when all members of American society have full "access to effective opportunities to acquire strong English language proficiency *plus* mastery of a second or multiple languages. 'English Plus' holds that there is a need for a vastly expanded network of facilities and programs for comprehensive instruction in English and other languages." English Plus rejects the ideology and divisive character of the so-called English Only movement. English Plus holds that national unity and American constitutional values "require that language assistance be made available in order to ensure equal access to essential services, education, the electoral process, and other rights and opportunities guaranteed to all members of society."[45]

What holds the EPIC groups together are the values expressed in a resolution that the founders adopted. Its preamble declares that "English is and will remain the primary language of the United

States" though "many U.S. citizens have native languages other than English . . . [and all] have not had an equal opportunity to learn English." Moreover, the ability to speak languages other than English enhances our "economic, political and cultural viability" and aids our "productivity, worldwide competitiveness, successful international diplomacy, and national security." Insofar as our "fundamental values and national documents ensure tolerance and respect for diversity and guarantee all persons equal protection under the law," and because "English Only and other restrictionist language legislation have the potential for abridging the citizen's right to vote, eroding other civil rights, fostering governmental interference in private activity and free commerce, and causing social disunity," EPIC is "committed to the principles of democratic and cultural pluralism and encourages respect for the cultural and linguistic heritages of all members of our society."[46]

In addition to the states of New Mexico, Oregon, Washington, and Rhode Island, some major cities—Atlanta, Cleveland, Dallas, San Antonio, Tucson, and Washington, D.C.—have adopted English Plus laws or resolutions. EPIC was organized as a direct response to U.S. English, although the idea of English Plus was articulated earlier, as a response to the attack on bilingual education by Secretary of Education William J. Bennett in a speech delivered in New York City on September 26, 1985. His address was a defining moment for both the Reagan Administration and the supporters of bilingualism.

ATTACK ON BILINGUALISM

Bennett opened with this statement: "Our common language is, of course, English. And our common task is to ensure that our non-English-speaking children learn this common language." Government has failed at that task, he said, because "too many children have failed to become fluent in English, and have therefore failed to enjoy the opportunities they deserve. Now is the time to get our policies back on track; now is the time to deliver on the promise of equal opportunity so solemnly pledged twenty years ago." Bennett attributed that failure to a 1975 decision by the Department of Health, Education, and Welfare "to require that educational programs for non-English-speaking students be conducted in large part *in the student's native language,* as virtually the only approved method of remedying discrimination." He blamed entrenched bureaucratic interests for "this fateful turn" in policy: "We had lost sight of the goal of learning *English* as the key to equal educational opportunity. Indeed, H.E.W. increasingly emphasized bilingual education as a way of enhancing students' knowledge of their native language and culture. Bilingual education was no longer seen so much as a means to ensure that students learned English, or as a transitional method until students learned English. Rather, it became an emblem of cultural pride, a means of producing a positive self-image in the student."[47]

Soon thereafter, the Spanish-American League against Discrimination (SALAD), a civil rights group in Miami, issued a response to Bennett. Its document "would become a blue-print for the English Plus approach to combating language restrictionism."[48] This manifesto read, in part:

> We fear that Secretary Bennett has lost sight of the fact that English is *a key* to equal educational opportunity, necessary but not sufficient. English by itself is not enough. Not English Only, English *Plus!* . . .
>   Bennett is wrong. We won't accept English Only for our children. We want English plus. English plus math. Plus science. Plus social sciences. Plus equal educational opportunities. English plus competence in the home language. Tell Bennett to enforce bilingual education and civil rights laws you enacted, or tell the President he cannot do his job. English Plus for everyone![49]

Thus began the conflict between English Only and English Plus, as Hispanic groups, notably SALAD and the League of United Latin American Citizens (LULAC), began using the term *English Plus* to express their alternative to official monolingualism. But while Bennett's comments and Reagan Administration policies may have expanded the scope of this conflict to the national government, the political sparks that ignited the English Only backlash predate the Bennett speech and can be traced to local controversies in California, Florida, and Virginia. Reaction to heavy-handed federal bilingual education mandates led Virginia in 1981 to enact the first state English Only law of the decade. The issue of bilingual ballots in San Francisco fueled a debate that ultimately resulted, in 1986, in the first statewide referendum on the issue, in California. And legislation codifying an official multiculturalism in Dade County, Florida, as early as 1973 provoked a backlash that gave rise to its replacement with an official English ordinance, the first such action by a county government.

English Plus proclaims the belief that the English language will, and should, always be the dominant language in the United States but that everyone, though especially non-English speakers, ought to be encouraged to speak other languages. English Only declares that English is, and should remain, the language of government and official communications, though its proponents do not oppose foreign language instruction or (transitional) bilingual education, or even providing emergency and legal services in other languages.

The shades of disagreement separating the two camps might not seem irreconcilable to the casual observer. But each side thinks its opponent is promoting a hidden agenda (separatism or racism), so the differences have become polarized into a deep ideological divide. This divide is normative, not economic, as an extremely perceptive essay by Ronald J. Schmidt points out: "For both sides, the conflict really is about power, but it is a conflict in which the stakes are seemingly much more important than a battle over jobs and other forms of material advantage. What is at stake, in this view, is the core identity of major groups in U.S. society, each of whom has reason to feel under attack from the other."[50]

For English Plus, then, bilingualism is a policy requirement for cultural legitimacy. For English Only, monolingualism is a social requirement for political stability.

1

SCOPE OF THE STUDY, METHODS, AND HYPOTHESES

In 1920 Nebraska was the first state to establish English as an official language by constitutional amendment. The earliest statutory enactment was in Illinois; its 1923 law designating "American" as the state's official language was revised in 1969 to make English the official language. In 1978 Hawaii made English and Hawaiian both official languages by a constitutional amendment. During 1981–90 ten midwestern and southern states established this policy by legislation, but more significant politically was the 1986 referendum vote in California amending the state constitution to codify English as the state's official language. Three referenda in 1988 in Florida, Arizona, and Colorado, along with one in Alabama in 1990, bring the number of official language enactments by state governments to eighteen (table 1.1).

In a counteroffensive against official English ("English Only"), advocates of multiculturalism and bilingualism ("English Plus") succeeded in winning support for their legislative agenda in four states. In 1989 legislatures in New Mexico and Oregon adopted resolutions, and a law was passed in Washington State.[1] Rhode Island also became an English Plus state when its assembly passed a law in 1992 stating that "it shall be the policy of the state of Rhode Island to welcome and encourage the presence of diverse cultures and the use of diverse languages in business, government, and private affairs in this state."[2]

Both sides claim victory in Hawaii. There is dispute about the status of Hawaii's constitutional amendment that English Plus proponents allege makes that state officially bilingual. The wording of

Table 1.1. States with Official English Language Legislation

Statute

Arkansas (1987)
Illinois (1969)
Indiana (1984)
Kentucky (1984)
Mississippi (1987)
North Carolina (1987)
North Dakota (1987)
South Carolina (1987)
Tennessee (1984)
Virginia (1981)

*Constitutional
Amendment*

Alabama (1990)
Arizona (1988)
California (1986)
Colorado (1988)
Florida (1988)
Hawaii (1978)
Nebraska (1920)

Resolution

Georgia (1986)

section 4 of the Hawaii constitution is explicit: "English and Hawaiian shall be the official languages of Hawaii, except that Hawaiian shall be required for public acts and transactions only as provided by law." While both languages are indeed official, the amendment gives primacy to English.

SCOPE OF STUDY

The official language laws of eleven states—Alabama, Arkansas, Colorado, Florida, Georgia, Illinois, Indiana, Kentucky, Mississippi, North Carolina, and North Dakota—are virtually identical and wholly symbolic. Section 3-3-31 of the Mississippi code, for example, reads: "The English language is the official language of the State of Mississippi." And chapter 145-12 of the general statutes of North Carolina states:

> English is the common language of the people of the United States of America and the State of North Carolina. This section is intended to preserve, protect and strengthen the English language, and not to supersede any of the rights guaranteed to the people by the Constitution of the United States or the Constitution of North Carolina.
> ... English is the official language of the State of North Carolina.

The laws of California, Hawaii, Nebraska, South Carolina, Tennessee, and Virginia go beyond symbolism since they imply or stipulate some kind of enforcement. Thus section 22.1-212.1 of the Virginia code declares that "English shall be designated as the official language of the Commonwealth of Virginia. School boards shall have no obligation to teach the standard curriculum, except courses in foreign languages, in a language other than English. School boards shall endeavor to provide instruction in the English language which shall be designed to promote the education of students for whom English is a second language."

Finally, an amendment to the Arizona constitution had the potential to be the most restrictive official language law in the nation, with an array of enforcement provisions, but it was ruled unconstitutional by a federal district judge. It may not be coincidental that Arizona voters barely approved the law, whereas the referenda in California, Colorado, and Florida passed by wide margins and delegated implementation to the state legislatures. California, however, like Arizona, also encourages individuals to use litigation to force compliance with the law. (For the language of all eighteen official English laws, see Appendix B.)

Of the eighteen official language enactments, ten were by statute; Georgia passed a resolution (without the governor's signature), and amendments were added to the state constitutions of seven states. All were initiated by the legislature except the most controversial laws of Arizona, California, Colorado, and Florida.

These resulted from citizens' initiatives based on grass-roots movements with direct assistance from the leading single-issue group, U.S. English.

Not much research exists on the movement to establish English as the official language of the United States. There are advocatory studies by those opposed, collections of primary documents, journalistic and historical accounts of U.S. language policy, reviews of legal precedents, research on California exit polls, cross-cultural studies on the United States and Canada, and formal models designed to produce an optimal resolution to the language problem.[3] Yet no one has conducted a systematic and empirical study of the states that have adopted official English language statutes. My purpose in writing this book is to fill that gap.

METHODOLOGY

My first step was to research legislative histories of the enactments. I collected biographical data on the members of the state legislatures and identified the sponsors and co-sponsors of the official English bills. The project began in December 1989 when I traveled to the state capitals of Arkansas, Indiana, Kentucky, Tennessee, Mississippi, and Illinois to visit the libraries or archives where journals of legislative proceedings are located in order to uncover the available information on committee deliberations and public hearings, floor debate, and roll calls. I did similar field research in Alabama, North Carolina, North Dakota, and South Carolina. Data on Georgia and Virginia were available at the Historical Society of Wisconsin Library in Madison. I also visited the capitals of Arizona, California, Colorado, and Florida to investigate whether official English bills had been introduced in the legislatures in those states. Finally, I traveled to Austin, to learn why no law exists in the key state of Texas despite the presence of a large Hispanic minority, and to Lincoln, to learn about the roots of Nebraska's 1920 state constitutional amendment.

To assess the political significance of the English language issue and to obtain background information on the controversy, I then reviewed reports in the national press, notably the *New York Times,* and in major dailies like the *San Francisco Chronicle,* the

Los Angeles Times, the *Miami Herald,* and the *Dallas Morning News,* as well as small-town newspapers that covered the deliberations of state legislatures. For this second step, I consulted local papers on microfilm at the state capitals and the better-known newspapers in files at the Center for Research Libraries in Chicago. For most states, this approach was not very productive, as there appeared to be little press attention to the official English question. In contrast, the degree of controversy in Arizona, Colorado, California, Florida, and Texas generated a good deal of news coverage in those states.

The third step involved follow-up telephone interviews with the sponsors and co-sponsors of the legislation, as well as other key legislators, where the documented history proved inadequate. The "key decision makers" were sent letters informing them of my research agenda and my intention to contact them for telephone interviews. I wanted their responses to six questions:

1. Was this legislation designed to address a local problem in your district, or elsewhere in the state?
2. Were you requested to sponsor this legislation by any organization or individual in your district, or elsewhere in the state?
3. Were you contacted by the organization U.S. English?
4. Did this legislation help you with your constituents, and were the voters in your district aware of your role in sponsoring this legislation?
5. Were you aware of any official publications of the state being printed in a language other than English?
6. Why didn't this law include more enforcement provisions?

My methodology is eclectic, insofar as many types of social science information are employed: historical documents, news and journalistic accounts, legal records and court decisions, and telephone interviews. At the mass level, quantitative data on voting patterns and public opinion are examined with statistical techniques. At the elite level, the legislative behavior of state representatives is analyzed in tabular form and through regression techniques. (To enhance the readability of this volume, the results of multiple and logistical regression models are placed in Appendix C.) Since my objective is to draw conclusions about what motivated states to enact official English laws, the multipronged analysis is guided by five hypotheses, based on race, ethnicity, class, politics, and culture.

HYPOTHESIS

The first hypothesis is racism. In the words of an advocate for the National Council of La Raza, English Only is "fundamentally racist in character."[4] Cries of racism abounded during the Arizona referendum campaign following the disclosure of a memo with anti-Spanish overtones by John Tanton, founder of U.S. English, but racist charges also were hurled in the Florida, California, and Colorado referenda campaigns.

The potential for conflict between Anglo and Hispanic groups is minimal in most states, since Spanish speakers constituted only 7.3 percent of the U.S. population in 1985. Elsewhere, however, including four states—California, Arizona, Colorado, and Florida—where English Only referenda were held, their numbers were substantial: Hispanics constituted 37.8 percent of the population in New Mexico, 22.8 percent in Texas, 22.1 percent in California, 16.8 percent in Arizona, 11.9 percent in Colorado, 10.6 percent in New York, and 9.8 percent in Florida.[5]

In south Florida, the Cuban presence, says Max Castro, represents "a sharp break with Miami's previous history." The situation is different in San Antonio, El Paso, and Los Angeles, where Spanish speakers have lived for decades: "The Latinization of Miami that occurred beginning in 1959 would not be experienced by much of the resident American population as a historical continuity with Florida's Hispanic past and Cuban connection. Rather, for a significant proportion of the resident population Latinization would be experienced as a traumatic rupture; an alien (and alienating) invasion; and ultimately as a 'takeover,' a transgression against the expected relation of domination/subordination between native and immigrant, newcomer and established resident, American and foreigner, Anglo and Hispanic." A study of perceived representation by ethnic groups in Dade County by Allen Bronson Brierly and David Moon offers corroboration that

"Anglo and Jewish respondents hold significantly lower opinions of their voice in local government when compared to Cuban and Latino respondents."[6] This situation would seem to offer the ideal ingredients for igniting political conflict between the growing Cuban and the heretofore dominant Anglo communities. This is exactly what happened in the 1989 congressional campaign in the Eighteenth District.

Cuban American Ileana Ros-Lehtinen ran as a Republican against an unknown Democratic candidate, Jewish lawyer Gerald Richman. Richman won his primary by publicizing this campaign slogan: "It's not a Jewish seat, or a black seat, or a Cuban seat, it's an *American* seat." That set the stage for a nasty general election campaign in which Cuban Americans cast 94 percent of their ballots for Ros-Lehtinen, while, in effect, everybody else voted for Richman. Dario Moreno and Nicol Rae explain the dynamics: "The electorate in Miami became divided along ethnic lines not because Cubans changed their voting behavior but because other groups rallied around the Democratic candidate in a futile attempt to 'stop the Cubans.' The tragedy of the 1989 special election was that Richman's coded call to U.S.-born voters ('this is an American seat') to stop the Cuban candidates . . . worked. In the general election, Richman carried all the non-Cuban groups in the district (Anglos, blacks, and Jews). According to one exit poll, he even won among Republican Anglos by 55 to 45 percent."[7]

Here racism is conceptualized as hostility by the majority toward a minority. Historically in the Deep South, racial fears were heightened in those areas where whites lived in close proximity to large concentrations of blacks. First asserted in the classic work on southern politics by V.O. Key, this idea is given empirical support in several studies, including those on voting by whites for George Wallace in 1968 and David Duke in 1990.[8] Similarly, as Bill Piatt observes, "the 'official English' movement is a socially acceptable way of tapping into nativist fears of being outnumbered by immigrants and fear of anyone different. The increasing Hispanic presence is viewed as a threat."[9]

Fear of racial minorities by the majority inevitably will extend to political elites. This occurred in the South during the 1950s, before blacks were fully enfranchised. An early study of the legislative reaction following the 1954 Supreme Court school desegregation ruling found that legislators from the Deep South, states that had sizable populations of black residents, were staunchly segregationist, whereas those from border states could afford to act more moderately on civil rights because blacks there were decidedly a minority and thus did not pose a threat to social and political norms.[10] For this hypothesis to be validated, political elites and the electorate should be more supportive of official English laws in areas populated by larger concentrations of Spanish speakers.

The second hypothesis is ethnic rivalry, conceptualized as conflict between minorities. Minorities who are roughly within the same class strata at the lower end of the economic structure will compete for social status, economic gain, and political power. In the past, ethnic voting reflected political rivalries among WASPs, Irish, and the white ethnics, as new waves of immigrants from different ethnic backgrounds left Europe for the cities of the Northeast.[11] Today, with more Spanish-speaking peoples immigrating to the United States, the potential exists for economic and political rivalries to divide the Hispanic and black communities.

After the appointment by President Clinton of Dade County prosecutor Janet Reno as the U.S. attorney general, the choice of Katherine Fernandez Rundle to be her successor provoked an outcry from prominent blacks, who demanded that a new state law school be established at Florida A&M University, the historic black institution, rather than at Cuban-dominated Florida International University. H.T. Smith, a black lawyer from Miami, declared that Cubans are really "white people whose native language is Spanish" and added that Rundle "is a Cuban-American, and relations between Cubans and blacks in Dade County have been strained at best and outright hostile at worst." Simply on these terms, it is more than plausible that blacks may resent the Cuban presence in Dade County, since, as Castro points out, "it is generally argued that blacks have suffered most from Hispanic/immigrant economic competition in Miami."[12]

Research by Paula McClain on municipal employment patterns by Hispanics and blacks indicates "a changing dynamic in the urban political landscape—the emergence of potential patterns of interminority group competition. In the future, the increasing presence of one group may have negative consequences for the political representation and political rewards of the other group."[13] The possibility of conflict between African Americans and Hispanics will be examined at the elite and mass levels. Were black legislators at the forefront of these efforts to codify English? Did black citizens express more support for official English than whites?

But there is a caveat to the racial hypothesis. Because blacks, more than whites, are sensitive to minority rights and because of their intimate experience with the civil rights movement, psychological and political constraints may affect their willingness to support a backlash against another minority. According to Castro, this consideration may have influenced the African American community of south Florida to split their vote 44–56 percent against the 1980 antibilingualism ordinance in Dade County, while 71 percent of non-Hispanic whites cast ballots in favor of the measure.[14]

The third hypothesis is economic class, here conceptualized as a reaction by groups of lower socioeconomic status. In his classic study of nativism, historian John Higham reminds us that blue-collar wage earners "eyed the foreigner for what he was at the moment—a cheap competitor, whose presence undoubtedly held down wages and bred unemployment in temporary local situations. And in a more general sense, workingmen could reasonably anticipate greater economic security through anti-foreign discriminations. . . . Consequently, every anti-immigrant agitation in the nineteenth century had drawn support from the urban laboring class." The historical account also suggests that periods of economic distress aggravated hostilities against foreigners and rekindled nativism.[15] An analysis of the anti-Chinese movement in California in the late 1800s concluded that "job shortages, accompanied by substantial Chinese competition for working class jobs, provided a strong impetus for [ethnic] conflict."[16]

From the perspective of political tolerance, it has been alleged that violations of the social order are more offensive to the masses than to the elites. In 1963 sociologist Seymour Martin Lipset coined the phrase *working-class authoritarianism* to explain how "the poorer strata everywhere are more liberal or leftist on economic issues. . . . But when liberalism is defined in non-economic terms . . . the correlation is reversed. The more well-to- do are more liberal, the poorer are more intolerant."[17] A lack of education, he felt, was the key reason for intolerance.

The fourth hypothesis is political. English Only may be a partisan and ideological reaction against Spanish speakers who tend to vote Democratic (Cubans are an exception). Since official English has great potential as a "cleavage" issue, it can be exploited by Republicans to attract the votes of disaffected Democrats— southerners, working-class people, and Catholics. During the past twenty-five years Republicans, notably Richard Nixon and Ronald Reagan, have campaigned by using "social" issues like abortion, pornography, capital punishment, affirmative action, school prayer, and gun control to establish their conservative credentials and attack Democrats for being too liberal and permissive.[18] Official English can be an especially appealing issue in places like Texas, Florida, and California, where the influx of millions of Spanish-speaking immigrants has imposed special burdens on state and local governments.

The California battle over English Only in the mid-1980s was closely tied to a backlash against bilingual education, spear-headed by then U.S. senator S.I. Hayakawa. A study of opinion polls led Jack Citrin to conclude that "the political right is the core of the 'official language' movement, but the movement attracts support from all along the ideological spectrum."[19] If this is true, then support for official English should be related to support for Ronald Reagan in 1984. The president's reelection offered the electorate a sharp choice between a conservative Republican and a liberal Democrat, Walter Mondale. And presumably GOP state legislators should be active sponsors of bills to codify English.

The fifth hypothesis is cultural and attributes English Only to a diffuse patriotic ("America First") mentality, conceptualized here as a generalized antiforeign sentiment rather than tangible fear of any particular immigrant group. The critics detect a closed-minded ethnocentrism. A *New York Times* editorial that followed the California referendum alleged that the campaign supporting passage of Proposition 63 "smacked of a mean-spirited, nativist irritation over the influx of Mexicans and Asians." James Crawford, an opponent of English Only, believes that a "cultural conservatism" provides an intellectual defense of the "Anglo-American" national culture and rationalizes attacks on bilingual education.[20]

There is logic to the view that English Only is the latest episode of nativism of the kind that surfaced in earlier periods of American history, simply because official English laws were not enacted because a Spanish minority constituted a threat to the established power structure. The notion that an Anglo majority is reacting to the growing population of Spanish speakers is a plausible explanation for what happened in Arizona, Colorado, Florida, and especially California. But the other eleven states that adopted English Only in the 1980s and 1990s are conspicuous for *not* having many Spanish-speaking people or any other non-English minorities. Less than 1 percent of the population in Alabama, Arkansas, Kentucky, Mississippi, Tennessee, Georgia, North Carolina, South Carolina, and Virginia is Hispanic. In Indiana the figure is below 2 percent, and North Dakota has fewer than ten thousand Hispanic inhabitants.[21]

LINE OF ARGUMENT

My work begins with two historical episodes that, though they predated the current agitation for official English, are analogous to the degree that language was codified as a patriotic expression in opposition to a linguistic minority. In Nebraska, the English-Only law followed World War I and was targeted against Germans (chapter 2). In Illinois, a 1923 statute proclaiming "American" to be the official tongue reflected anti-British sentiments (chapter 3). After exploring these cases, I will proceed to show a linkage between nativism during the 1920s, as manifested in the National Origins Act of 1924, and support for the 1980s official English laws.

Lengthy case studies of how referenda were utilized to enact official English laws in Florida and California (chapter 4) as well as in Arizona and Colorado are contrasted with the movement's failure to achieve legislative success in Texas (chapter 5). This group of states is distinguished by sizable numbers of Spanish speakers. Public attitudes toward English Only and mass electoral behavior are explored in chapter 6, to illustrate the fact that support for these laws reaches consensus levels.

Since the electoral context is amenable to appeals from the official English movement, some questions logically emerge: Which political elites brought this issue onto the policy agenda? Why did they do so? The first is addressed by means of a comparative analysis of the legislative process and the socioeconomic and political attributes of senators and representatives in fourteen state legislatures (chapter 8). Some clues about legislative intent are gotten from mini-cases (chapter 7), beginning with the statutory enactment in Virginia (1981) and then proceeding with events in eight more southern and midwestern states.

The book concludes with a summary of the historical record and empirical findings in order to assess each of the five hypotheses that drive the analysis. My goal is not to determine why the English Only movement surfaced at the present juncture in U.S. history but to assess whether it is the latest manifestation of nativism in American culture.[22] The evidence argues in the affirmative, but the story is more complicated than that.

In fact there are two distinct political scenarios by which official English laws were established. Stage 1 is nativist; stage 2 reflects partisan politics. This leads me to speculate about future political developments in a stage 3. My discussion concludes with a normative statement on whether rational argument can overcome the irrational fears of activists on both sides of the controversy.

2

WARTIME HYSTERIA:
THE NEBRASKA EPISODE

The first official language laws, passed in Nebraska and Illinois, came at the height of the 1920s nativism that followed in the wake of World War I and reached a climax with the enactment of federal quotas on immigration. Did like motivations underlie those laws? Were the issues raised in the public debate similar to those being heard today? Were the laws historical oddities or indicators of a broad-based political backlash? In this chapter Nebraska is given detailed scrutiny; chapter 3 offers a discussion of Illinois and the National Origins Act of 1924. It is commonplace for opponents of English Only to characterize the movement as the latest nativist backlash against foreigners, this time Hispanics. If this is true, then parallels should exist between the 1920s and 1980s that can be empirically validated.

NEBRASKA

Article I, section 27, of the Nebraska constitution reads: "The English language is hereby declared to be the official language of this state, and all official proceedings, records and publications shall be in such language, and the common school branches shall be taught in said language in public, private, denominational and parochial schools." Compared with the symbolic declarations of most official English laws today, this 1920 amendment more thoroughly proscribes the use of non-English languages by government and the schools. Even this wording, however, masks the intensity of the Americanization campaign that gave rise to the adoption of the amendment. While Germans may have been the specific target group, a general antiforeign and antialien attitude motivated the political establishment of Nebraska to pass an array of restrictive laws. The educational system was used as a tool to democratize the newcomers and to unify the state. Most important, the debate over enacting the Nebraska law was virtually duplicated in the arguments made during the 1980s debate over English Only laws.

1919 ENGLISH LAWS

The thirty-seventh session of the Nebraska legislature, meeting from January 7 to April 18, 1919, approved three measures to stop the influence of foreign languages.[1] Since Republicans had huge majorities in the senate (thirty Republicans to three Democrats) and the House (eighty-five to fifteen), and all legislative sponsors but one were members of the GOP, the actions gained overwhelming approval.[2] Democratic senator John W. Robbins, in agreement with his Republican colleagues, introduced Senate File no. 15 to repeal sections 1099, 1100, and 1101 of the Revised Statutes of 1913, which dated back to 1879, and "to declare an emergency." Easily passing the senate (29–0) and the House (87–0) and signed into law by the governor on February 14, Robbins's bill ended the requirement that county board proceedings and land sales by county treasurers be published in German, Swedish, and Bohemian language newspapers.[3]

⋅   The second measure by Republican senators Fred G. Johnson and Perry Reed was Senate File no. 237, which required that all public meetings be conducted in English.[4] It also passed the senate (25–0) and the House (67–6) with ease and was enacted on April 17, 1919.

Enacted on April 9, 1919, was Senate File no. 24, co-sponsored by Senators H.E. Siman, Perry Reed, Benjamin J. Ainlay, and Fred G. Johnson, all Republicans. It stipulated that "no person, individually or as a teacher, shall, in any private, denominational, parochial or public school, teach any subject to any person in any language than the English language." A single exception was allowed: "Languages, other than the English language, may be taught as languages only after a pupil shall have attained and successfully passed the eighth grade as evidenced by a certificate of graduation issued by the county superintendent of the county in which the child resides." Anyone violating this statute faced a misdemeanor charge carrying a fine of twenty-five to one hundred dollars or confinement in the county jail for a period not to exceed thirty days.[5] Overwhelming majorities of the senate (32–0) and House (80–2) favored this very restrictive legislation, which became known as the Siman Language Law.

Two years later, however, this law, chapter 249, was replaced with an even more restrictive statute; it was also the subject of an extensive debate at the Constitutional Convention convened on December 2, 1919, to consider amendments to the Nebraska constitution. The convention debated Proposal 77 and Proposal 326, both of which codified an official language.[6]

Proposal 77 was introduced by Walter L. Anderson of Lancaster County and endorsed by ten American Legion posts across the state; it was referred to the Bill of Rights Committee. Proposal 77 would amend section 2 of Article IX of the Nebraska constitution to prescribe the use of the "American" language:

> Ability of the people to freely communicate with and understand each other is essential to a republican form of government, and a common language being therefore a necessity to the people of this state, the right of the people to such a common language shall never be denied or in any way impaired or abridged. To that end, the American language—the language of the Declaration of Independence, of the Federal Constitution and of this Constitution—is hereby declared to be such common language and the official language of this state, and all public proceedings, record and publications shall be in such language and no other, and no person shall be taught in or taught any other language in any school, public or private, until such person shall have attained the age of fourteen years and shall be able to understandingly read, write and speak such American language.

Anderson, who chaired the Bill of Rights Committee, could not get majority support for his measure. Instead, the committee recommended the indefinite postponement of Proposal 77 and reported a substitute, Proposal 326, which eventually was adopted as section 27 of Article I of the Nebraska constitution. Anderson, Albert Byrum, and Wilbur F. Bryant dissented from the majority report, but only Anderson issued a minority report to carry his fight to the floor of the convention. The debate over Proposal 77 provides key insights into the concerns that led the delegates to pass the first official English law in the United States.[7]

THE CONVENTION DEBATE

After taking note of "the number of petitions that have come in from the American Legion Posts," Anderson read the text of Proposal 77. Saying he was willing to modify or eliminate the age requirement, Anderson turned to the real issue: "If a majority of the Convention thinks we should call it the English language rather than the American language, I will agree with that, but I like to call it the American language, and I like to call this country America, and I like to call the flag the American flag, for I am for one country, one language and one flag, and I am for America, I am for the American flag, and I want to be for the American language."

Continuing, he said, "You have all heard the argument that, since the Siman law has been held constitutional [in *Nebraska District of Evangelical Lutheran Synod of Missouri v. McKelvie*, 1919], we should not stir up anything or put anything of this kind into the Constitution, but should leave it to the legislature." He was wary of politicians, though, and warned his colleagues, "We do not want to go on for the next ten years electing representatives to the legislature on the platform of whether they are for or against the Siman law." Such "intrinsic matters," he added, should be in the constitution, "where a legislature cannot change them over night."

Anderson was also worried that politicians might waffle on this issue, since the committee substitute, Proposal 326, had

a sentence, well qualified, for every man to carry back to his constituents and talk two ways on:
You can go back home and tell the man who wanted the American language, that it has to be taught, and that you

voted for a substitute which said that the common school branches shall be taught in the American language, and you can tell the man who wanted to keep alive the old language and who wanted to keep little Italys and little Bohemias in this Constitution, that there is not a thing in the Constitution, and that you did not vote for anything that will prevent the teaching of Bohemian or German in the same school room.

Anderson also alleged that the provisions of Proposal 326 would allow evasion of the law, owing to the failure to insert the word *only* (to refer to the use of English) in the substitute. This omission, he asserted, was deliberate: "They did not want it there and one or two of them said that the reason they were voting for that form was that it permitted a foreign language to be taught at the same time and in the same school room and by the same teacher and possibly the English language that did comply with the Constitution might be taught for only five minutes." Anderson asked the convention to give floor consideration to Proposal 77 and not the "denatured" substitute. What Anderson wanted, that students be taught solely in English, is not very different from the view expressed today by the opponents of bilingualism who prefer the "immersion" method to achieve English proficiency as quickly as possible.

Several delegates rose to answer Anderson's charges. John Wiltse made three points. First, he saw "no reason why, at this late day in the history of our country, we should undertake to change the name 'English language' to 'American language'" because "there is no such thing as the American language unless we refer to the language of the American Indian." Second, he believed that the age requirement would "prohibit any parent in the State of Nebraska from having his children taught Bohemian, French, Spanish or any other language except English." Speaking for himself, he said that he "would like to have my family taught to speak some other language besides the English language." Third, Wiltse made a prophetic point, echoed by foreign language instructors in the 1980s debate: "There may be a time in the history of our people when it will be necessary, for business reasons, for the young men and young women of this state to be able to speak some other language besides the English language. They tell me that in the European countries, nearly every pupil has to learn the language of some other country in order to carry on and transact the business that comes before him sometime in his career." Then Wiltse, like many who opposed the constitutional amendment, felt obliged to defend himself on patriotic grounds. He stated that "no man can make any stronger claim than I can of being purely American stock." He expanded on that theme:

> Early in the year 1623 the ancestors of my family landed on the Atlantic shore, and I think no man can accuse me of being disloyal to my country or saying that which would be against its interests. For one, while I want every man in this state to speak the English language, I want all public records to be kept in that language, I insist that the English language be taught as the law provides it shall be, but I am not willing to go far enough to say that if you want to hire a private tutor in your family and instruct them in some foreign language, that you cannot do it. This proposal would prohibit us from doing that.

Wiltse's comments show how the official English debate has been fundamentally transformed from the 1920s to the 1980s. Wiltse was a "liberal" who opposed restrictions on the private use of foreign languages but favored public records in English, whereas today the advocates of bilingualism favor government subsidies to maintain bilingualism and cultural diversity. Elaborating on this point, Wiltse objected to the words *public proceedings* in Proposal 77: "If it means matters that concern the public, like court proceedings, I would favor it, but if it is going to interfere with church services, and if it is going to prevent private meetings of our friends who want to meet occasionally in a social manner, I would oppose it."

He made the same point with respect to the clause "all . . . publications shall be in [the English] language," saying:

> It would take away every German, Bohemian and Polish paper from every German, Bohemian and Polander in this state. If they want such a publication they must get one from outside of the state. I am not willing to go that far, but I am

willing to go far enough to say that every legal publication in the State of Nebraska, and every legal publication in every county, and that every legal proceeding and every court proceeding, and every notice of administration shall be published in the English language. I am not willing to say that every paper published in Nebraska must be in the English language, because I cannot see any good purpose to be served by it.

Then Wilbur Bryant, though he dissented from the majority report, opposed Anderson's use of *American* because, he said, "our language is defined in our dictionaries as 'English.'" Thus Bryant would support a change of wording in the original Proposal 77 should the Committee of the Whole consider the measure. His next point, that fluency in English is necessary for participation in a democracy, is made over and over by those who favor official English laws today. Bryant said that Proposal 77 "only concerns the people that are brought up here, being taught the English language before they are taught any other; that they shall learn that first, so they will think in that language. Our language is adapted to a republic, and a republic where the people make their own government, and it is adapted to discussion." Noting that all but one of his own children "can talk German, and I am glad of it," Bryant concluded that Proposal 77 "is trying to have common people brought up in a language that is adapted to our institutions."

The next speaker, Aaron Wall, agreed that Bryant "reflected the views of the Committee on portions of this proposal, that they did not know, would not know, and the world would not clearly understand, and it would always be referred to with the duty of defining just what would be meant by the 'American language.'" Confusion would reign if too many dialects were encouraged, because "if each state or territory or nation was permitted to adopt the particular language suitable to their taste, or their use, [then] such conduct and such operations might lead to an unsatisfactory conclusion in this great, broad country of ours." The committee realized, Wall added, "that the world understands . . . that our language is known as the English language, and that it is spoken by more people than any other language, and we do not want to forget that definition or that understanding."

Fundamental to the argument of opponents of official English today is that such laws violate civil liberties, and Wall intimated the same thing. He told the convention that, while the committee agreed that the proceedings of the federal and state governments ought to be in English, "we were seriously in doubt as to how far we might be contravening the rights of the foreigners that we had invited, in urgent terms, to come and join with us under the flag of our country and become American citizens, telling them before they came that they might live in communities, that they might have their schools, and instruct in their language, and they might observe the rights they had in the old and mother country from whence they came."

The committee was wary of supporting Anderson, he added, because his proposal might mean "that those old mothers and fathers, cultured perhaps in a foreign language, uncultured in the English language, that came here bringing their histories and literature with them, and who brought their Bibles and their hymn books and were able to instruct their children in faith and in morals and in good citizenship and the noble, lofty ideals of Americanism, that they would be deprived of the use of that language they brought with them." In sum, the supporters of a watered-down version of Proposal 77 took the distinction between public and private actions very seriously.

Wall called Anderson's concern that teachers would give only scant attention to teaching in English "a trivial consideration" that questioned the integrity of a lot of people. Still, Wall felt obliged to defend his own honor and that of the committee majority by calling the substitute "just as patriotic as the signers of the petitions [World War I veterans] that have been referred to in the remarks we have heard. I believe every member of that Committee is actuated with the same high impulses and noble intentions as are the gentlemen who have sent their petitions to you, and there was no thought of disregarding the petitions, and no thought of disrespect towards the petitions." While the critics in 1920, like those today, argued that advocates of official English do not have a monopoly on patriotism, those opposed to the majoritarian view, then as now, found themselves on the defensive and compelled to express their loyalty to country and flag.

During this round of debate, brief commentary was heard from three other speakers. Thomas Lahners offered a novel illustration from World War I to explain his opposition.

> This is a free country, gentlemen, and we should stand first above all for the English language. What made us so strong in this last war? Did we not all do all we could and were we not proud of our boys, and what they did for us? I have heard it said by a man who was in the trenches and came back wounded, that "When we had the Germans on the run and they knew they could not do anything, we heard them pray in the German language in the trenches. What did we American soldier boys say to them?" We said, "Boys, do as we command you to do." Our soldier boys spoke the German language as well as Germans do.

Lahners then made his obligatory statement—"I am an American born citizen and I stand up for my country"—before announcing that he could not support the proposal.

Advocacy for Proposal 77 was voiced by F.C. Radke, who, like the 1980s advocates of official English, argued that earlier generations of immigrants learned English, so why, he said, should newcomers be treated any differently? Radke drew this comparison in his own family. First he recalled how his immigrant grandmother "came over when she was more than sixty years old and acquired a knowledge of the English language, as did my mother, and so should everyone who comes here, acquire the language of this country. That is what this proposal tries to accomplish." But he also had three cousins "who were born in Cedar County, and today cannot write a love letter or any other kind of a letter in the American language. They must write them in German or have their young sister write for them. That is the situation. I do not oppose the acquiring of other languages, but, gentlemen, let us make it mandatory to acquire the language of our country first."

Then A.R. Oleson spoke, reminding the convention that "I have stood, long before this war, for over twenty years ago, or nearly twenty years, when I was a member of the Senate, for taking out of the public schools of this state the teaching of all foreign languages, so that my conviction, gentlemen, did not come about by reason of this war, but I took the broad ground that the public school was no place for the teaching of any foreign language at public expense." Those desiring to learn foreign tongues should attend private school or get private instruction, he added, "but when you say to me that when my children have complied with the course of instruction in the English language in the public or private or parochial schools, that they cannot in private schools, acquire a knowledge of another language, I say that is going too far and I am against it." Oleson's opposition to Proposal 77 was based on its infringement of his rights as a private person, not because he was any less than a good citizen:

> I am foreign born myself, but I stand for this country and for its language just as strong as any man on the floor of this Convention, and so do my children who are born in this country, and, while I want them to acquire the full rudiments of the English language and comply with all the rules and regulations pertaining to that language in the public schools, yet I want permission to teach my children some other language in case they wish to acquire it, by private instruction or otherwise, and I do not want this state nor the Constitution of this state, as Proposal No. 77 proposes to do, to deny to me that right when I have fulfilled my duty to my children and to the state.

To diffuse the growing opposition to Proposal 77, Anderson then responded: "There is nothing in this that prevents Mr. Wiltse's tutor in his own family teaching any foreign language that he desires to have taught. There is nothing in this that prevents Judge Wall's parents, foreign born and foreign speaking, from teaching their own language in their own home, but this proposal prevents teaching in schools and in flocks and getting them together and having a center of a foreign language."

When the president called the question, Anderson's motion was defeated handily, with a 28–64 vote. Later the convention endorsed the substitute, Proposal 326, but not before Anderson and his allies offered amendments. Byrum, who also dissented from the committee report, moved to amend Proposal 326 to read: "The English is hereby declared to be the official language of this state, and all official proceedings, records and publications shall be in such language, and *no person shall be taught in or taught any other language in any public, private, denominational or parochial school until such person shall be able, understandingly, to read, write and speak the English language*" (amendment in italics). Byrum stated that his change "does carry it a little further than they have seen in their wisdom to go, and it so fixes it that we shall recognize the English language not only as being the language of this country, but we shall, in the education of our children, require that every child, no matter what language he may be in the habit of using, before he can study a foreign language in any of the schools of the state, become acquainted with the language of this country."

Pointing to the committee substitute, he declared that "it does not say nor it does not require, in my opinion, that the common school branches shall not be taught in some other language." That was assumed by some committee members, but "when they were requested to put that in plain words . . . they refused." Explicit wording was needed, he argued, because "I want to know if you are willing to go on record saying here and now that you are in favor of the language of this country, and that you are not only in favor of it, but you are in favor of putting it into the Constitution, so that every child from this time on, before he can study a foreign language, shall understand something of the language of this country, not some other country."

Why was that necessary? For today's advocates of official English the most compelling argument is the effect of a common language in forging national unity and social cohesion, but for Byrum language was a bulwark of American traditions and institutions: "In my judgment, in this free republic of ours, any child or person, I don't care whether he be young or old, if he wants to understand our traditions, if he wants to become acquainted with our institutions, and the reason for which we have these institutions, he must do so by and through the English language and no other, because no other language will give him the reasons why we have these institutions. It is the only way he can properly study the traditions of this country."

The motion by Byrum was supported by Anderson, who agreed that "the committee proposal does not say that [the child] absolutely must learn [English] first." He reaffirmed that his proposal would have no effect on the older generation:

> We have let them come together in their societies and converse frequently in their own language, for the preservation of their own language and because of the sentiment attached to it, and now to bluntly and suddenly throw them out speechless, I do not think it is right. We will grow out of this before long, and there is no need to cause the old people any inconvenience or trouble; but let the children that are growing learn the English language and let us make sure that they learn first the native language, that is the English language and you can not be sure of that until you have something that will enforce it.

Then Anderson mounted an attack on what the 1980s critics allege is the "hidden agenda" behind bilingualism: "These old languages die hard; you cannot talk to an American who is advocating that they shall be allowed to teach these things, or to a German or a Bohemian, if there is such a hybrid any more, who is advocating that, but before he gets through talking to you he will be talking about 'our language.' 'We must be allowed to keep our language alive.' What language? 'Why, the Bohemian or Slovenian or German,' or whatever he is talking about."

In other words, linguistic minorities fracture the body politic and the sense of community. Clearly the belief expressed by Anderson in 1920 is accepted today by people in the official English movement and promoted with equal fervor. Anderson said,

> The idea we want them to get is, that there is no language but the American or the English language which he should talk. The first principle of a subjugated state is that they be allowed to keep their own language. . . . In all the years that Bohemia has been under the control of German Austria, they have kept their own language. They had not migrated into another country and accepted another country's protection, and

another country's flag and then tried to keep the language of
their own country. The business of these little language centers is to keep alive the language of the mother country,
which is the language they were taught in their childhood,
and that is what we want to get away from in this country, so
that there shall not be any child grow up in this country that is
first getting the language of the country that his parents came
from, instead of getting his own native language.

Here, sixty years before the modern debate over bilingualism, was
the kind of statement favoring social cohesion through language
loyalty, coupled with a fear of the persistence of linguistic ghettos,
that was heard so often in the 1980s.

The next to rebut Anderson was Jerry Howard, who stated
that "if our nation is to be thoroughly fortified . . . the citizens of
the nation must be able to comprehend more than one language."
He prefaced his remarks by saying that he "was not born in this
country as you will possibly judge from my accent. However, I am
proud of it. I became an adopted citizen of this republic without
any mental reservation whatsoever, and I challenge anyone to be
more patriotic, for patriotism is in the air nowadays." The story
he then told the convention was that he wrote to Secretary of State
William Jennings Bryan (a Nebraskan) to apply for a position
as consul in any city of Ireland. "I got an answer inquiring 'Did
I understand any modern language, the German language?' and
I think a couple of others. I wrote back and I said the only language I could express my ideas in was the language which was
used in the country of my adoption, but if the language of my
ancestors was considered a modern language possibly I might pass
an examination in that. The answer further said that if I did not
understand the German language, I could not be made a consul to
Cork or Dublin or anywhere else."

Then Howard lectured his colleagues about true meaning of
patriotism:

It is comical, and . . . it would be comical if it was not so
abusive and so insulting to see every fellow stand up and put
his hands in the corners of his vest, like I have mine, and declare his patriotism.

> I had some of the women down here to this Convention
> before a committee, telling about some of the men who did
> not understand the English language who had volunteered to
> go to the front and I know some of them who did go there.
> This is all camouflage and it is all political camouflage and
> just a cheap patriotism.

Just before the roll-call vote was taken, George G. Junkin asked, "In the word 'publication' in the second line, how far did the Committee expect that improvement to go?" Anderson responded, "I think my original draft said 'all public proceedings and publications shall be in such language' and it was changed to 'all official proceedings,' etc., for the reason that the word 'publication' should be modified by the 'official,' and consequently should not go farther than official publications. Tax lists and county commissioners' proceedings and matters of that kind ought all to be in English."

The 27–59 roll-call vote against the substitute to the committee version of the legislation did not quiet Anderson, who then moved that Proposal 326 be amended so that it read: "The English is hereby declared to be the official language of this state, and all official proceedings, records and publications shall be in such language, and the common school branches shall be taught in said language, *and no other*, in public, private, denominational and parochial schools" (amendment in italics). Anderson proposed the amendment because "it takes out any question of doubt," and again he referred to those who would play both sides of the political fence. Anderson asked for a roll-call vote on his motion, and this time he lost by the narrowest of margins (43–44).

At this point Charles H. Epperson moved for the indefinite postponement of the committee report on procedural grounds, noting that the convention had adopted a rule to keep legislative matters out of the constitution. R.S. Norval concurred, but almost all the speakers who joined this debate were against postponement.

John A. Davies asked the committee "whether or not it considers this proposal in any way weakening or strengthening the legislative enactment on this subject which is already on the statute books, and whether or not it would, in any way, affect the Supreme Court interpretation on that subject?" Charles J. Thielen, a member of the Bill of Rights Committee, said that the issue had been considered and that "we concluded that it added nothing one way or the other." Norval interjected: "We provide here that the English is to be the official language, that the official records and proceedings shall be kept in English. That was not done in the act of the legislature that was passed upon by the Supreme Court and known as the Siman law, and I think this proposal, as it has been reported by the Committee, should be adopted."

Charles W. Sears then reaffirmed a point made earlier by Anderson, saying that "it is true that the last session of the legislature passed the Siman Language Bill, but it is just as true that the next session of the legislature may be called upon to repeal it, as the same forces that were opposing the Siman Language Bill will be there in the same strength that they were here in opposition to it." Sears wanted to make the prohibition part of the constitution.

But Lewis K. Alder returned to the original question of putting legislation in a constitution; he favored postponement. William Kieck, however, offered a contrary view: "This might be said to be legislation, but it is a very important subject, and the Siman Law as you all know, does not have anything in regard to official proceedings or official publications, and it is a very important subject, and if it is a little legislation it should go into the Constitution of Nebraska."

Harry L. Keefe rose to support Kieck's position. "I believe, Mr. Chairman and members of this Committee, that having interviewed something over three thousand of these men [veterans], I know something about their wishes and desires, and I can say to you candidly . . . the conditions are met entirely by the provision of this amendment, and I wish to say to those who are suggesting legislative matter in the Constitution in this late hour, that this is not purely legislation. This is laying down a fundamental principle that will be good one hundred years from now, just as much as it is today."

On the other hand, Wilbur Bryant declared his intention to vote to postpone because, though he had originally favored Proposal 77, "I think that this thing has been emasculated until it has reached the insipidity of skimmed milk and crackers, and I can see nothing to it. So far as official proceedings being printed in

English, that is the official language by the common law, and the enactment of a statute, and there is no danger of anyone trying to pass a law to have court proceedings in any other language, and I think all this is just useless."

What is significant about Bryant's reaction is that in the debate of the 1920s no one questioned the wisdom of mandating English for governmental publications, including those opposed to the prohibition on teaching foreign languages, whereas during the 1980s, with bilingual ballots and bilingual educational programs safeguarded by federal law, some people stridently opposed any kind of official English law. The issue today is larger than life and fought almost entirely on symbolic grounds. A key difference between the 1920s and 1980s debates is that, although Italians, Bohemians, and Germans were specifically targeted by the Nebraska law, opponents did not issue countercharges of ethnic discrimination.

Critics of official English laws today commonly allege that the vagueness of such legislation may give rise to abuse when the measures are implemented. That kind of argument was raised by Davies, who asked the meaning of the phrase "all official proceedings, records and publications": "To what extent does that go? To court proceedings, or to official documents in a foreign language, or to wills that are offered for probate that may be written in a foreign language? I speak not in any criticism of the measure, but merely for information as to how far this provision relating to court proceedings goes, to the question of signatures of documents which may be filed in some foreign language?"

Norval responded: "A will, when it is signed by the testator and witnessed, is not an official document. When it is duly admitted to probate it is then to be recorded in English and it thereby becomes an official document." Other examples he cited were delinquent tax lists and court proceedings, but Davies persisted, asking about, "for instance, the introduction of a deed in court, and signed in some foreign language?" To that Norval answered: "No, it is not a part of the record until after it is received." Then Davies offered another illustration: "But, for instance, a marriage license was recently refused I believe in some court in Nebraska on the strength that the names of all the witness were not signed in English." Norval did not agree with that decision: "That would not affect its validity at all, it is not a part of the record until it is received." Anderson agreed: "Regarding a signature," he said, "that some of us might sign by a mark which is admitted as a signature, ʼso that even if it was in some foreign language that we could not understand, it would still be a signature."

The next person to speak against the postponement was Nathan P. McDonald, who had drafted the committee substitute measure and now tried to explain the group's thinking on the matter. He recalled that the committee, feeling that Proposal 77 went too far, voted to postpone it indefinitely. He "thought that the matter was worthy of consideration further," and thus he incorporated the "vital matters" of Proposal 77 into Proposal 326, which was then approved. He had "no objection to fixing that substitute so that it would limit instruction in the common branches to the English language." Furthermore, he recollected, "it was suggested to the Committee that the next legislature or the legislatures to come might be importuned to repeal or amend that law in such a way that would make it ineffective. We think that it might be a wise thing to put that beyond the power of the legislature or any other body and put it in this Constitution which we will submit to the people, and if the people approve of it, it would put the matter forever at rest."

Another consideration was before the committee, said McDonald: "I thought that it was fundamental that the common school branches of this country ought to be taught in the English language alone, and I think that is the reasonable interpretation of this amendment. We are all proud of our liberties, proud of the institutions under which we live, but I, for one, believe there is no language spoken by man that breathes the spirit of American liberty like the language that has come down to us from our Anglo-Saxon forefathers, and that is the English language."

Those comments provoked a final question from A.R. Oleson: "Will this eliminate the Latin phrases and maxims that are often used in the judicial opinions of our Supreme Court?" "I do not think so," McDonald answered, but before the roll was called, Anderson interjected a word of compromise to influence his ally Bryant: "Mr. Bryant made some remark that I did not get the full purport of, but I thought it was something to the effect that he was intending to vote for the indefinite postponement, but I know where his heart is and I know this is not the proposal I brought in and I know it is not the proposal that a great many of the boys, the AMERICAN LEGION POSTS have endorsed, but I believe half a loaf is better than none."

On the call of the roll, Epperson's motion to postpone indefinitely was defeated 9–80. Proposal 326 later passed its second reading by the Committee of the Whole on a 77–0 vote and awaited final approval. When the day for that arrived, Anderson, deferring to the judgment of McDonald, asserted that "it now means just what it would mean if the words 'and no other languages' were put in, that it now means that the teaching of all and every part of the common school branches in any other than the English language is prohibited and that no court would construe it to be otherwise." He declined to offer additional amendments, and on a third reading, Proposal 326 was approved by an 85–0 vote.

In a special election held on September 21, 1920, the voters of Nebraska approved the constitutional amendment. A pamphlet to inform the electorate gave a one-line explanation for the new section: "The purpose of the amendment is to insure to the youth of the state a knowledge of the language in which the spirit of our institutions is expressed and to promote true Americanism."[8] This action did not end the dispute, however; it surfaced again when the next legislature convened in 1921.

1921 ENGLISH LAWS

When the fortieth session of the legislature convened on January 4, 1921, Senate File no. 160 was introduced by R.S. Norval, a Republican who had supported official English as a delegate to the Nebraska Constitutional Convention.[9] But the outcry provoked by an amendment to his bill prompted Norval ultimately to vote against the measure. Still, it easily passed the Senate and House, which suggests that feelings bordering on hysteria had galvanized the advocates of English Only in the aftermath of World War I.

Senate File no. 160 would repeal the 1919 Siman Language Law and replace it with a law designed to accomplish what the convention had refused to do, namely mandate English as the only language of instruction in the schools. The senate Committee on Education, University and Normal Schools, and Library, however, added a new provision (section 4) applicable to private organizations, which caused Senators R.C. Harriss, J.C. McGowan, and D.H. Cronin to file a minority report asking that no. 160 be indefinitely postponed. Later they were joined by Senators George C. Humphrey, Eric Johnson, Otto Ulrich, John Wiltse, and R.S. Norval—all Republicans—in voting against the bill, but twenty-two others passed the measure with the required two-thirds vote. Such a proportion was needed to pass the legislation because it contained an emergency clause.

Six senators in the 1921 session had been delegates to the 1920 convention; they split 3–3 on File no. 160 even though five had voted for Proposal 326 (one abstained) to constitutionalize English as the official language. This fact coupled with Norval's opposition shows that no. 160 represented a decided shift to the political Right. Three legislators entered into the minutes their reasons for voting no.

Harriss declared: "The drastic provision of S.F. No. 160 will likely be declared unconstitutional by the higher courts. If they are declared unconstitutional we will then not have as good a law as we have in the Siman Law which in my judgment should remain intact." Norval agreed: "Believing that some of the provisions of this Bill as amended are unconstitutional and violate the rights of the people, I vote 'No.'" Wiltse, who had opposed Proposal 77 at the convention because it affected teaching in private contexts, expressed the same view here: "I believe the Siman Law meets all public requirements and will in a reasonable length of time cure every evil the authors of S.F. No. 160 have in mind. I believe S.F. No. 160 goes much further than is necessary in restricting the privileges of the people and much further than the public demands. I am opposed to passing criminal laws with an emergency clause attached, because the people should have an opportunity to know a law's provisions before they become liable for violating them." The bill passed the senate with the controversial committee amendment (section 4 below), and later the House added an amendment to section 3 (italicized below). As enacted as chapter 61 of the 1921

Session Laws, the four key sections (of a total of eight) read as follows:

> Sec. 1. The English language is hereby declared to be the official language of this state, and all official proceedings, records and publications shall be in such language, and the common school branches shall be taught in said language in public, private, denominational and parochial schools.
>
> Sec. 2. No person, individually or as a teacher, shall, in any private, denominational or parochial or public school, teach any subject to any person in any language other than the English language.
>
> Sec. 3. Languages other than the English language may be taught as languages only, after a pupil shall have attained and successfully passed the eighth grade as evidenced by a certificate of graduation issued by the county superintendent of the county or the city superintendent of the city in which the child resides. Provided, that the provisions of this act shall not apply to schools held on Sunday or on some other day of the week which those having the care and custody of the pupils attending same conscientiously observe as the Sabbath, where the object and purpose of such schools is the giving of religious instruction, but shall apply to all other schools and to schools held at all other times. *Provided that nothing in this act shall prohibit any person from teaching his own children in his own home any foreign language.*
>
> Sec. 4. It shall be unlawful for any organization, whether social, religious or commercial, to prohibit, forbid or discriminate against the use of the English language in any meeting, school or proceeding, and for any officer, director, member or person in authority in any organization to pass, promulgate, connive at, publish, enforce or attempt to enforce any such prohibition or discrimination.[10]

The language of section 1 repeated the official English provision of the state constitution. Section 2, which the convention had rejected, reiterated that provision of the 1919 Siman Law that no person could teach in any language but English in any school—public, private, denominational, or parochial. Section 3 did what the convention had refused to do (but for which a provision was incorporated in the 1919 Siman Language Law)—that is, apply an age criteria, stating that only students who had passed the eighth grade could be taught a foreign language. This version allowed two exceptions to the ban, however, one for "Sunday school" and one for persons who taught their own children—not a group of un-related children—in their own home. Penalties for violations were set in section 5, section 6 provided for "severability" in the event any provision was invalidated by a court, and section 7 formally repealed chapter 249 (the Siman Law) of the 1919 Session Laws. The final part, section 8, decreed that an emergency existed, so the laws would immediately take effect.

Chapter 61 of the 1921 Session Laws was signed into law on April 15, two days after clearing the House. In the lower chamber the only significant action involved an amendment to section 3 by the Committee for General File. The original form of section 3 included the statement "Provided that nothing in this act shall prohibit any person from teaching his own children in his own home any foreign language, or of employing a private teacher to so teach them." The Committee of the Whole voted 65–31–4 to de-lete the last phrase, apparently to bar any possibility that a teacher would be hired by parents to teach a group of children foreign language at home.

Five representatives made statements for the record to ex-plain why they intended to vote against the bill.[11] One was Peter Hakanson, who went to the heart of the matter: "I wish to explain my vote for this reason, we now have compulsory education and only the American language can be taught, and Senate File No. 160 will prohibit the people from worshipping their God after the dictates of their own conscience in as much as private schools and colleges where teachers and preachers may be educated as forbid-den, there will be no one to teach or preach the word of God to a people that cannot understand the American language." On third and final reading, the bill was approved on a 70–28–2 vote, but cu-riously, Hakanson, alone among the five, deviated from his stated position and voted yea. He offered no explanation.

The only person from the majority who made a statement for the record was James W. Lundy. He simply stated that "the Ameri-can language only should be taught in grade schools in Nebraska."

But three dissenting members made their feelings known in stronger terms. F.L. Anderson, from Knox County, said: "I regard religion more important than language, more vital to development of moral citizenry. This bill places languages above religion, prohibiting schools for religious instruction six days of the week, except they be conducted in English." The same concern provoked Ernest H. Gifford: "I cannot reconcile myself to vote for a bill that forbids religious instruction in a foreign language on any day except Sunday. I endeavored to amend the bill so it would not interfere with religious instruction, and it was voted down." Henry Behrens, who had recorded his comments against the key amendment earlier, made the caustic remark that "we have a language law on our statute books now that is very simple to take care of the situation, this agitation is for the war profiteers to cover up their crimes."

LITIGATION POLITICS

Ultimately the objections of the minority carried the day, in court. The Siman Language Law, chapter 249 of the 1919 Session Laws, was challenged in a lawsuit that reached the U.S. Supreme Court in 1923. Few legislators probably anticipated that the law would be reversed, since the Nebraska Supreme Court had upheld the old Siman Law, a fact noted many times in the Constitutional Convention debate. That case, *Nebraska District of Evangelical Lutheran Synod of Missouri v. McKelvie*, decided on December 26, 1919, upheld the ruling of district judge Arthur C. Wakeley of Douglas County, who held that chapter 249 of the 1919 Session Laws was constitutional.[12]

Some local church corporations that operated parochial schools, certain private schools, and foreign language–speaking parents joined the plaintiff. The court summarized their complaint:

> Since the officers and members of the respective churches are largely made up of foreign language speaking people, if the act is enforced their children will be unable to obtain instruction in religion and morals in accordance with the doctrines of the religious denominations to which the parents

belong, in the language of their parents; that many of the
children cannot understand English, and cannot understand
such instruction in that language; that in the parochial
schools below the seventh grade the language of the parents
is used in order to teach English, and that the children cannot
learn English if they do not receive rudimentary education in
the tongue the parents use; that property rights in the school
buildings and grounds, and in the good will of the schools,
will be destroyed.

But the court took judicial notice of other facts about foreign-
born Nebraskans:

The operation of the selective [military] draft law disclosed a
condition in the body politic which theretofore had been ap-
preciated to some extent, but the evil consequences of which
had not been fully comprehended. It is a matter of general
public information, of which the court is entitled to take judicial knowledge, that it was disclosed that thousands of men
born in this country of foreign language speaking parents and
educated in schools taught in a foreign language were unable
to read, write or speak the language of their country, or
understand words of command given in English. It was also
demonstrated that there were local foci of alien enemy sentiment, and that, where such instances occurred, the education
given by private or parochial schools in that community was
usually found to be that which had been given mainly in a
foreign language.

The purpose of the Siman Law was "to remedy this very apparent
need, and by amendment to the school laws make it compulsory
that every child in the state should receive its fundamental and
primary education in the English language." The court observed
that in 1919 similar measures were adopted by the legislatures of
Iowa, Kansas, Maine, Arkansas, Washington, Indiana, Wisconsin,
and New Hampshire.

After reviewing the state's compulsory education laws, the
court turned to the themes of self-government and citizenship. Undoubtedly the court's sentiments are shared by many people today,
especially the 1980s advocates of official English legislation:

> The ultimate object and end of the state in thus assuming control of the education of its people is the upbuilding of an intelligent American citizenship, familiar with the principles and ideals upon which this government was founded, to imbue the alien child with the tradition of our past, to give him the knowledge of the lives of Washington, Franklin, Adams, Lincoln, and other men who lived in accordance with such ideals, and to teach love for his country, and hatred of dictatorship, whether by autocrats, by the proletariat, or by any man, or class of men.
>
> Philosophers long ago pointed out that the safety of a democracy, or republic, rests upon the intelligence and virtue of its citizens. . . . The state should control the education of its citizens far enough to see that it is given in the language of their country, and to insure that they understand the nature of the government under which they live, and are competent to take part in it. Further than this, education should be left to the fullest freedom of the individual.

The court brushed aside the claim that the act interfered with parents who wished to give their children religious or moral instruction in a foreign language, saying that the compulsory education laws "only require compulsory education for children not less than seven, nor more than sixteen years of age, and for a period of not less than twelve weeks in certain districts, and a longer period in others." So the legislature could not have intended "to bar its parents, either in person, or through the medium of tutors or teachers employed, from teaching other studies as their wisdom might dictate."

The court took issue with the plaintiff's argument favoring "bilingual" education, likely one of the earliest if not the first effort to win legal acceptance for using foreign languages to teach English proficiency. The court seemingly endorsed the "immersion" method, without benefit of the kind of educational research that, according to today's proponents, validates the efficacy of bilingual education. Instead the justices relied on common sense and logic when they declared:

> The assertion that it is necessary to teach Polish in order to teach English does not seem well founded. . . . We think we

are not bound to draw the conclusion that because children, when they first attend school, cannot understand or speak English, they must be taught the language of their parents, whether Polish or Bohemian, in order that they may learn English, otherwise no children of foreign speaking parents attending the public schools, wherein no other language than English is spoken, could ever learn the language. It is common knowledge that the easiest way to learn a foreign language is to associate only with those who speak and use it.

Finally the court upheld the Siman Language Law and rejected claims of constitutional violations based on the exercise of "police powers" by the state. It reasoned that if government can safeguard the public in other ways, for example, "'to protect the minor from impoverishing himself by contract, it surely is not an arbitrary exercise of the functions of the state to insist' that the fundamental basis of the education of its citizens shall be a knowledge of the language, history and nature of the government of the United States, and to prohibit anything which may interfere with such education."

Three years later, in 1922, the Nebraska high court was asked to rule in another case, in which it upheld criminal penalties against a schoolteacher, thereby setting the stage for a landmark decision by the U.S. Supreme Court. Again the Siman Language Law was at issue.

In *Meyer v. State*, defendant Robert T. Meyer, who had been charged with violating the Siman Law, found guilty, and fined twenty-five dollars, appealed to the high court.[13] Meyer was a teacher in a parochial school operated by the Zion Evangelical Lutheran Congregation, and between 1:00 and 1:30 on May 25, 1920, he taught the German language to a ten-year-old boy who had not yet passed the eighth grade. As the text he used a book of biblical stories written in German.

The court described the defendant's argument:

> That the teaching of the German language from this book containing Bible stories served a double purpose, in that it both taught the children the German language and also familiarized them with the Bible stories, and that the teaching, so characterized, was religious instruction. It must be conceded,

even under that argument, that two subjects were being taught—one the German language and one a religious text. If the law prohibited the teaching of the German language as a separate and distinct subject, then, certainly, the fact that such language was taught from a book containing religious matter could not act as a shield to the defendant. The teaching of the German language, as a subject, would come within the direct prohibition of the law, regardless of what text might be used in the book from which the language was taught.

For the court the key issue was "Does the statute interfere with the right of religious freedom, by prohibiting the teaching of a foreign language, when that language is taught with the idea and purpose of later using it, at some other time or place or in the school itself, in religious worship?" No, the court ruled, because

> the salutary purpose of the statute is clear. The legislature had seen the baneful effects of permitting foreigners, who had taken residence in this country, to rear and educate their children in the language of their native land. The result of that condition was to be inimical to our own safety. To allow the children of foreigners, who had emigrated here, to be taught from early childhood the language of the country of their parents was to rear them with that language as their mother tongue. It was to educate them so that they must always think in that language, and, as a consequence, naturally inculcate in them the ideas and sentiments foreign to the best interests of this country.

In other words, learning a foreign language inherently meant that children were learning un-American values.

To the counterargument that the law infringed on English-speaking citizens who might wish to have their children taught a foreign language in school, the court presumed a lot: "Other citizens, in their selection of studies, except perhaps in rare instances, have never deemed it of importance to teach their children foreign languages before such children have reached the eighth grade."

The reasoning in *Meyer v. State* caused Justice Charles Letton to dissent in part from the majority opinion. Meyer had alleged that the state failed to show that his teaching occurred during the regular school hours or that his instruction was a course of study as prescribed by the compulsory education act. That students were "assembled in the school for the purpose of receiving instruction" was enough to support the offense against Meyer, the court argued. Then it added: "So far, then, as it may have been indicated in the former opinion in *Nebraska District of Evangelical Lutheran Synod v. McKelvie, supra,* that the law was aimed to apply only to those school hours which should be set apart for the teaching of the so-called common school branches, or set apart as 'regular school hours,' we believe that opinion should be modified." The majority saw efforts by the parochial school to evade the Siman Act:

> After the decision in the case of *Nebraska District of Evangelical Lutheran Synod v. McKelvie, supra,* in which it was said that the statute aimed only at the teaching of foreign languages during "regular school hours," the church authorities, by resolution, changed the afternoon school hours so that they covered the period of from 1:30 to 4 o'clock, instead of the 1 to 4. The morning hours remained the same. Pupils, however, as before, each day assembled at 1 o'clock in the afternoon and were taught German, in the manner we have described, until the hour of 1:30, at which time regular school was said to commence.

Even though attendance during the half-hour period was not compulsory, the trial court had asked the jury to determine if the change of hours was an evasion of the law. The Nebraska Supreme Court agreed that, "in the light of the evidence, the only verdict which could have been expected was the one returned by the jury, finding the defendant guilty of the offense charged."

The dissent by Justice Letton (who had authored the majority opinion in *Nebraska District of Evangelical Lutheran Synod of Missouri v. McKelvie*) was joined by Justice C.J. Morrissey. Morrissey rejected the notion that state police powers may "interfere with the fundamental right of every American parent to control, in a degree not harmful to the state, the education of his child, and to teach it, in association with other children, any science or art, or any language which contributes to a larger life, or to a higher and broader culture." Letton endorsed a contrary view of foreign language acquisition, which, he said, parents should be allowed to take advantage of: "Educators agree that the period of early childhood is the time that the ability to speak and understand a foreign or a classic language is the most easily acquired. Every parent has the fundamental right, after he has complied with all proper requirements by the state as to education, to give his child such further education in proper subjects as he desires and can afford." He also questioned the rationale for the Siman Law: "It is patent, obvious, and a matter of common knowledge that this restriction was the result of crowd psychology; that it is a product of the passions engendered by the World War, which had not had time to cool."

The landmark U.S. Supreme Court ruling of June 4, 1923, in *Meyer v. Nebraska* overturned the Nebraska high court decision, but a close reading of the majority opinion does not indicate that the decision was a conclusive victory for foreign language instruction.[14] This case is often cited by the opponents of English Only today, when in fact the issue was decided on narrow grounds. Moreover, the majority actually endorsed state-mandated teaching in the English language.

The majority opinion by Justice James Clark McReynolds agreed with the essence of Letton's dissent. The issue, McReynolds wrote, "is whether the statute as construed and applied unreasonably infringes the liberty guaranteed to the plaintiff in error by the Fourteenth Amendment [due process clause]." Established doctrine requires that liberty "may not be interfered with, under the guise of protecting the public interest, by legislative action which is arbitrary or without reasonable relation to some purpose within the competency of the State to effect."

First the law adversely affected Meyer insofar as he "taught this language in school as part of his occupation. His right thus to teach and the right of parents to engage him so to instruct their children, we think, are within the liberty of the [Fourteenth] Amendment." Second, that the state "may do much, go very far, indeed, in order to improve the quality of its citizens, physically, mentally and morally, is clear; but the individual has certain fundamental rights which must be respected. The protection of the Constitution extends to all, to those who speak other languages as well as to those born with English on the tongue. Perhaps it would be highly advantageous if all had ready understanding of our ordinary speech, but this cannot be coerced by methods which conflict with the Constitution—a desirable end cannot be promoted by prohibited means."

From the larger perspective of whether the state could mandate teaching in English, however, the Court said: "The power of the State to compel attendance at some school and to make reasonable regulations for all schools, including a requirement that they shall give instructions in English, is not questioned. Nor has challenge been made of the State's power to prescribe a curriculum for institutions which it supports. Those matters are not within the present controversy. Our concern is with the prohibition approved by the [state] Supreme Court."

Nor was the law unique to Nebraska: twenty-one other states had enacted similar laws regulating foreign language use, though only those of Ohio, Iowa, and Nebraska had been challenged. The very day the Supreme Court decided *Meyer v. Nebraska*, the precedent from that case was used to reverse rulings by the Ohio (*Bohning v. Ohio; Pohl v. Ohio*) and Iowa (*Bartels v. Iowa*) Supreme Courts against teachers who taught German to parochial school pupils below the eighth grade and to nullify the decision in *Nebraska District of Evangelical Lutheran Synod of Missouri v. McKelvie*.[15]

A dissenting opinion in *Meyer* and the four companion cases was authored by Justice Oliver Wendell Holmes Jr. and joined by Justice George Sutherland. It was Holmes's view that the Nebraska statute was "a reasonable or even necessary method of reaching the desired result." This result, namely, was to inculcate the English language: "Youth is the time when familiarity with a language is established and if there are sections in the State where a child would hear only Polish or French or German spoken at home I am not prepared to say that it is unreasonable to provide that in his early years he shall hear and speak only English at school. But if it is reasonable it is not an undue restriction of the liberty either or teacher or scholar." While Holmes understood the objection raised, nonetheless, he wrote, "it appears to me to present a question upon which men reasonably might differ and therefore I am unable to say that the Constitution of the United States prevents the experiment being tried." In other words, Holmes felt the law was a reasonable means to a desirable end, and thus he articulated a position of judicial restraint, saying that the Court should defer to the judgment of the state legislatures in this matter.

The terms of the debate in the 1920s thus were similar to what is being voiced today, but differences do exist. In the 1920s, there was no dissent, even from the critics, concerning the propriety or legality of mandating English in the public domain. While advocates saw that proposal as affirming the obvious, for those of foreign extraction, it was reasonable and patriotic. Any questions involved defining the boundary between private and public and making sure the state law did not intrude into family life. The debaters, though testy at moments, did not succumb to name-calling or scapegoating, yet the 1921 Nebraska law represented a foreboding sign.

The 1921 law, which mandated English in social, religious, and commercial settings, was a dangerous departure from what the 1919 legislature and the 1920 convention had contemplated. Proponents said that constitutionalizing the English language was necessary so that politicians could not rescind the law, but the irony is that the very next legislature chose to extend English Only regulations to private settings. That development suggests that, once agitation over emotive symbolic issues begins, it is difficult to constrain those political forces. They were slowed, if only temporarily, by the *Meyer v. Nebraska* ruling, but within a year of that decision the nativists turned their energies to dealing with the problem at a more fundamental level: federal immigration restrictions.

3

ANTECEDENTS OF NATIVISM: THE 1920S AND THE 1980S

The driving force of nativism during the 1920s led to the enactment by Congress of the National Origins Act of 1924, which imposed strict quotas against people from southern and eastern Europe, as well as Asia and Africa, while favoring emigration from England and northern European countries. In this chapter I take a close look at the congressional debate over that legislation, both to show that nativist feelings were openly expressed in the House of Representatives and to document the extent of anti-immigrant sentiment by each state congressional delegation. Once those facts are established, I will attempt to determine whether any linkage exists between the states that most fervently backed curbs on immigrants in the 1920s and those states that enacted official English laws during the 1980s. Before proceeding, I will first chronicle how and why Illinois established "American" as its official language in 1923. Clearly the Illinois episode shows that Walter L. Anderson, the prime mover for codifying American—not English—in the Nebraska Constitutional Convention of 1920, was not alone in his sentiments. Illinois, however, was the only state to take that action.

NATIVISM

John Higham's classic historical account defines *nativism* as "an intense opposition to an internal minority on the ground of its foreign (i.e., 'un-American') connections."[1] Underpinning this generalized feeling were two specific themes. One, its antiradical sentiment, was first manifested by the reaction to the French Revolution and resulted in the Alien and Sedition Acts of 1798. The second was anti-Catholic paranoia, as reflected in the "No-Popery" agitation of the 1820s and Know-Nothingism of the 1850s. But fear of the immigrant was a contributing factor during the mid-1800s: "Many Americans believed that the influx of aliens threatened their established social structure, endangered the nation's economic welfare, and spelled doom for the existing governmental system." As Higham points out, however, both antiradical and anti-Catholic strains of nativism "aimed from the outset to define the nation's enemies rather than its essence."[2]

The essence of nativism developed later. The belief that "the United States belongs in some special sense to the Anglo-Saxon 'race'" offered an interpretation of the source of national greatness."[3] This "racial nativism" or "Anglo-Saxon nationalism" gained intellectual and emotional strength following the Civil War. It erupted with political force, under the aegis of the American Protective Association (APA), during the economic troubles of the 1880s and 1890s and reached its peak of influence in the state and congressional elections of 1894. Though the APA was primarily anti-Catholic, it voiced support for immigration and suffrage restrictions as "the nativistic sentiment of the period," because "large numbers of the immigrants coming to the country at the time were adherents of the Catholic Church."[4]

The Immigration Act of 1891 lodged responsibility for this problem with the federal government, which began building the Ellis Island facility in New York Harbor, and also included the first provision for deporting aliens. But restrictionists were unsatisfied and continued to lobby, without success, for a law to require literacy tests of immigrants. The next outburst of nativism accompanied World War I: now German Americans were subjected "to the plain and simple accusation in which every type of xenophobia culminated: the charge of disloyalty, the gravest sin in the morality of nationalism." The crusade against "hyphenated Americans" widened and enveloped President Woodrow Wilson and former president Theodore Roosevelt. Roosevelt denounced divided loyalties as "moral treason" and demanded allegiance to his maxim, "the simple and loyal motto, AMERICA FOR AMERICANS."[5] That kind of sentiment, when coupled with wartime hysteria, led to the Immigration Act of 1917. This act included a literacy test; adult immigrants who were unable to read a simple passage in some language (not just English) could be excluded from the United States.

The end of World War I only worsened this nativist outburst, and, writes Higham, "the survival of 100 per cent Americanism under peacetime conditions is one of the great keys to the storm of xenophobia that followed in the wake of battle. An unappeased demand for the kind of conformity which only an extremely belligerent nationalism might provide flowed on for years, making World War I a major turning point in American nativism." At first nativism had a benign purpose when the "Americanization" movement promoted education and the teaching of English as tools for uplifting immigrants and socializing them in civic virtues. But a more patriotic edge developed with the Red Scare after the Russian Revolution of 1917. Following the end of the Americanization crusade, which failed in its efforts to assimilate the immigrants totally, nativists turned their energies to keeping them out. "While the movement for the redemption of the alien ebbed in 1920, the old drive for the rejection of the immigrant passed all previous bounds."[6]

ILLINOIS

The 1923 Illinois statute shows that codifying an official language as an expression of national identity is not unique to the modern era. Senate Bill 15 was introduced by Democratic state senator Frank J. Ryan, an Irishman from Cook County, to establish "American" as the official language of Illinois.[7] Its preamble gave a strident anti-Tory defense:

> WHEREAS, Since the creation of our American Republic there have been certain tory elements in our country who have never become reconciled to our Republican institutions and have ever clung to the tradition of king and empire; and

WHEREAS, The assumed dominance of this tory element in
the social, business and political life of America tends to
force the other racial units, in self defense, to organize on
racial lines, thus creating nations within a nation and fostering those racial and religious differences which lead to
disunion and disintegration; and

WHEREAS, The supreme problem of American statesmen,
and supreme desire of American patriots, is to weld the racial
units into a solid American nation in the sense that England,
France and Germany are nations; and

WHEREAS, The name of the language of a country has a
powerful influence in stimulating and preserving the national
ideal; and

WHEREAS, The languages of other countries bear the name
of the countries to which they belong, the language of Germany being called German; of France, French; of England,
English; and so on; and

WHEREAS, Our government, laws, customs and ideals as
well as our language differ materially from those of England,
now therefore;

Section 1. *Be it enacted by the People of the State of Illinois,
represented in the General Assembly*: The official language of
the State of Illinois shall be known hereafter as the "American" language, and not as the "English" language.[8]

The senate Judiciary Committee reported a shorter and more
restrained version, which emphasized themes of "social integration" and omitted references to "racial" conflict. It read:

WHEREAS, Since the creation of our American Republic
there have been certain tory elements in our country who
have never become reconciled to our Republican institutions
and have ever clung to the tradition of king and empire; and

WHEREAS, America has been a haven of liberty and place of
opportunity for the common people of all nations; and

WHEREAS, These strangers within our gates who seek economic betterment, political freedom, larger opportunities for
their children, and citizenship for themselves, come to think
of our institutions as American and our language as the
American language; and,

WHEREAS, The name of the language of a country has a powerful psychological influence upon the minds of the people in stimulating and preserving national solidarity; and,

WHEREAS, The languages of other countries bear the name of the countries where they are spoken; therefore,

Section 1. *Be it enacted by the People of the State of Illinois, represented in the General Assembly*: The official language of the State of Illinois shall be known hereafter as the "American" language.[9]

In the floor debate, Senator Ryan told his colleagues that "in Washington today there is a bill before Congress asking that the American language be recommended to the people of the United States. This is one country, with one flag, and should have one language."[10] He presented documents "from all the universities in the country . . . recommending this very strongly to the people of the state of Illinois, and congratulating the state of Illinois on being the first state to take up this measure. It is time that we should teach more Americanism than we do now." At this point Senator James J. Barbour (R-Cook Co.) took issue with the concept of an American language:

I would like to know what the American language is. I go away from this state and some one says to me: "Where are you from?" "From Illinois." "What language do you speak there?" "The American language." "What is that?" "I don't know what it is, it is something that Senator Ryan got up." I am going to vote "No" on this bill. I have been criticized in the public press for being appointed upon a sub-committee to get up a bill for making the American language the official language of Illinois. I don't want to be made a fool of any more, and I vote "No."

Replying to Barbour, Senator Frank O. Hanson (R-McLean Co.) said that "a good many of the colleges of the country have endorsed it; a good many of the Americanization organizations of the country are for it, because a good number of the foreigners wonder why our language is not called the American language." Senator Harold J. Kessinger (R-Kane Co.) agreed and cited "the play 'So This is London?' which shows strikingly the difference there is in the common every day items of speech, and the difference between the two languages. If any one should ask me what language we speak in Illinois, I for one will not be ashamed to say that I speak the American language." When Senator Otis F. Glenn (R-Jackson Co.) said that such a law should be passed at the federal level, Kessinger rejoined that in Washington "they say it is up to the states." He continued, "We are all good when it comes to 'passing the buck.' I am not anti-English but I am not pro-English either."

In his own defense, Ryan claimed that "this bill calls for the American language [and] that is all. It wants to educate us Americans in the American language, and not in any other language. As stated a moment ago, the language and the flag go hand in hand." Then the senator waxed poetic:

> There's no other land like my land,
>   Beneath the shining sun;
> No other flag like my fair flag,
>   In all the world—not one;
> One land, one tongue and one people,
>   To one flag loyal, true—
> No red shall wave over my land
>   Without the white and blue.

> There's a granduer [*sic*] in my land's mountains,
>   Contentment in her vales;
> There's wealth in her broad prairies,
>   There's freedom in her gales;
> In my land all men are equal,
>   Her flag proclaims it, too—
> No red shall wave over my land
>   Without the white and blue.

> There's majesty in Old Glory,
>   Hope in each stripe and star,
> It heralds freedom, liberty,
>   To nations, near and far,
> Unsullied and triumphant,
>   Glorified, she floats anew—
> No red shall wave over my land
>   Without the white and blue.

His ending—"No language not American to go with the American flag"—was affirmed, though with less rhetorical flourish, by Senator Rodney B. Swift (R-Lake Co.), who announced his vote in favor of the bill "after realizing that the English language since the day the Pilgrims landed on the shores of Massachusetts has taken its course, and the language of this nation has taken its course. Not long ago I couldn't find my way about London by asking directions. Why? Because I didn't speak the English language. We do talk the American language, perhaps not always as we should, but we do talk a language that we call the language of this continent, of the Western hemisphere."

Senate Bill 15 was enacted by overwhelming margins in the Illinois senate (32–3) and later in the lower chamber (103–7). It remained on the books until the Illinois General Assembly in 1969 approved an amendment offered by a Democratic state representative from a Chicago suburb to substitute "English" for "American." The revision was also passed by near-unanimous votes in the state senate (49–1) and house (129–4).[11]

The sponsor of the 1969 amendment said that the notion of an American language is "technically erroneous" and a "mistake of history," because the 1923 law was motivated by "Anglophobia hysteria." In fact, he believed that the bill had been introduced at the urging of Chicago mayor "Big Bill" Thompson. Thompson, a Republican, gained notoriety when he once declared that he would punch the king of England in the nose if he ever came to Chicago! When the sponsor was asked why he did not simply eliminate the statute from the code, he responded that the language of the United States should be English, that "the lack of a uniform language can be divisive to a country," and that English is thus necessary to "unify the state."[12]

FEDERAL LANGUAGE BILL

No state followed the lead of Illinois, although on February 1, 1923—as mentioned in the Illinois senate floor comments by Frank Ryan—a like-minded Anglophobia prompted Congressman Washington J. McCormick (R-Mont.) to introduce such a bill (House Resolution 14136) in the Sixty-seventh Congress. Establishing "American" as the official language of the United States,

McCormick declared, "would supplement the political emancipation of '76 by the mental emancipation of '23."[13] He continued:

> America has lost much in literature by not thinking its own thoughts and speaking them boldly in a language unadorned with gold braid. It was only when Cooper, Irving, Mark Twain, Whitman, and O. Henry dropped the Order of the Garter and began to write American that their wings of immortality sprouted. Had Noah Webster, instead of styling his monumental work the *American Dictionary of the English Language*, written a "Dictionary of the American Language," he would have become a founder instead of a compiler. Let our writers drop their top-coats, spats, and swagger-sticks, and assume occasionally their buckskin, moccasins, and tomahawks.[14]

If the commentary in the *Nation* is any guide, intellectual opinion ridiculed the McCormick proposal:

> The trouble with this country is these here foreigners coming in and learning English out of grammar-books instead of picking up American on the vacant lots where the boys would given them the merry-ha-ha if they pulled any of the high-and-mighty. We got to shake the real Americans out of the feathers and make them get behind a line of patter that doesn't sound as if it came through a nose with a monocle sitting just off to starboard. It is time to tell these here foreigners and high-brows where they get off.[15]

Similarly, an editorial in the *New York Times* offered an oblique observation about the pending legislation: "What stirred up the pure mind of the Montana Representative to this needed reform we do not know. Perhaps he was moved to resentment by the news from London that the sightseeing omnibuses had engaged specially trained interpreters to make everything plain to American tourists. It may be that he had heard with indignation of the need of publishing along with English editions of leading American novels a glossary, to explain our untutored ways of speech to the ignorant islanders." In the first section of McCormick's bill, it noted with regret, "he betrays some doubt whether it will not be necessary to

have a 'more particular standardization of the American language.'
It is a work which he implies that Congress itself may hereafter
undertake. Certainly, to convert it for a period of years into a sort
of American Academy analogous to the French, tracing out labori-
ously the history of each word and settling good usage, might
provide it with a less harmful occupation than it finds for much of
its time." The editors had little doubt about what motivated the
congressman: "The whole cannot be denied to be a noble application of the spirit of a hundred per cent Americanism in everything.
We must cut loose from allegiance to foreign grammar, and avoid
as we would the plague all entangling linguistic alliances. It is a
great honor to Montana that this fertile and patriotic suggestion
comes from one of her Representatives in Congress. Westward the
star of empire over language takes its way. Main Street will have to
look to its laurels."[16] House Resolution 14136 was referred to the
Judiciary Committee, where it died, so the first attempt to establish
an official language by federal law is simply a footnote in history.

What followed in 1924, however, was landmark legislation
aimed at stemming the tide of emigration from southern and
eastern European nations. The National Origins Act was the climax
of antiforeign sentiment and remained on the statute books virtually unchanged until the 1960s.

NATIONAL ORIGINS ACT OF 1924

The precursor to the landmark 1924 act was the Quota Act of
1921, a stopgap measure to expire one year later, which imposed
the first immigration quotas in U.S. history by specifying that no
more than a number equaling 3 percent of the foreign-born population of each nationality residing in the United States in 1910
could be admitted in any year. It thus introduced the concept of national origins quotas.

The 1924 act, sometimes called the Johnson-Reed Act after
its sponsors, Representative Albert Johnson (R-Wash.) and Senator
David Aiken Reed (R-Pa.), was more restrictive. To take effect
after a period of transition, the act provided for an annual quota of
150,000 for Europeans and a ban on Japanese immigration (the
law unofficially was known as the Japanese Exclusion Act).

Quotas would be based on the contribution of each nationality to the *total* U.S. population in 1920, not the number of foreign-born residents.[17]

The 1924 act was passed by overwhelming and bipartisan majorities in the Senate (62–6) and the House (323–71). In the House, upward of 80 percent of Democrats and Republicans voted for final enactment of the National Origins Act of 1924. Analysis of voting patterns shows a regional differential in the support for immigration restrictions (table 3.1).

Almost two-thirds of northern Democrats but all the southern Democrats favored that legislation. What seems curious, but lends credence to the nativist interpretation offered here, is that states (mostly southern) with populations of foreign-born residents and Catholics *below* the national average cast 98 percent of their votes for enactment. A strong correlation existed between the percentages of Catholic and foreign-born in forty-eight states in 1920, and undoubtedly both factors contributed to this nativist outburst.[18]

One indication that the hostility was directed against foreigners, not Catholics per se, is the voting behavior of congressmen from Louisiana. In 1920 the foreign-born population of Louisiana was only 2.6 percent, as compared with the national average of 13.2 percent. But members of the Catholic Church represented 33 percent of Louisiana's total population; this was almost double the national average (18 percent) and ranked Louisiana as fifth highest among the states in the proportion of Catholic residents. Yet all voting representatives from Louisiana—including Catholics—joined their southern brethren to support the 1924 act (and also to oppose the Begg Amendment, a key amendment that was designed to allow aliens a measure of due process before deportation).[19]

Of the seventy-one opposing votes, sixty-six came from representatives in states with percentages of Catholics and foreign-born residents above the national average. The majority of no votes were by congressmen from the Northeast, and they were joined by a small number of legislators from midwestern (mainly industrial) states. New York accounted for twenty-four votes in opposition; twenty-eight more were added by New Jersey, Massachusetts, Pennsylvania, and Connecticut (table 3.2).

Table 3.1 Voting on Begg Amendment and Final Enactment of the National Origins Act of 1924

| | Begg Amendment | | | Final Enactment | |
	Yeas	Nays		Yeas	Nays
Total Vote					
	198 (51%)	193 (49%)		323 (82%)	71 (18%)
Party Affiliation					
Republicans					
	146 (76%)	47 (24%)		161 (83%)	33 (17%)
Democrats					
	49 (25%)	146 (75%)		160 (81%)	37 (19%)
Southern Democrats					
	1 (1%)	92 (99%)		94 (100%)	0
Northern Democrats					
	48 (47%)	54 (53%)		66 (64%)	37 (36%)
Farm Labor					
	1			1	
Socialist					
	1				1
Progressive					
	1			1	
Percentage of Foreign-Born in State					
Above National Average					
	149 (82%)	33 (18%)		118 (64%)	66 (36%)
Below National Average					
	49 (23%)	160 (77%)		205 (98%)	5 (2%)
Percentage of Catholics in State					
Above National Average					
	143 (82%)	32 (18%)		110 (63%)	66 (37%)
Below National Average					
	55 (25%)	161 (75%)		213 (98%)	5 (2%)

Sources: U.S. Department of Commerce, Bureau of the Census, *Abstract of the Fourteenth Census of the United States, 1920* (Washington, D.C.: GPO, 1923), 103; idem, *Religious Bodies, 1926*, vol. 2, *Separate Denominations* (Washington, D.C.: GPO, 1929), 1257.

Table 3.2   Opposition Votes in House of Representatives to the National Origins Act of 1924, by State

State	Opposition Votes
Connecticut	5
Illinois	6
Maryland	1
Massachusetts	8
Michigan	3
Missouri	1
Nebraska	1
New Jersey	9
New York	24
Ohio	2
Pennsylvania	6
Rhode Island	3
Wisconsin	2

Sources: roll call vote from *Congressional Record—House* (April 12, 1924), vol. 65, part 6, pp. 6257-58; states for each representative voting against bill from *Congressional Directory*, 68th Congress, 1st session, 1924 (Washington, D.C.: GPO, 1924).

Thus, support for immigration restrictions was greatest in those states where political leaders faced almost no threat of electoral reprisal from foreign-born constituents. This situation offers an interesting parallel with the politics of English Only today. In four states with a substantial minority of Spanish speakers, the legislature failed, or more accurately refused, to enact official English bills that were introduced, whereas the legislatures in eleven other states with small concentrations of Hispanics were easily able to pass those statutes.

THE BEGG AMENDMENT

Final enactment of any legislation reflects a bundle of political compromises made during the legislative struggle. While the votes against the 1924 act represent the ardent "liberals" who opposed any immigration restrictions, the yea votes are not an accurate indicator of *core* nativist sentiment in the House of Representatives. A careful reading of the congressional debate suggests that a closely divided vote (198–193) on the amendment offered by Congressman James Begg (R-Ohio) on April 12, 1924, is most relevant to gauge the intensity of antialien feelings by legislators, not only for the voting cleavage indicated on that roll call but also for the kinds of sentiments expressed on the House floor.

Some commentators have mistaken this provision of the law as strengthening the administrative power of the government.[20] Its legislative history, however, suggests the contrary—that "liberals" of that day included this proviso to assist aliens living in the United States in their fight against deportation. Whereas *all* the voting representatives from thirty-five states supported final enactment of the 1924 act, a vote against the Begg Amendment by 100 percent of a delegation occurred only in fifteen states. There were 122 more representatives who voted "liberal" on the Begg Amendment but who nonetheless favored the immigration quotas of the 1924 act.

The original version of section 23 of the 1924 act read as follows: "In any proceeding under the immigration laws the burden of proving the right of any individual to enter or remain in the United States shall, as between him and the United States, be upon such individual."[21] On the floor a committee amendment changed *individual* to *alien*, and then Congressman Begg offered his amendment as a substitute:

> Whenever any alien attempts to *enter* the United States the burden of proof shall be upon such alien to establish that he is not subject to exclusion under any provision of the immigration laws; and in any deportation proceeding against any alien the burden of proof shall be upon such alien to show that he entered the United States lawfully, and the time, place, and manner of such entry into the United States, but in presenting such proof he shall be entitled to the production of his immigration certificate, if any, or other documents concerning such entry in the custody of the Department of Labor. [emphasis added]

Begg said the bill was not intended to deal with people now in the country but to regulate the flow of new immigrants, and he added that the original wording of section 23 "is contrary to the practice and the basic principles of the United States in guaranteeing everybody, when accused of any crime, the right of a supposition of innocence until they are proven guilty." At that time, like the present day, however, processing immigration claims was not considered to be a criminal matter requiring due process, as Congressman John F. Miller (R-Wash.), who would vote against the Begg Amendment, put it: "It is not the guilt or innocence, it is the right of a man to remain in this country. To your question I will say yes; it is right [to place the burden of proof on the alien]." Begg rejoined that "the man's presence in the United States is all the evidence that is required to-day to be conclusive proof that he is entitled to be here unless the Government of the United States can show that he is an alien smuggled into this country."

Then the key sponsor of the 1924 act, Albert Johnson, announced that the Immigration Committee, which he chaired, would agree to the substitute amendment: "When I find a provision being challenged from a constitutional standpoint, and from the viewpoint that as written it may be dangerous, I am willing to take a more modified provision in the hope that we are playing fair with all hands."

To undercut the argument about presumption of innocence, Walter Newton (R-Minn.), who opposed the Begg Amendment, referred to precedent from earlier laws aimed at Orientals. He explained "that there is now a provision in the Chinese exclusion act making it incumbent upon the Chinaman in any proceedings under the act to establish his right to remain here. The United States courts have held that provision to be valid." At that point Congressman Ogden Livingston Mills (R-N.Y.), who supported the amendment, expressed his concern that if "the [immigration] commissioner decides in favor of deportation, all that the courts will do is to review the case to see whether the man has had a fair hearing, and will not go into the question of the guilt or innocence; in other words, the courts leave much to the discretion of the commissioner." He added, "Now before you commit a grave injustice, before you open wide the door of opportunity for possible injustice to thousands of individuals who may be subject to deportation owing to personal enmity or personal suspicion or unjust charges, I submit that at least a conclusive case should be presented to this

House showing the need for a reversal of what we have always considered the basic principle of justice in this country, that each man is presumed to be not guilty but innocent until it is shown to the contrary."

Then Congressman John Edward Raker (D-Calif.), another opponent, recalled that the "Supreme Court of the United States within the last month, affirming the Chinese act, has held that it is not unconstitutional." He proceeded to read a section from that law, which provided that "any Chinese person or person of Chinese descent arrested under the provisions of this act, or the acts hereby extended, shall be adjudged to be unlawfully within the United States unless such person shall establish, by affirmative proof to the satisfaction of such justice, judge, or commissioner, his lawful right to remain in the United States." Raker's understanding of the law was that "deportation is not a criminal proceeding; it is a civil proceeding, and therefore the law relative to charging one with crime never applies in a deportation proceeding."

The congressman was making reference to the Chinese Exclusion Act of 1882, amended in 1884 and 1888. One of the 1884 amendments required "all such permanent residents to acquire a 'reentry certificate'—that period's version of a green card—before traveling to China if they planned on re-entering the United States."[22] The 1884 amendment, known as the Scott Act, banned the return to the United States of any Chinese person who had gone back to China. It was this provision that gave rise to the Supreme Court case referred to by the opponents of the Begg Amendment, *Chae Chan Ping v. United States*.[23]

Ping was a Chinese laborer who had lived in San Francisco for twelve years. He returned to China, with the required reentry certificate in his possession, but was prevented from returning to the United States. Ping was blocked pursuant to the 1884 Scott Act, and he sued, but the high court upheld the Scott Act in a majority opinion that held that the "highest duty of every nation [is] to preserve its independence . . . whether from the foreign nation acting in its national character or from the vast hordes of its people crowding in upon us."[24]

The Begg Amendment applied only to aliens seeking to enter the United States, but Congressman Raker wished to retain the "burden of proof" requirement for those aliens who already resided in the country, noting that "testimony before the committee shows and the Secretary of Labor has said that within the last year alone over 300,000 men had entered the United States unlawfully."[25] If, he continued, you begin deportation proceedings against such a person, an alien could not refuse to respond, because "under this provision he would have to testify. And why? He was in the United States, and you can get the record of every port of entry in the United States, and then if he has overcome the burden of proof he is entitled to remain."

NATIVIST SENTIMENT

Nativist sentiment was expressed during the debate on the Begg Amendment, when Congressman John Robsion (R-Ky.) requested unanimous consent "to correct the gentleman from New York," Fiorello La Guardia (R), who, Robsion said, "utter[ed] the vicious, contemptible slander against the mountain people of Kentucky" by stating "directly and by insinuation that we had no schools in the highlands of Kentucky, the people were on starvation, aliens could not learn or see any examples of law and order, and they would not have opportunity to learn much of our American institutions or Americanism."

First Robsion declared: "All of our working people are 100 per cent American and they stand as a unit for this, the Johnson bill. They know that unless the hordes of immigrants are checked and America ceases to be the 'garbage can and dumping ground for the world' their wages will be reduced and living standards greatly lowered." On temperance, he continued: "While Kentucky and the mountains of Kentucky are strengthening the eighteenth amendment and other laws, we find the great State of New York repealing its law-enforcement code. . . . It was voted out in every county of my district more than 20 years ago, and I doubt if as many—and I am sure that no more—teetotal abstainers can be found in any section of the country. There is about as much difference in my district and the gentleman's district from New York City, according to my information, as there is between the Sahara Desert and the Atlantic Ocean."

Concerning crime, Robsion said that "in practically every instance" murders for robbery are "committed by some one who has come to us from other sections. We do not have any 'black-hand' organizations. You can not hire a man killed for a few paltry dollars. We have no Tong wars. We have no buildings blown up with dynamite and innocent lives taken." Obviously implying that much violence occurred in the Empire State, Robsion concluded: "It is a joke for the gentleman from New York City to speak disparingly [*sic*] as to any part of our country."

The congressman from Kentucky then turned to immigration: "It has been said that the hope of the perpetuity of our institutions lies south of Mason and Dixon's line, where we have the pure strain of the Anglo-Saxon stock; and if this be true, the backbone of this hope is in the highlands of West Virginia, Virginia, Kentucky, Tennessee, Georgia, North Carolina, and South Carolina. Here lives the purest strain of Anglo-Saxon blood." Robsion ended his diatribe by saying that "the gentleman says an alien could not learn Americanism in the mountains of Kentucky. There is nothing but Americanism in the mountains. In the great city of New York groups of foreigners in recent years marched under the red flag of anarchy. There is no room in the mountains of Kentucky for the red flag. We know there but one country, one loyalty, and one flag." After La Guardia was repeatedly denied his request for unanimous consent to respond, the debate returned to the Begg Amendment.

Robsion's invective against La Guardia, who would later become mayor of New York City and so thoroughly personified the urban, ethnic, and hyphenated American, succinctly captured the essence of nativist thinking—that personal vices and social pathologies had resulted from unrestricted immigration from abroad. Ten years earlier the first federal law to regulate narcotics use was targeted at immigrants, particularly the Chinese, and by 1924 the view that southern and eastern Europeans came from inferior stock gained pseudo-scientific credibility from research alleging that Southern Europeans had higher rates of insanity, crime, disease, and "social inadequacy" generally, as compared to people from Northern European countries.[26]

VOTING ON THE BEGG AMENDMENT

The Begg Amendment, though it would appear, prima facie, to be a repressive aspect of the 1924 National Origins Act, was actually

a "liberal" provision, insofar as it weakened the original committee version by applying only to aliens seeking to enter the United
States, not those already in the country. This would explain why,
when House Resolution 7995 was reported by the Committee of
the Whole for a House vote, La Guardia cast his vote to support
the Begg Amendment, despite his later vote against the 1924 act.
So the 193 representatives who voted against the Begg Amendment reflected hard-core opposition to aliens, even those who then
resided in the United States.

Analysis of voting on the Begg Amendment shows the decisive impact of regional origin (see table 3.1). At first glance the
outcome looks like a party vote, since three-fourths of Republicans
favored the amendment and three-fourths of Democrats opposed
it. But the obvious masks the significant impact of regional forces.
Whereas 76 percent of Republicans and 47 percent of northern
Democrats voted for the Begg Amendment, 99 percent of southern
Democrats opposed it.

Nonvoting representatives also tended to be clustered in the
same states that provided most of the yes votes.[27] (By contrast,
there were only seven nonvoting House members from twelve
southern states.) That the majority of representatives who cast yes
votes or abstained on the Begg Amendment represented northeastern and midwestern states suggests that they may have been under
pressure from foreign-born constituents when forced to deal with
this volatile issue.

Of representatives who voted on the amendment, all members from Arkansas, Florida, Georgia, Louisiana, Mississippi,
North Carolina, South Carolina, Texas, and Virginia voted against
it, as did nine of ten from Alabama and all but two (the only two
Republicans) from Tennessee. During the period 1981–90, of the
Deep and Border South states, all except Texas and Louisiana approved official English language laws.

PARALLELS IN TIME

To evaluate whether any linkage exists between the 1920s nativism and the 1980s pattern of official English law adoptions, I
performed a statistical analysis using logistical regression (see Ap-

pendix C, table C.1). This technique differentiates between the states that have and have not enacted English Only laws. For that purpose, fifteen states with laws were coded "1," and thirty-one others were coded "0," as the dependent variable. Because Alaska and Hawaii did not exist as states in 1924 and since the Nebraska and Illinois (and also Hawaii) enactments reflected the ethnic politics of a different era, these four states were excluded from this examination. I derived regression models using various combinations of eight socioeconomic and political variables to assess the racial, ethnic, class, political, and cultural (or nativist) hypotheses:

1. SPANISH: Percentage of Spanish-speaking residents in 1980 (racist)
2. BLACK: Percentage of black residents in 1980 (ethnic)
3. INCOME: Median family income in 1979 (class)
4. COLLEGE: Percentage of residents aged twenty-five and over with a college education in 1980 (class)
5. POVERTY: Percentage of families below the federal poverty line in 1979 (class)
6. REAGAN: Percentage of the two-party vote for Reagan in 1984 (political)
7. POPULATION: Total state population in 1980 in units of 10,000 (cultural)
8. RURAL: Percentage of residents in towns under 2,500 population in 1980 (cultural)

I used these variables to analyze referenda voting in the five states, legislative behavior by political elites, and public opinion as manifested in survey data. From these generally comparable statistical analyses, I sought to determine whether the same political forces underlie the pattern of enactments among the states as have influenced the political and legislative processes within the states.

To validate each hypothesis, I anticipated that each variable would have a specific relationship to the pattern of official English adoptions among the states:

Hypothesis 1 (racist): Support for official English laws will be greater in states with larger percentages of Spanish-speaking people.

Hypothesis 2 (ethnic): Support for official English laws will be greater in states with higher percentages of black residents.

Hypothesis 3 (class): Support for official English laws will be greater in states with larger percentages of people below the poverty line, generally lower median family incomes, and smaller percentages of people who completed a college education.

Hypothesis 4 (political): Support for official English laws will be greater in states where larger percentages of votes were cast for Ronald Reagan in 1984.

Hypothesis 5 (cultural): Support for official English laws will be greater in states with higher percentages of people in rural areas but smaller total populations.

The results of the baseline eight-variable logistical regression model (Appendix C, table C.1) indicate that only the variable COLLEGE is statistically significant at the .05 level, and its negative sign means that states with lower percentages of college-educated residents tended to adopt official English laws during the 1980s.[28] Thus, the effect of COLLEGE corroborates the reverse class hypothesis.

To evaluate a historical linkage, I derived a new variable (HR1924) based on the records of votes on the 1924 National Origins Act. It is the percentage of the voting members of each state delegation in the 1924 House of Representatives who *opposed* the Begg Amendment. A further hypothesis is therefore needed:

Hypothesis 6 (cultural): Support for official English laws will be greater in states whose delegations in the House of Representatives in 1924 voted against the Begg Amendment to the National Origins Act.

I evaluated the impact of HR1924 in a reduced five-variable model, along with the four other variables having the most theoretical significance for this study: SPANISH, BLACK, COLLEGE, and REAGAN (see Appendix C, table C.1).

While the results again show that only COLLEGE reaches the .05 significance level, HR1924 comes closer (its value being

.09) than the other variables in meeting that threshold, suggesting that it would be a significant predictor in a final two-variable logistical regression model (Appendix C, table C.1).[29] The results of that model point to especially COLLEGE but also to HR1924 as statistically significant predictors in a model that is equally as effective as the prior five-variable and eight-variable models in the reduction of error achieved.

This statistical analysis therefore gives some credence to the historical hypothesis. Just as the most intense opposition to aliens during the debates over the National Origins Act of 1924 came from southern congressmen, so the opposition to "new" immigrants has been reflected most fully by southern legislatures. Today, as before, the South has not experienced a mass influx of foreign-born immigrants. So the historic legacy of nativism coupled with relatively few educated elites may partly explain why many southern states passed official English language laws from 1981 to 1990.

Case studies of the legislative enactments by this large group of states, which I will explore in chapter 7, provide indirect evidence that cultural influences may have played a role in the South and the Midwest simply because the alternative hypotheses, specifically racism and partisan politics, can be rejected for the most part. Certainly racism, and likely partisanship, would have a stronger bearing on English Only in the subset of states with sizable concentrations of Spanish speakers as well as two-party competition (both being absent at the local level of southern society). Analysis of those questions begins in chapter 4, which is devoted to the policy process in Florida and California.

4

REFERENDUM POLITICS: THE BEGINNINGS OF AGITATION IN FLORIDA AND CALIFORNIA

The beginnings of the recent controversy over official English can be traced to issues of local concern in Florida, California, and Virginia. In 1980 proponents succeeded in gaining voter approval for the first countywide English Only law in Dade County, Florida. At about the same time, agitation in San Francisco over the use of bilingual ballots in elections resulted in an advisory referendum that called for a halt to the practice. The Virginia episode, which concerned federal bilingual education mandates, is discussed in chapter 7.

In Florida and California, local skirmishes gave rise to grass-roots movements to codify English as the official language of the states, and that was achieved in both cases by referenda. Since this pattern of enactment is atypical in the group of states with official English laws, it raises some important research questions. Were bills considered in the state legislatures of the two states, and if so, why and by whom were they defeated? Was partisanship a factor, and did the scope of conflict over English Only affect a wide or a narrow range of interests in the states? What arguments were exploited by each side in the public debate, and did the popular press take a stand on the issue?

FLORIDA

Miami seemed destined to become the field of a battle between the English Only and English Plus forces. It was a city, writes Max Castro, in which "the Hispanic population grew from a small minority in the 1960s (5.3 percent in 1960) to a significant community (23.6 percent in 1970), overtaking the black American population (15 percent in 1970) to become the largest minority in the city." According to Joanne Bretzer, by the mid-1980s within the metropolitan area Hispanics gained control of "six mayoral seats, ten of twenty-eight positions on the state legislative delegation, and city commission majorities in Miami, Hialeah, West Miami, and Sweetwater," in addition to winning two congressional seats in south Florida.[1]

Beyond the force of numbers and political influence, the change from an Anglo-dominated town was sudden and far-reaching. The ethnic succession, says Castro, "was especially radical because it represented a sharp break with Miami's previous history." Moreover, "what made the newcomers to Miami a special challenge to the natives was not merely (or basically) the power of numbers. Unique among Latin American immigrant groups . . . Hispanics in Miami (and particularly Cubans) were establishing not only a surpassing demographic and cultural presence, but also a strong economic base."[2]

Anglos were acutely aware that things were changing fast. Not only did Miami create the first bilingual public school program in 1963, but in 1976 the *Miami Herald* became the only major U.S. newspaper to publish a daily edition in Spanish (*El Heraldo*). In everyday life, as Joan Didion observes, Latinos sustained their identity by speaking their native tongue:

> The sound of spoken Spanish was common in Miami, but it was also common in Los Angeles, and Houston and in the industrial cities of the northeast. The difference was that in the other cities, Spanish was the language spoken by people who worked in the car wash and came to trim the trees and cleared the tables in restaurants. In Miami, Spanish was spoken by the people who ate in the restaurants, the people

who owned the cars and trees, which made, on the socioaudi-
tory scale, a considerable difference. . . . What was so unusual
about Spanish in Miami was not that it was so often spoken,
but that it was so often heard.[3]

In 1973 the Metro–Dade County Board of County Commissioners passed a declaration that Dade County was bilingual and
bicultural and created an Office of Latin Affairs, though no Hispanics were members of the board. In designating Spanish as the
second official language, the board's resolution took note of the
fact that "a large and growing percentage of Dade County is of
Spanish origin . . . many of whom have retained the culture and
language of their native lands, [and therefore] encounter special
difficulties communicating with governmental agencies and
officials." The resolution continued, "Our Spanish-speaking population has earned, through its ever increasing share of the tax
burden, and active participation in community affairs, the right to
be serviced and heard at all levels of government."[4]

The situation was ripe for some kind of backlash, but what
precipitated the reaction was public concern about the crime wave
and rioting that resulted after criminals and asylum inmates
released by Fidel Castro in the 1980 Mariel boat-lift began
arriving in Miami. The new influx of Cubans as well as increased
Haitian immigration to south Florida led to the formation of the
group Citizens of Dade United. When the Metro-Dade commissioners refused to rescind the 1973 resolution on biculturalism,
this organization collected more than enough names for a ballot
initiative.

The groundswell of opposition to the 1973 ordinance arose
virtually overnight during the summer of 1980, as a *Miami Herald*
reporter described:

> Marion Plunske heard Emmy Shafer on a WNWS radio talk
> show on July 8. The two women started their campaign the
> next day and the Citizens of Dade United registered as a po-
> litical action group on July 21. From the start the campaign
> seemed to run itself.
>
> In just over four weeks the groups gathered 44,166 sig-
> natures, nearly twice as many as they needed to put the

ordinance on the ballot. Exulting in their strength, they brought another 25,767 signatures to the supervisor of elections on Sept. 16.

"It was like giving gold away," Shafer said in late October. On one day alone she received over 300 phone calls from people who wanted to sign the antibilingualism petition.[5]

On November 4, 1980, Dade County voters passed Ordinance 80-128 by a 59.2–40.8 percent margin. Analysis by the *Miami Herald* determined that 71 percent of non-Hispanic whites favored the proposal, whereas 56 percent of blacks and 85 percent of Hispanics opposed it. "Little else beside ethnic group—not age, not sex, nor education, nor choice of presidential candidate made much difference in how people voted on the ordinance." Fifty-four percent of Reagan voters and 52 percent of Carter voters stood together in supporting the referendum. Among the whites who voted for it, a majority indicated they would be pleased if the referendum "would make Miami a less attractive place for Cubans and other Spanish-speaking people," and more than three-quarters said they would leave Dade County "if it were practical."[6]

The ordinance was opposed by the *Miami Herald*, and "the Greater Miami Chamber of Commerce, a key element of the white Anglo elite, spent $50,000 in opposition. In contrast, the antibilingual forces spent less than $10,000 in their successful campaign." At base, while the vote in favor was sizable, "the antibilingual movement, both in terms of leadership and electoral support, was almost exclusively a creature of one ethnic sector of a triethnic community: whites of other than Hispanic descent, who voted in favor of the proposal in massive numbers."[7]

The key provisions of Ordinance 80-128 follow:

Section 1. The expenditure of county funds for the purpose of utilizing any language other than English, or promoting any culture other than that of the United States, is prohibited.

Section 2. All county governmental meetings, hearings, and publications shall be in the English language only.

Section 3. The provisions of this ordinance shall not apply where a translation is mandated by state or federal law.

Section 4. If any section, subsection, sentence, clause, phrase, words or provision of this ordinance is held invalid or unconstitutional, the remainder of this ordinance shall not be affected by said holding.[8]

In addition to barring the use of public funds to support bilingualism, the ordinance stipulated that all public meetings and documents had to be in English, which meant that no Spanish, Yiddish, Creole, or French translations of information about bus routes, job openings, or recreational opportunities could be provided to the Hispanic, Jewish, Haitian, or French Canadian residents. While 911 emergency services were not affected, signs throughout Dade County (including those at the local zoo) were posted only in English, the county stopped allocating money for the annual Spanish Heritage Week celebration, and advertisements to lure Latin American tourists had to be printed in English even though they appeared in Central and South American newspapers.[9]

Beginnings of Conflict

In 1984 Metro-Dade commissioner Jorge Valdes, a Cuban and the only Hispanic on the county board, got the ordinance amended to allow translations for tourism promotion, emergencies, and public services to the elderly, handicapped, or ill, and he also included a section declaring English to be the official language in Dade County. But Valdes always favored repeal of the measure for symbolic reasons. "What we have left is a piece of paper that says we are anti-bilingual and anti-bicultural," he said. "Basically, what this ordinance does is hurt the feelings of a large segment of the population. All I want to do is say Dade won't be pro-bilingual or anti-bilingual."[10]

The controversy over official English began in earnest in 1987, when Commissioner Valdes announced that he would propose the repeal of the 1980 English Only ordinance. What prompted this reconsideration was a June 11 zoning meeting in which Manuel Vega, a flower peddler who had been operating illegally, was badly treated. Though Vega appeared before the commission to ask for permission to operate, he could not speak English, and because of the ordinance Dade County could not hire full-time interpreters. The attempted translation by zoning director Rafael Rodon was uneven, and Vega was unable to answer adequately the complaints raised by local residents. In the end the commissioners voted 6–1 against his request.[11]

Since five of the nine Metro-Dade commissioners faced re-election in September 1988, none relished tackling this issue. Those opposing repeal of the ordinance promised retribution. "If they repeal it, we are going to get another anti-bilingual ordinance on the ballot, and if Jorge doesn't like the 1980 ordinance, he is sure not going to like the 1988 ordinance, I can guarantee him that," declared Terry Robbins, head of Dade Americans United to Protect the English Language. "It's as though native Americans don't exist in Dade County," she said. "It's as though the Cuban people of this community are the only ones who contribute to the health and welfare, they're the only ones who have problems, they are the only ones who should be taken care of. Well, we are mad as hell. We're not going to take it any more. This is still the United States of America."[12]

Emmy Shafer, president of Citizens of Dade United during the 1980 referendum drive, wrote a letter on June 16, 1988, to the political leadership: "I am hereby notifying each of you commissioners and mayor that we will absolutely not stand for any repeal of the anti-bilingual ordinance that 60 percent of Dade County's voters voted for in 1980. Anyone on the commission advocating a repeal will go down in defeat along with Commissioner Valdes."[13] After a barrage of telephone calls against repeal, leaders of the Hispanic community, including members of the Latin Chamber of Commerce, persuaded Valdes to drop his plan.

Legislative Inaction

Advocates of English Only measures had to resort to popular initiative because previous attempts in the state legislature had died quick political deaths. The four bills of 1981 and 1982 were identical, and their one-sentence preambles declared: "The Legislature recognizes that commonality of language should be a thread binding a state and nation together, and wishes to prevent polarization of our citizens into different cultural and ethnic subsections or entities which would interfere with this concept of unity."[14] These bills were more restrictive than any of the measures enacted by the eighteen states, arguably even more so than the controversial Arizona referendum. Besides codifying English, they would have repealed the 1973 Dade County bilingual and bicultural ordinance. The official summary provided to assist the lawmakers said that such a bill

> Provides that English shall be the official language of the state and that all official publications and contracts shall be in English. Requires that all official county and municipal publications, contracts, and governmental activities be in English and specifies that no county or municipality shall be declared officially bilingual or bicultural.
>
> Provides that all public signs and directions, legal notices, public records and meetings, and traffic signs shall be in English.
>
> Requires that all examinations for licensure for professions regulated by the Department of Professional Regulation be in English and deletes provision for examination of certain immigrants in their native tongue.[15]

In 1981 state senator Joe Carlucci (D-Jacksonville) sponsored Senate Bill 389, and state representative Robert O. Melby (R–St. Petersburg) authored House Bill 275. Action on the Carlucci bill was indefinitely postponed by the Governmental Operations, Economic, Community and Consumer Affairs Committee; in the House, the same fate awaited the Melby bill in the Governmental Operations Committee.[16]

The next year Melby filed House Bill 347. Referred to the Governmental Operations Committee and also the Appropriations Committee, it eventually arrived on the House calendar, where it died. The companion measure, Senate Bill 675, was sponsored by Senator Thomas F. Lewis (R–North Palm Beach). His bill, first sent to the same committee that buried the 1981 measure, was re-referred to the Rules and Calendar Committee, but that committee took no action.[17]

Then in 1985, five representatives co-sponsored House Bill 183 and House Joint Resolution 184: Grover C. Robinson (D-Pensacola), Everett A. Kelly (D-Astatula), Charles R. Smith

(D- Brooksville), Sam Mitchell (D-Vernon), and John W. Lewis (D-Jacksonville). Available evidence indicates that both measures were simply declarations that English should be Florida's official language.[18] House Bill 183 was referred to the Judiciary Committee, where the Subcommittee on Court Systems and Miscellaneous reported negatively, and the bill died in the full committee. That committee also received House Joint Resolution 184, and the same subcommittee temporarily postponed consideration.[19]

Finally, in 1986 Representatives Robinson, Smith, John Lewis, and Mitchell joined forces, along with Alfred J. Lawson Jr. (D-Tallahassee), to co-sponsor House Bill 277. This bill, similar to what ultimately would be enacted by referendum, comprised two statements: "The English language shall be the official language of Florida" and "The Legislature shall enforce the provisions of this section by appropriate general law." This purely symbolic gesture gained a favorable report from the Judicial Committee but then died on the House calendar. It had progressed further through the legislative process than had any previous measure.[20]

During 1981–86 the ratio of Democrats to Republicans averaged 29:11 in the 40-member senate and 79:41 in the 120-member House. The fact that no bill was introduced in the 1987 session likely indicates that the proponents of official English had given up hope of getting positive action from the legislature. But Democratic control was not a barrier to enacting official English legislation, because only one of the nine sponsors of such measures was a Republican. It is noteworthy that none of those Democrats (nor Republican senator Thomas Lewis) were elected from Dade County. Indeed, most came from the northern reaches of the state, which had smaller populations of Spanish speakers. Two legislators were from Jacksonville, and those who represented Pensacola and Vernon had districts in the northwestern panhandle. So the legislative majority blocked consideration of these bills that originated with its own partisans.

Florida English Campaign

The statewide official English campaign got a boost in March 1987, when the organization Florida English opened an office in Tampa and hired one employee. "We're in a new era right now," said activist Patricia Fulton. "We're taking this issue to the people. It needs to be settled, on the books." In a later interview, Fulton recalled, "The Legislature put the language issue in a drawer. They didn't want to deal with it." She said, "If you won't do it, we'll do it."[21]

The reaction from Hispanics was predictable. "They want to legislate the language we should speak, and that's a violation of our First Amendment rights," said Alan Alvarez, a staffer with the Spanish-American League against Discrimination. "Having an official language is like having an official religion, an official God, or an official color of hair." The executive director of Florida English felt otherwise: "We really have a problem when we have entire communities of adults who can't speak to each other," said Tom Kirby. "It's common sense. If English is the common language of this country, then we can't really participate in society without knowing English."[22]

According to Patricia Fulton, residents saw a "threat" in the growing numbers of Spanish people. "We get letters from people in South Florida who are frustrated, who feel like they're in a foreign city," she said. "It's like, whoops, I just stepped off into South America. You stop a person on the street in a Hispanic neighborhood to ask for direction and they won't speak English. It's unsettling." That view was not idiosyncratic; one survey found that 67 percent of Floridians believed that U.S. immigration policy should be tougher.[23]

The Florida English Campaign did not establish a close relationship with Dade Americans United to Protect the English Language, since Terry Robbins, who chaired the latter group, generated some controversy when she asked the Community Relations Board to sponsor a public forum, saying it was time for a "bloodletting" on the issue, though she did apologize for using that term.[24]

In September 1987 the results of a statewide poll by U.S. English were reported, showing that 86 percent of Floridians supported the group's position. The Washington-based polling firm of Hamilton, Frederick and Schneiders asked respondents: "It has been proposed that Florida adopt an amendment to the state constitution to make English the official language of Florida. Do you strongly favor, somewhat favor, somewhat oppose, or strongly oppose this?" Only 10 percent were opposed; Hispanics divided 64–36 percent in favor; and residents of Dade and Broward Counties were overwhelmingly supportive (72 percent and 83 percent respectively).[25]

By early 1988 the Florida English Campaign had collected around 200,000 signatures toward its goal of 342,939 (the deadline was August 9), and the opposition went to court. Mark Gallegos, president of the Hispanic National Bar Association, filed a brief with the Florida Supreme Court on behalf of Unidos, a Miami-based coalition of Cuban organizations, to determine whether the ballot language was constitutional.

"It's nothing but divisive. Making English the official language will not resolve the problems they complain about," Gallegos said. "The problem is, they have a hidden agenda," stated Paul Siegel, another lawyer. "It's a symbolic way of saying, 'We don't like hearing all this Spanish spoken in this state.'" Len Kaminsky, who administered the Haitian Refugee Center in Miami, offered a similar assessment: "A lot of racists can convince themselves they're not racist. But it is racist. It's, 'Let's close the border and have America be for Americans.'"[26]

While non-English speakers believed that the measure attacked the new immigrants, Mark LaPorta, a Miami Beach physician who became state chairman of the Florida English Campaign, said that its purpose was "to prevent the second Tower of Babel." He added, "The Florida English Campaign that I chair is not racist, is not xenophobic and is not provincial." In a later interview Dr. LaPorta elaborated: "Since 1980, we're looking at a wave of immigration that has no end in sight. If that's true, there will be pressure not to learn English. The linguistic ghettos can expand. If nothing comes of it now, it could prevent something happening in the future. If the people who were building the Tower of Babel had prayed a little before, maybe God would not have given them all those languages."[27]

But an editorial in the *Tallahassee Democrat* called the initiative "divisive" and "a slap in the face to those who do speak Spanish, or other foreign languages." The writer countered, "Many residents of the United States are arrogant when it comes to languages. They expect English to be spoken in every foreign country they visit, but take no time to learn other languages them-selves."[28]

Florida English used social clubs, senior citizens' groups, and radio talk shows to publicize its movement. The organization added a novel tactic during the primary elections on Super Tuesday in March 1988 by setting up tables outside the polling places to gather signatures. The cause was also helped by rumors about Miami store clerks and city hall employees who could not or would not speak English. "I think those stories from [Dade County] have helped us," observed Eileen Trawinski, Florida English coordinator in Pinellas County. "People say, 'Hey, we don't want this kind of problem.' This is America, and some of the attitudes of people in Dade County have certainly not been American, but very un-American," commented Trawinski. In Martin County, news accounts of up-risings by Cuban inmates in federal detention centers helped Florida English, according to coordinator Cathie Kuhnmuench.[29]

In March 1988 Commissioner Jorge Valdes resurrected his attempt to repeal the Dade County antibilingual ordinance, now with the argument that adoption of the statewide referendum made it unnecessary. Terry Robbins disagreed: "We're going to pack the chamber," she said, and she explained that the constitutional amendment would have no impact unless implementing legislation was enacted. Given the refusal of the state legislature to deal with the issue previously, "we don't know if it's going to be something that's just stuck on the books," declared Robbins.[30]

Countermobilization

By June the Florida English Campaign had amassed 482,116 sig-natures, above the required number, which boded well for the group's position on the referendum. The simple language of the proposition read:

> *The following new Section is added to Article II of the Florida Constitution.*
>
> *Section 9.* English is the Official Language of Florida.
>
>   (a) English is the official language of the state of Florida.
>
>   (b) The Legislature shall have the power to enforce this section by appropriate legislation.[31]

Just five months before election day, the opposition became
mobilized as English Plus, to publicize a counterargument that official English would send a negative message to foreign tourists
and cause economic hardship for the state. "If there are negative
attitudes about residents, what does it say to tourists, to foreign in-
vestors?" asked Sylvia Andrade, the coordinator of central Florida
teachers who were networking with English Plus. English Plus,
which raised fifty thousand dollars during a Spanish radio mara-
thon in mid-July, planned a media blitz to explain the economic
risks should the amendment pass. Lawyer Jon Weber contended
that the vague wording of the measure could end AIDS education
for non-English speakers, stop tourism promotions, prohibit witnesses to crimes from testifying in court except in English, and
create an expensive enforcement bureaucracy. "The amendment
seems like apple pie," Weber explained. "We're going to try to tell
voters to look inside before they bite." For the most part, the opposition consisted of the American Civil Liberties Union, the Greater
Miami Chamber of Commerce, and Greater Miami United (a triethnic community relations coalition), with leadership provided by
English Plus and Speak Up Now for Florida.[32]

The implications for bilingual education were obvious and
never far below the surface of the public debate. Three research
studies of English acquisition by immigrants were publicized by
the *Miami Herald*, including one by the RAND Corporation that
showed that "the transition to English begins almost immediately
and proceeds very rapidly" and that, "contrary to what many believe, the integration process among Mexican immigrants and their
offspring is very similar to that of European immigrants."[33]

Teachers of English to Speakers of Other Languages
(TESOL), with ten thousand members nationwide, opposed official
English on the grounds that it represented a rejection of cultural
pluralism and individual rights. "It's a terrible message to those
who are trying so hard to learn English," said Christine Grosse,
president of Florida TESOL. Florida English, like U.S. English,
supported "transitional" bilingual programs to facilitate English
learning but feared the long-term effects of children using languages other than English. "I can see the advantage of using a
child's native language at first," said Patricia Fulton, state coordinator for U.S. English and director of communications for Florida

English. "What we are concerned about is the use of the foreign language as a political tool, as a guise, as a subterfuge so that the child doesn't really make the transition."[34]

Early in August 1988 the Division of Elections verified that 359,266 signatures had been collected by Florida English, but an administrative error caused some turmoil as the deadline for petitions approached. Signatures equaling 8 percent of the votes cast in the 1984 general election had to be collected in ten of Florida's nineteen congressional districts, but Martin County deputy elections supervisor Carol Hanna had overcounted the number of verified signatures in her county by about 1,300, which left the campaign short in the Twelfth District. A final petition drive got the needed signatures, and 366,555 signatures were verified with only twenty-four hours to spare. But the leader of a recently formed group, Speak Up Now for Florida (SUN), was not admitting defeat. Alfredo Pedroso promised, "We're just going to keep right on rolling."[35]

Other prominent Hispanics, however, foresaw the inevitable and chose not to become embroiled. "We all think it's a losing battle," said banker Raul Masvidal, who refused to head a drive to raise funds to oppose the proposition. "I don't see the practical effects of leaving the ring with a black eye after getting punched around for the next two months." Apparently Masvidal reflected the view of many Hispanics who did not see official English as any threat. "The fact is, they're not going to stop people from speaking Spanish," he said. "The day-to-day life of the average Floridian is not going to change."[36]

In fact, what caused Metro-Dade commissioner Valdes to drop his attempt to repeal the 1980 ordinance was resistance from important Hispanic leaders. When WQBA-AM commentator Fernando Penabaz invited Dr. LaPorta of Florida English on his radio call-in program, no controversy was provoked. "I thought fireworks would fly," Penabaz said. "There was practically no reaction. There's an I-don't-give-a-damn attitude. They feel that since this is a Cuban community, they're going to continue speaking Spanish anyway."[37]

The difficulty of recruiting the Hispanic leadership was underscored by Jon Weber, executive director of English Plus. "It was like talking about the diminution of the ozone layer," he said. "It was just something that didn't seem real to them." Weber, however, also recognized the strategic problem that would result if the opposition was entirely Hispanic. "If this is a Hispanic versus non-Hispanic campaign, we're not going to win," he said. "Our job is getting people to think about the broader issues."[38]

Despite the misgivings of some leading Hispanics, in mid-August a group of six hundred met in Lake Worth to map a statewide strategy against the referendum. SUN publicized the facts that nearly two million foreign tourists had spent more than one billion dollars in Florida the previous year and that the state had exported more than eleven billion dollars' worth of goods, mainly to Venezuela, Colombia, Brazil, and the Dominican Republic. SUN also raised the specter of intrusive governmental powers. Jeffrey Browne, a member of SUN, said that what the referendum backers "really want to do is ban any foreign language in any public forum," and they would even have airport signs in English only.[39]

In September the results of another commissioned poll, announced by Linda Chavez, president of U.S. English, before the Florida Economics Club, were used to discredit the economic counterarguments. Not only did the poll find that 81 percent of those surveyed supported the constitutional amendment but also that 74 percent disagreed that "the proposal is a discriminating attack," 81 percent disagreed that it "would hurt Florida's efforts to stimulate trade and business with Spanish-speaking countries," and 80 percent disagreed that "tourism would be hurt because Spanish-speaking tourists would think they wouldn't be welcome here."[40]

Though the sample underrepresented the target population (80 percent of those surveyed were non-Hispanic whites and 7 percent were Hispanics), Chavez called the amendment "an incredibly popular idea" and brushed off charges of racism, noting that three of the six directors of U.S. English were immigrants. "Clearly, we are not a group of nativist Americans that want to keep America pure," she said. In a later interview Chavez added that although official language laws were "largely symbolic," they would help taxpayers: "In Canada, where the society is a mix of French- and English-speaking people, the government spends $505 million in language programs," she said. "Our country faces potential massive costs if we move to official bilingualism."[41]

The adversaries of official English made the point that the Florida English Campaign had deliberately kept most voters uninformed about the impact of Amendment 11. "Supporters of the amendment are carrying out a silent campaign. They don't want the public to be aware of the ramifications of the proposal," said Vanessa Garcia Serra, director of English Plus. While English Plus alleged that it did not oppose an official language per se, the manner of enforcement "by appropriate legislation" was reason for concern. Garcia Serra wondered: "Will this appropriate legislation take us back to a time when drinking fountains in the park were reserved for whites only? I don't need to tell you the dangers of this."[42]

Not to be outflanked, English Plus also commissioned a statewide poll by Howard M. Burkholz and Associates in July 1988. The survey found that 80 percent of Floridians favored the amendment, just 10 percent were opposed, and support was in the 81–82 percent range for men, women, liberals, and conservatives—the level among moderates was 75 percent—though again non-Hispanic whites (at 85 percent) favored the amendment more than did blacks (at 66 percent) or Hispanics (at 54 percent). The last finding has been disputed on grounds of sample bias, because "the evidence is that the overwhelming majority of Hispanics voted against the amendment."[43]

Just as the poll by the Florida English Campaign disputed the economic arguments by its opponents, so this English Plus survey indicated that 59 percent of Floridians agreed that "bilingual education helps students learn English more quickly." When asked whether "English is being threatened by the state's bilingual services," a plurality of 44 percent disagreed. Max Castro, Margaret Haun, and Ana Roca summarized the poll results: "The symbolic issue of the primacy of English as the nation's language elicits broad and overwhelming support from all demographic sectors except Hispanics. . . . But that support, which should be read largely as an affirmation of English as the nation's language, does not translate into voter support for specific language-restrictionist policies."[44]

The political battle was not an evenly matched contest in numbers or finances. According to state reports, as of September 29, 1988, the Florida English Campaign had spent $122,720 on its crusade as compared with only $53,255 by English Plus.[45] So again the opposition turned to the federal courts. In mid-October a complaint was filed that the petitioners had violated the Voting Rights Act of 1965 by circulating the petitions only in English in seven counties (Dade, Hillsborough, Hardee, Hendry, Collier, Glades, and Monroe) where more than 5 percent of the residents had limited knowledge of English.

U.S. district judge James Kehoe in Miami was asked by four registered voters—two Cubans, one Mexican, and one Puerto Rican—to nullify more than sixty-three thousand names collected in six of the bilingual counties on the grounds that they were denied information about the petition process. The suit against Florida's secretary of state, Jim Smith, was prompted by a court decision in Colorado that invalidated signatures on that state's official language referendum petitions on similar grounds. In Florida, as in Colorado, the defendants argued that the 1965 act applied to elections, not petition drives.[46]

It so happened that the attorney general, Democrat Robert Butterworth, was responsible for defending the secretary of state even though he formally had announced a position against the referendum. Smith also opposed the measure. "I just can't figure out what it's really going to accomplish," he said. "I think English is the official language in this state and I don't know why it needs to be in the constitution." And Florida's most prominent Republican, Governor Bob Martinez, of Cuban ancestry, was not sympathetic either. "We don't select a religion for Americans. We don't select a race for Americans. And we have not selected a language for Americans. If you pass it, the only thing you'll get is hard feelings," he said.[47] In the end Judge Kehoe ruled that a petition drive was a private activity and not covered by the Voting Rights Act.

A *Miami Herald* survey of residents of Dade and Broward Counties in mid-October found that Hispanics and non-Hispanics agreed overwhelmingly that English should be the language of public life but disagreed entirely on Amendment 11. Overall, 75 percent of all registered voters felt that Amendment 11 was necessary, although eight of ten Hispanics over age thirty-five were worried that they might need emergency help and no one would understand them. On the other hand, "young Dade Hispanics use English frequently—a mastery highly valued by their Spanish-speaking elders. In this regard, Dade Hispanics are like previous immigrant groups: The younger generation is fluent in English." While these findings, according to the newspaper, "cut against key theories underpinning Amendment 11," the pollsters did find that widespread use of Spanish was irritating to Anglos. One-half of the English-only speakers said that language was a factor shaping their decisions on where to live and shop.[48]

The *Miami Herald* included daily news coverage of the English question as November 8, election day, approached. On October 31 an article called attention to educators' concerns, not so much about existing bilingual programs as about the psychological impact of the amendment on children. "It would make some kids afraid or ashamed to speak their own language," said Mercedes Toural, supervisor of bilingual programs for Dade County schools. Another article focused on the amendment's "vague agenda" and asked, "What does it *really mean?*" To Chesterfield Smith, the prominent Miami attorney who helped draft the 1967 Florida constitution, its vagueness was dangerous. "Who knows how this thing will be interpreted?" he declared. "It's just garbage. I agree that every American should know English, but I oppose this amendment, because I don't want garbage in the Constitution."[49]

Federal Intervention

A final effort to halt the voting came in a surprise move by the Bush Administration. The Justice Department, in the wake of two adverse decisions by judges in Miami and Denver, requested a ruling by the Eleventh Circuit Court of Appeals in Miami that the petition drive had in fact violated the 1965 Voting Rights Act on the grounds that petitions circulated in six of Florida's seven bilingual counties should have been in Spanish. "For non-English-speaking voters to participate in the electoral process, they need to have petitions in their own language in order to understand what they are being asked to sign," the brief stated. Without bilingual petitions, the process is "fraught with potential for misrepresentation and fraud." But attorney Mark Dienstag, representing the Florida English Campaign, took issue with the action. "We'll just have to strap on the guns and shoot it out," he said. "Their brief doesn't quote from any of the recent decisions." Moreover, he continued, "This is just a matter of the Justice Department quoting the Justice Department. It would've been nice if they had looked up some law."[50]

The three-judge panel voted 2–1 not to block the referendum; appellate judge Peter Fay of Miami, a Ford appointee, and senior district judge Clarence Algood of Birmingham, Alabama, a Carter appointee, were in the majority, and appellate judge R. Lanier Anderson of Macon, Georgia, a Kennedy appointee, dissented. "It is hard to imagine that in passing the act, Congress could have intended that private citizens seeking to further their own political goals through the initiative-petition process be subject to specific language requirements," argued the majority opinion. "Rather, the interests of both the First Amendment and the Voting Rights Act can be harmonized by limiting the latter to those activities involved in casting a vote and not to political speech." The dissent made the contrary argument. Said Judge Anderson: "I am persuaded that the initiative petitions at issue are 'materials or information relating to the electoral process' within the meaning of . . . the Voting Rights Act and that the state of Florida has 'provided' these materials within the meaning of the statute." A year later the U.S. Supreme Court rejected the appeal and, without comment, let stand the ruling of the Eleventh Circuit Court of Appeals.[51]

On November 8, Amendment 11 passed overwhelmingly, with 83.9 percent of the vote statewide, carrying all sixty-seven counties of Florida. The margin was 61.5 percent in Dade County and ranged between 81.3 percent and 90.5 percent in the other six designated bilingual counties: the vote in the bilingual counties of Collier, Glades, Hardee, Hendry, and Monroe Counties was above the statewide percentage; in Hillsborough County it was 81.3 percent. The Florida English Campaign made known its plans to establish a lobbyist in Tallahassee to pressure the state legislature to increase state funding for English instruction, ensure that driver licensing tests were given in English, and review bilingual education programs to make sure that students really learned English.[52]

On the eve of the election, a conciliatory note was struck when a joint statement was issued by Florida English Campaign coordinator Mark LaPorta and Jon Weber, executive director of

SUN. They called for more state money to teach English to immigrants and urged that "laws and regulations should not be used to coerce, punish or encumber the rights of people who do not speak English." Entirely unexpected was their agreement to seek repeal of the Dade County antibilingualism ordinance, which was no longer necessary. News reports described "pandemonium," as backers of Official English tore the microphone away from LaPorta and a man yelled, "You're selling us out!"[53]

What Policy Impact?

In the aftermath of the referendum vote, the Latino community reported a rise in anti-Hispanic incidents across south Florida. "What has happened is that people have taken the law into their own hands and are enforcing it as they see fit," said Osvaldo Soto, president of the Spanish-American League against Discrimination (SALAD). In one highly publicized incident, the manager at a Publix supermarket in Coral Gables suspended a cashier for speaking Spanish on the job. Another involved the Mount Sinai Medical Center in Miami Beach, where the employee handbook required workers to speak English.[54]

News speculation about whether the law would have any policy impact irritated its supporters. "They are beginning to say, 'Nothing will change, it's just symbolic.' That's what gets us angry," charged Terry Robbins, chair of Dade Americans United to Protect the English Language. On the other hand, Steve Workings, governmental affairs director for U.S. English, observed, "It has had very little effect in the other states, but as we have said, it's not likely to change the lives of very many people." And news reports indicated that there was a developing consensus among political elites that the law only required what was already practiced in Florida, namely that all public meetings, records, and official documents use the English language. Apparently a deal was struck between Cuban Republican legislators from Miami and the Democratic leaders of the legislature to block enactment of any enforcement provisions of the new law.[55]

Effective or not, the symbolism of "English Only" remained, and on May 18, 1992, the Dade County Commission voted unanimously to repeal its 1980 English Only ordinance. Six Hispanics, four blacks, and three whites constituted the commission, which had been chosen the previous month in a court-ordered district election, replacing a system of at-large elections that had favored white incumbents. The 1980 ordinance was passed by a commission that was predominantly white at a time when Dade County was only one-third Hispanic; time marched on, though, and the 1990 census reports that 57.4 percent of the county's residents speak a language other than English at home.[56]

So much has Miami society changed that the Spanish-speaking majority has no plans to reestablish an official policy of bilingualism. "I don't need to ask for an ordinance recognizing what is already a reality," remarked Osvaldo Soto, a Cuban-born lawyer and president of SALAD, the primary organization that pushed for repeal of the Dade County antibilingualism measure. He added: "We realize that English is the language of this country, but by the same token we're saying that there are now a million plus people in South Florida who either do not speak English or don't speak it well, and why should we penalize them?"[57]

The new linguistic minority was now the devil's advocate. "These Cubans apparently don't adhere to the principle that in Rome you do as the Romans do," said Enos Schera, vice president of Citizens of Dade United. "They have already established another Cuba inside Dade County, and now they are forcing Spanish down our throats." And Christopher Doss, field director for U.S. English, appeared on radio talk shows to argue that repeal of the 1980 ordinance would make Dade County a Spanish-speaking "enclave within the United States, an apartheid enclave for Cubano culture and language, like Transkei in South Africa." Moreover, he continued, "if we allow this version of apartheid to be used as a model for multiculturalism in Florida, we certainly will see that model replicated in other parts of the country."[58] At the time of this writing, backers of official English are threatening to take the issue to court.

CALIFORNIA

Legislative efforts to codify the English language in California date from the late 1970s, but none were successful. Unlike the case in Florida, in California it is readily apparent that Republicans were the prime movers behind the official English bills but were obstructed by their minority status in both chambers of the state legislature (table 4.1).

From 1979 through 1986, the ratio of Democrats to Republicans averaged 24:16 in the forty-member senate and 49:31 in the eighty-member House, so the political obstacles to gaining enactment of English Only legislation were formidable.

In 1979–80, Assembly Constitutional Amendment 5, sponsored by Dave Stirling (R-Whittier), would have added a section to the state constitution stating that "the English language shall constitute the official language of this state."[59] It died in committee.

In the next session, sixteen Republicans from both houses were joined by Senator Rose Ann Vuich (D-Fresno) to co-author Senate Joint Resolution 21, urging the federal government to establish English as the official language of the United States. The Senate Rules Committee voted 3–0 to report the measure without recommendation to the floor, where it passed on a 22–7 roll-call vote. All seven no votes were cast by Democrats, but eight Democrats joined fourteen Republicans to favor a watered-down version. (All but three GOP senators voted yes, whereas seven other Democrats abstained, with one seat vacant.) But ultimately this measure also died in a standing committee of the Assembly.

Table 4.1   Party Affiliation of Sponsors of Official English Bills in California

Session	Bill	Assembly Members		Senators	
		R	D	R	D
1979–80	A.C.A. 5	1			
1981–82	S.J.R. 21	8		8	1
1983–84	S.J.R. 7			1	
1985–86	A.B. 201	20	2	3	1
	A.C.A. 30	1			

Sources: California Legislature: 1979-80 regular session, *Assembly Final History*, pp. 5, 1960; 1981–82 regular session, *Senate Final History*, pp. 4–5; at Sacramento: 1983–84 regular session, *Senate Final History*, pp. 1493; 1985–86 regular session, *Assembly Final History*, pp. 4–5 and *Senate Final History*, p. 1958.

Much of the original wording of Senate Joint Resolution 21, which was eliminated by its chief sponsor, Senator Ollie Speraw (R–Los Angeles), would later surface in the language of the official English referendum of 1986. What Senate Joint Resolution 21 had contained was a simple declaratory statement to be transmitted to the president and vice president, the Speaker of the House of Representatives, and all U.S. senators and representatives from California:

> WHEREAS, A Constitutional Amendment has been proposed in the United States Senate to designate English as the official language of the United States; and
>
> WHEREAS, The English language has traditionally been the means of communicating and sharing ideas among our country's diverse cultural groups; now, therefore, be it
>
> Resolved by the Senate and Assembly of the State of California, jointly, That the Legislature of the State of California urges the United States Senate and House of Representatives to support an appropriate Constitutional Amendment which should include, but need not be limited to, a clear declaration that the English language shall be the official language of the United States.[60]

The Bilingual Ballots Issue

What successfully fueled the English Only movement in California was a battle that erupted during 1983 in San Francisco over the use of trilingual ballots (Chinese, Spanish, English). A federal lawsuit based on the 1975 amendments to the 1965 Voting Rights Act (section 4[f][1]) led to a 1980 "consent degree" by which the registrar of voters agreed to furnish trilingual ballots, voter pamphlets, and poll watchers and to conduct a voter registration drive for Spanish and Chinese citizens who did not speak English. The incumbent registrar of voters, however, had to be removed amid charges of racism before the implementation process could begin.[61]

Controversy began when San Francisco supervisor Quentin Kopp, a conservative Democrat from a white, upper-middle-class district, proposed that notices be inserted in Chinese and Spanish in voters' handbooks urging voters to learn English and explaining how to get English lessons. In March the Board of Supervisors approved Kopp's plan but then sent the measure back to committee after lobbying by Henry Der, leader of the organization Chinese for Affirmative Action. But Kopp, who chaired a group called the Committee for Ballots in English, announced that a drive would begin to collect signatures to put an advisory question on the ballot. Kathryn Woolard reported, "The recently established U.S. English organization quickly joined forces with Kopp. Working primarily at shopping centers in White, middle class areas, the organization garnered 14,400 signatures in less than a month. The Registrar of Voters certified the validity of 12,400 of these signatures, well above the 9,679 needed to place the measure on the ballot."[62]

Kopp's referendum would request the federal government to change the law so that cities would not have to provide election information in any language except English. "There is no way for our new citizens to move into the political, social and economic mainstream in our society without proficiency in English," said Kopp. "What good is served by translating election materials into a foreign language if the person is unable to comprehend the discussion of issues and candidates taking place in English?" To that, Der retorted: "We would all like not to have bilingual ballots. But until English learning opportunities are adequate, non-English speaking citizens should not be punished for not knowing English perfectly."[63]

The San Francisco Democratic Central Committee endorsed bilingual elections and cited the 1848 Treaty of Guadalupe Hidalgo, which ended the Mexican War, as requiring the United States to recognize language rights of Spanish speakers in territories gotten from Mexico.[64] Guy Wright, columnist for the *San Francisco Chronicle*, whose articles regularly opposed bilingual ballots, took issue with that view, calling it "an old myth that refuses to die." He later stated that "the Hispanic chip-on-the-shoulder toward English and the Anglo culture goes back at least to the Mexican War. A mythical rationale has evolved for making Spanish an official language of the United States, starting with a claim that the treaty ending that war guaranteed the right to vote in

Spanish. That is totally untrue. Further, there were only 75,000 Mexicans in the territory Mexico ceded."[65]

Kopp was opposed by many of his partisans, including Mayor Dianne Feinstein, virtually all other city supervisors, "all the Democratic clubs, including the Gay and Black organizations, and the powerful speaker of the California Assembly, Black politician Willie Brown." A statement from Joaquin Avila, president of the Mexican American Legal Defense and Education Fund (MALDEF), called voting for Proposition O "a vote to disenfranchise an important sector of the Hispanic community. Studies show that bilingual ballots are mostly used by the Hispanic poor, elderly and under-educated. These citizens may not have the opportunity and time to better their English, but they too have a right to vote."[66]

On November 8, election day, Proposition O won 62 percent of the vote. It carried high-income areas of the city and particularly the "West of Twin Peaks" neighborhood represented by Kopp. It was "rejected in the Chinese areas and the Latino area of the Mission, although by a remarkably narrow margin. But only in one other identifiable neighborhood, Haight-Ashbury, then still the home of many new-left radicals, was there a clear-cut rejection of Prop 'O' (61%)." More surprising, the referendum carried "normally progressive neighborhoods such as Eureka Valley and Potrero Hill. Election analysts calculated that gay as well as Black areas of the city failed to take a stance against 'O,' with 51% of those voters supporting the measure."[67]

San Francisco's enactment of Proposition O reinvigorated the efforts to get statewide action by the legislature. In 1983–84, the only Official English bill introduced in the regular session was Senate Joint Resolution 7 by Senator Speraw, essentially an abbreviated form of Speraw's 1981 measure. It would have had the legislature petition Congress to amend the U.S. Constitution to declare English "the official language of the United States." On February 15, 1984, following two hours of testimony, including commentary by former U.S. senator S.I. Hayakawa, that the "English language is a great unifying force in the United States," Senate Joint Resolution 7 failed on a 2–3 vote to be cleared by the Rules Committee for floor debate. Opposing senator Nicholas Petris (D-Oakland) said: "I dispute vigorously that language unites us." He recalled when English-speaking blacks were denied their rights. "I fear the climate that such a resolution would generate. It would revive the old attitude of hostility and suspicion against anything that isn't American."[68]

Proposition 38

By August, however, hundreds of thousands of Californians had supported an initiative to put an advisory referendum on the ballot. Pursuant to the Voting Rights Act of 1965, amended in 1982, ten (of fifty-eight) California counties had a language minority (Hispanic in every case) that lacked adequate English proficiency to participate in elections and whose voting-age population comprised more than 5 percent of the total number of voting-age citizens in the county. Fresno, Imperial, Kern, Kings, Madera, Merced, Monterey, San Benito, Tulare, and Yuba Counties were obliged to provide bilingual voting materials. Moreover, a state law required that the forty-eight counties not subject to the federal statute had to post certain election materials in each precinct in Spanish or other languages unless the secretary of state determined that the precinct lacked a large enough language minority to warrant posting materials in a language other than English.

The English Ballot Initiative more than qualified for the November 6 ballot: 628,000 signatures on petitions were obtained. The wording of the measure included this rationale against bilingual ballots:

> Section 1. Findings and Declarations.
> We the People of the State of California do hereby find and declare that:
>
> (a) The United States has been and will continue to be enriched by the cultural contributions of immigrants from many countries with many different traditions.
>
> (b) A common language, English, unites our immigrant residents, fosters harmony among our people, promotes political stability, permits interchange of ideas at many levels and encourages societal integration.
>
> (c) The United States Government should foster similarities that unite our people, the most important of which is the use of the English language.

(d) Multilingual ballots are unnecessary since immigrants seeking citizenship must pass an examination for literacy and proficiency in English.

Section 2. Transmittal.

The Governor of the State of California, within thirty (30) days of enactment of this statute, shall sign and cause to be delivered to the President of the United States, the Attorney General of the United States and to all members of the United States Congress a written communication which incorporates the findings and declarations in Section 1 and includes the following language:

"The People of the State of California recognizing the importance of a common language in unifying our diverse nation hereby urge that Federal law be amended so that ballots, voters' pamphlets and all other official voting materials shall be printed in English only."[69]

The petition drive was orchestrated by the California Committee for Ballots in English, chaired by Stanley Diamond (later of U.S. English), S.I. Hayakawa, and businessman J. William Orozco. Their statement favoring Proposition 38, provided by the secretary of state to inform the electorate, said: "Citizens who have limited or no knowledge of English do not have access to essential information for independent decision-making." Moreover, it stated that "applicants for United States citizenship must pass a test for literacy and proficiency in English," that foreign language ballots "create tensions and ill will among neighbors" insofar as previous immigrants "resent special treatment for other immigrants," that "San Francisco spent $150,000 for ballots in three languages" and for California "in 1982, the cost of foreign ballots exceeded $1,200,000," and that such ballots "are discriminatory; only Hispanic, Asian American, American Indian and Alaskan native languages are targeted for special treatment in the law."[70]

Cesar Chavez, leader of the United Farm Workers, launched a campaign at the end of September to defeat all four referenda on the November ballot, including Proposition 38, which he said would "disenfranchise American citizens." Also that month, Hispanic and Chinese opponents tried to obtain a court order to block the secretary of state from counting the ballots. But Sacramento superior court judge J.M. Sapunor rejected their claims, saying: "The initiative reached the ballot at the request of more than half a million voting petitioners from all walks of life. They should not be so easily frustrated."[71]

Among the leading opponents of the English initiative were Robert T. Matsui, Esteban Edward Torres, and Don Edwards, three Democratic members of the U.S. House of Representatives, from the Third, Thirty-fourth, and Tenth Congressional Districts of California respectively. Their anti-38 statement for the California ballot pamphlet argued that the "grossly inflated bilingual ballot costs can't be substantiated," that the "allegation of noncitizen voters is completely distorted and unfounded," that bilingual ballots "have long been successful" and have "propelled minority citizens into a meaningful role in the electoral process," and that the Voting Rights Act "protects *all* citizens from voting discrimination, not just Hispanics and Asian Americans." The requirement of English proficiency for citizenship, in their opinion, was inadequate, since "federal laws require only a fifth grade level of English to become a naturalized citizen." Voting assistance, therefore, is especially needed "in California, where so many state and local propositions are written in such complex language that they confuse even native-born, English-speaking college graduates."[72]

Three California Polls taken during September and October found increasing public awareness of the English Only question. Among those who had seen or heard something about Proposition 38, a plurality supported passage (table 4.2). Other questions asked in the California Poll of early September found that 54 percent agreed that it was a good thing for different immigrant groups within the United States to preserve their own foreign languages (23 percent disagreed), but, by a 61–36 percent margin, respondents also believed that citizens who could not read English should not be allowed to vote in U.S. elections. The California Poll taken during late October found that nearly three of four voters knew something about Proposition 38, and among this subgroup of respondents, supporters outnumbered opponents by more than two to one.[73]

That ratio held up in the balloting on November 6: statewide, Proposition 38 got 70.7 percent of the vote, with 29.3 percent of

Table 4.2   California Polls on Proposition 38

	Late Oct. 1984	Early Oct. 1984	Early Sept. 1984
Have not seen/heard	27%	37%	43%
Have seen/heard	73%	63%	57%
Favor	48%	42%	40%
Oppose	20%	16%	13%
Undecided	5%	5%	4%

Source: Mervin Field, "Voter Awareness Rises on Propositions 40, 41," *San Francisco Chronicle*, Nov. 3, 1984, 14.

the voters opposing adoption. In every California county the majority voted for enactment, and the electoral margin ranged from a low of 56.5 percent in San Francisco County to a high of 84.3 percent in sparsely populated Colusa County. In Los Angeles County 66.6 percent voted for the English Ballot Initiative. In nine of the ten counties qualifying for bilingual ballots under federal law, the level of support was *above* the statewide average. For this group, the yes vote ranged from a low of 72.9 percent in Fresno County to a high of 79.5 percent in Madera County. (The exception to this trend was Imperial County, where 68.1 percent of the voters voted in favor of the measure.)[74]

This overwhelming mandate led Mervin D. Field, who directs the California Poll, to the obvious conclusion that many voters believed that "voters should be able to read English."[75] The *San Francisco Chronicle* agreed:

> This state is often portrayed as one in which the bilingual and trilingual ballot is much valued. The great majority of voters obviously do not agree with this view.
>
> The voters, we believe, accepted the electoral manual argument that non-English ballots are too costly, are not necessary and may even impede the full participation of newcomers in the society at large. We have heard and made the same arguments ever since multilingual ballots were forced upon us almost a decade ago. . . .

It is unfortunate that neither the local proposition of 1983 nor the statewide vote of this week will terminate the multilingual nuisance. Both measures were advisory, indicating the will of the people but not carrying the force of law. They were, more or less, popularity polls. Changing the law will require federal law amendment. We can only hope that the message is getting through.[76]

Following the directive of Proposition 38, Republican governor George Deukmejian wrote to the president, attorney general, and members of Congress. The Voting Rights Act would not expire until 1992, though, and Representative Don Edwards, who led the opposition to the proposition and chaired the Constitution and Civil Rights Subcommittee of the House Judiciary Committee, made known his objections to acting before then. "We'll look at the letter with great respect, but we'd be hesitant to open the issue up again," he said. "We'd be loathe to bring it up because others might try to push other amendments that would be devastating to the best (voting rights) bill we've ever passed."[77]

The success of Proposition O in San Francisco in 1983 and Proposition 38 in 1984, coupled with the failure of the state legislature to pass an official English law in 1985, set the stage for the popular referendum that took place in November 1986. Vowing that "we're no longer going to let them chip away at our language," state assemblyman Frank Hill (R-Whittier) introduced two bills in the 1985–86 legislative session. "Keep in mind we have an official state bird (the valley quail), an official state reptile (desert tortoise)," he observed. "It seems to me there isn't any reason why we shouldn't have an official state language."[78]

One bill, Assembly Constitutional Amendment 30, sought to add a section to the state constitution:

SEC. 6. (a) English is the official language of the State of California.

(b) The Legislature may enforce this section by appropriate legislation.

(c) Any person who is a resident of or doing business in California shall have standing to sue the State of California to enforce this section, and the courts of the State of California shall have jurisdiction to hear cases brought to enforce this section.[79]

The other measure authored by Assemblyman Hill (Assembly Bill 201) was co-sponsored by twenty-three Republicans from both houses and three Democrats. It proposed that a one-line section 276 be added to the Government Code of California: "The English language is the official language of the State of California."[80] Both measures died in committees of the Assembly.

Local Skirmishes

During the same period, episodes of community conflict over official English broke out in Fillmore, which lies about twenty miles from the Pacific coastline in Ventura County, northwest of Los Angeles, and in Monterey Park, a San Gabriel Valley city within Los Angeles County. Hispanics comprised not quite half of the ten thousand residents of Fillmore but more than three-fifths of the school population. What caused the agitation was the practice in some schools of non-Hispanic children getting about twenty minutes of bilingual instruction daily along with children not fluent in English. A community group called the ABC Committee viewed this practice as wasteful, and at a city council meeting, a spokesperson asked for a resolution to declare that "the English language is the official language of the City of Fillmore." On April 23, 1985, Councilman Gary Creagle formally introduced such a resolution, and in reaction, Hispanics began boycotting a market whose owners had backed the ordinance. In August, when the city council refused to repeal its policy, about four hundred Hispanics rallied, and former mayor Ernest Morales told the gathering: "We don't want [English Only] to go beyond Fillmore. We want it to stop here." But the current mayor, Hulbert Cloyd, took issue with Morales. "Are the signs on the road going to be in Japanese, Chinese, Oriental, or Spanish, Anglo?" he asked. "There could be another Quebec in the United States of America," he continued. "Who would want that?"[81]

In June 1986 the city council of Monterey Park, a city of fifty-eight thousand whose population was 40 percent Asian and 37 percent Latino, approved a resolution urging the adoption of English as the nation's official language and greater enforcement of immigration laws, but four months later it voted 3–2 to rescind that policy. Councilman Cam Briglio supported the original measure but offered the motion for repeal because he did not "want to divide the community anymore." One council member who voted no was Barry Hatch, author of the measure. "The resolution still lives in the voting booths," he said, referring to a proposition then on the state ballot. "How could a winning team feel bad about losing a scrimmage?"[82] The Coalition for Harmony in Monterey Park, which was formed the previous year to defeat another proposal to make English the official language of the city, had presented the council with a petition signed by more than forty-five hundred people asking that the latest English Only measure be rescinded.

Proposition 63

The successful 1986 drive for Proposition 63, amending the California constitution to declare English the state's official language, was spearheaded by the California English Committee (CEC). Chairman of the CEC was Stanley Diamond, a sixty-year-old retired military reserve officer from San Francisco and aide to former U.S. senator S.I. Hayakawa. Hayakawa, now eighty years old and the honorary chair of the CEC, was born in Canada and had seen the frictions between English and French Canadians. Interviewed in October 1986, Hayakawa said that he "feared the same thing could happen here." When asked if he saw a Latino separatist movement akin to the Quebec French separatists, Hayakawa answered: "No, but I will say this much—when you go to a LULAC (League of United Latin American Citizens) convention, you get a much more rabble-rousing kind of speaker and much stronger statements of ethnic solidarity than from other groups I have encountered."[83]

One of a few politicians to endorse official English was U.S. senator Pete Wilson, a Republican. Making reference to Canada, he announced that he would vote for Proposition 63 "simply because I think nationally it is unwise to encourage any duality. . . . There is not only no harm but a good deal of wisdom in stating that English will be the official language." Wilson also said he was against bilingual ballots but not the "reasonable" use of bilingual materials for advertising, consumer contacts, and street signs. And like those who opposed Proposition 63, Wilson sensed hostility toward immigrants: people, he said, know the "border is out of control."[84]

Just as Wilson was almost alone among politicians in voicing those sentiments, so the number of organizations that formally backed Proposition 63 were also relatively few: the California Republican Party, California Republican Women Federated, the American Legion, the California Farm Bureau Federation, and the California State Grange.[85]

Besides Hispanic organizations like the Mexican American Legal Defense and Education Fund (MALDEF), the League of United Latin American Citizens (LULAC), and the National Council of La Raza (NCLR), ethnic groups aligned in opposition to official English included the Chinese-American Citizens Alliance, the Japanese-American Citizens League of San Francisco, the Korean-American Coalition in Los Angeles, and the Armenian National Committee of Southern California. The executive director of the Armenian National Committee, Berdg Karapetian, noted that after the Turks occupied Armenia "there was forceful pressure to change the Armenian language and adopt Turkish" and added: "We feel this kind of proposition could lead to that." Not until mid-August did the Asian and Latino groups and civil libertarians coalesce as the Californians United Committee against Proposition 63. Republican governor George Deukmejian, whose parents emigrated from Armenia, announced his opposition because "in practice, English is already California's dominant language, and there is no compelling reason to add such a provision to the state Constitution." Such an action, he said, "would also cause fear, confusion and resentment among many minority Californians, who see the measure as an effort to legislate the cultural superiority of native English-speaking people. Without questioning the sincere motives of its sponsors, the initiative as drafted is insensitive to our state's ethnic diversity, which is one of our great strengths."[86]

Democrats lined up solidly against the referendum. Attorney general John Van de Kamp called Proposition 63 "an open invitation to hundreds of hurtful and frivolous lawsuits." He told a legislative committee: "I would certainly hope that no sensible court would entertain such notions here in California, but I can guarantee to you today that some zealous defender of 'pure Americanism' will raise each and every one of them in court—and set neighbor against neighbor in the process." Among other prominent Democrats opposed to Proposition 63 were Mayor Tom Bradley of Los Angeles, Mayor Dianne Feinstein of San Francisco, U.S. senator Alan Cranston, Assembly Speaker Willie Brown, senate president pro tem David Roberti, and superintendent of public instruction Bill Honig. Even Los Angeles police chief Daryl F. Gates announced a position against the referendum. In fact, Gates joined the attorney general and Speaker Brown to author the official ballot argument against Proposition 63. Chief Gates was afraid that the law might force his department to eliminate services like the Spanish telephone hot line and multilingual storefront police stations in Chinese, Korean, and Spanish neighborhoods.[87]

The Los Angeles City Council voted 12–1 for a proclamation stating that Proposition 63 is "contrary to our most basic principles of equality and opportunity" and "will result in a sense of inferiority, debasement and shame in one's own heritage." The San Jose City Council also voted 8–1 to condemn the measure.[88] With the exception of the *San Francisco Examiner*, a solid phalanx of media outlets voiced objections to the referendum, including "the *Los Angeles Times, Los Angeles Herald Examiner*; the *San Diego Tribune*; the *San Diego Union*; the *San Francisco Chronicle*; the McClatchy newspapers; the Sacramento, Fresno and Modesto *Bees*; the *Stockton Record*; plus scores of other daily and weekly papers and magazines in the state. In addition, all major television channels and radio stations editorially opposed Proposition 63—*all*."[89]

Other groups that formally opposed the measure included the League of Women Voters of Los Angeles and the California League of Women Voters, the American Civil Liberties Union, and the California Labor Federation (AFL-CIO). In late September the twenty bishops and archbishops of the California Catholic Conference declared that Proposition 63 would "enshrine prejudice in the law," would "open the way for endless and costly lawsuits against bilingual programs and services," and would "cause disharmony between ethnic groups."[90]

Upon hearing about the announcement from the Catholic hierarchy, Stanley Diamond responded: "We'd be ever so grateful if (the bishops) would read the amendment and the ballot arguments. If so, I'm sure they would retract their statement." He added that advocates of Proposition 63 "are the strongest supporters of bilingual education; what we want are bilingual education programs that bring immigrant children into an English-speaking setting as quickly as possible."[91]

The *Los Angeles Times* gave much coverage to the official English campaign, though ultimately the paper also stood against adoption of the referendum. An editorial on September 25 argued that inadequate funding for English proficiency classes showed the hypocrisy of the official English campaign: "People who try to make a case that immigrants to California don't want to bother learning English the way earlier generations of immigrants did need only visit a school district anywhere in the state. Schools are swamped by the enormous demand for adult-education classes in English and, to the state's great shame, they are turning away applications by the thousands because the budget for classes in English as a second language (ESL) is too small."[92]

A week later the *Times* unleashed a barrage of criticism of Proposition 63, calling it a "mean-spirited, deceptive and dangerous constitutional amendment that would invite costly litigation. It must be defeated." This editorial made many of the arguments heard against official English laws: "Even if Proposition 63 had no legal effect, and a vote in favor of it was merely symbolic, the initiative would be insulting and demeaning to the thousands of foreigners and immigrants who live in California and help enrich the state both culturally and economically. Despite the many studies that prove how badly these people, and their children, want to learn English—and are doing so despite obstacles like insufficient funding for English-language classes by the state and federal governments—Proposition 63 would do nothing positive to help them."[93]

Moreover, the referendum was not "harmless, and even innocuous," as the proponents had suggested; to the contrary, "what they do not point out is that the language of their proposed amendment is so loosely written that it could, once approved by the voters, result in many complex and expensive lawsuits. Not only does the proposition's language order the Legislature to 'take all steps necessary to insure that the role of English . . . is preserved and enhanced,' but it would give any California resident or business the right to sue the state in order to enforce the amendment." The effect of such language, the editorial continued, "would be to invite litigation, and not just on complex and admittedly controversial issues like bilingual education in the public schools. It could even result in lawsuits challenging multilingual government services that any reasonable person would agree are necessary, like Spanish-speaking operators for Los Angeles' 911 emergency telephone number or translators in the state's courts." The advocates of the measure say that they do not intend to pursue such litigation, but "what is to prevent less responsible people from using the proposed amendment's vague language to stir up legal mischief?" In conclusion, the *Times* admonished the voters: "Californians are just too smart, too generous, too open-minded and too confident to let themselves be fooled into approving such an unnecessary and trouble-causing amendment to their Constitution. They should vote no on Proposition 63 in overwhelming numbers."[94]

Californians did speak in overwhelming numbers, but in the affirmative. The California English Campaign collected 1.1 million signatures, far above the required 670,000; it was the second largest total in state history, and public opinion favored the referendum by large margins.[95] A *Los Angeles Times* poll in early September found 70 percent in favor, 22 percent opposed, and 8 percent undecided. Despite the opposition of Asian and Latino organizations, 54 percent of Latinos surveyed said they would vote for the measure (with 31 percent opposed and 15 percent undecided), though the level of support was higher among blacks (65 percent) and whites (73 percent).[96]

Things turned nasty as election day approached. In mid-September the opposition called for an investigation by the California Fair Political Practices Commission, charging that the California English Campaign had received a $385,000 loan from the U.S. English Legislative Task Force although the Task Force reported making a loan of only $289,600 to the California campaign. "The campaign reporting practices of the California English Campaign are as deceptive as the initiative itself," said Lenny Goldberg, campaign manager for Californians United against

Proposition 63. But Stanley Diamond replied that his adversaries were comparing data from different reporting periods. "These guys use scare tactics and dirty tricks," he said. "They ought to look at the records more carefully."[97] It was later reported that the California English Campaign amassed more than $500,000 during its first fourteen months. It received contributions totaling $264,877 between April 17, 1985, and June 30, 1986, along with a loan of $338,000 from the U.S. English Legislative Task Force.[98]

At the beginning of October, Stanley Diamond and S.I. Hayakawa complained about the "rude treatment" they got from the Democrats on a special two-house subcommittee of the state legislature. Senator Art Torres (D–Los Angeles) told Diamond, "You and Sen. Sam (Hayakawa) may be wonderful human beings, but you don't control the kooks who are supporting you." And Assemblyman Louis Papan (D-Millbrae) remarked to Hayakawa, "You are being used and it's wrong. . . . Your motives may be good, but you're hurting California and our society." To that, Hayakawa shot back: "I'm not being used by anybody. . . . The whole thing is my damned idea." It was prompted by the "misguided idea to try to impose French in the non-French-speaking provinces of Canada." So upset was Diamond that he promised retribution. "After that experience, I thought, 'Let our state senators and assemblymen who are up for election, let them go to the public on this issue, so the voters will know where they stand,'" he said. "We have 70 percent of the voters in this state with us on this."[99]

Two weeks before the November 4 balloting, seventy-one-year-old Norman Cousins, who for thirty-five years had been editor of the *Saturday Review*, resigned from the advisory board of U.S. English. In his letter to its executive director, Gerda Bikales, Cousins said he originally was supportive "because I believe it to be a mistake to equate cultural pluralism with a multilingual society." Now, he said, "I . . . recognize that Proposition 63 has a negative symbolic significance" and, moreover, "that legislation is not the proper or effective means for dealing with this problem. . . . Not until we provide educational facilities for all who are now standing in line waiting to take lessons in English should we presume to pass judgment on the non-English-speaking people in our midst." This action by Cousins prompted yet another editorial from the *Los*

Angeles Times, which borrowed heavily from his letter of resignation to "urge the defeat" of Proposition 63.[100]

The *Times* also made inquiries and learned that other members of the twenty-one-member advisory board of U.S. English had only vague understandings of what the debate in California was all about. When interviewed, author Gore Vidal responded: "They didn't ask my advice about the language of this proposition—if they had, I would have advised against it. . . . Obviously, this amendment is out to get the Hispanics—that's clear and I would disagree."[101] Other *Times* articles scrutinized the views and background of John Tanton, focusing on his record as president of Zero Population Growth from 1975 to 1977.

Despite the barrage of negative publicity during the final weeks of the campaign, opinion polls found little slippage in support for the referendum, even among Spanish speakers. A *Los Angeles Times* poll of October 21 found, among Latinos, that 51 percent favored the measure, 41 percent were opposed, and 8 percent were undecided. "On this issue Hispanics have separated from their so-called leaders," declared Diamond. "They all feel English is the route into the American mainstream."[102]

The opponents claimed that most Latinos did not comprehend the true implications of the measure. "They don't really understand what the initiative does," Senator Torres said. "But when you point out some of the details, especially that the courts can be used to harass them in a variety of ways," then, he predicted, voters would be opposed. A 1985 study by political scientists Bruce Cain and Rod Kiewiet found that 69 percent of Latinos favored bilingual education and 60 percent supported bilingual ballots. Cain accounted for the paradox: "This is a classic case of a proposition being worded in such a way as to seem to be nothing more than motherhood and apple pie."[103]

One week before election day the *Los Angeles Times* published commentaries from both sides of the issue, showing how English Only versus English Plus embodied a clash of cultures. The first was an essay by Richard Rodriguez, the author of *Hunger of Memory: The Education of Richard Rodriguez* (1982), a book about his experience as a Spanish-speaking child growing up in an

English-speaking society. He wrote about what the past, specifically the Mexican War, means for Hispanics: "In recent years, Mexican-Americans have been compared to black Americans, but Mexicans are preoccupied with memory in ways that make us more like the American Indian. For like the American Indian, the Mexican-American harbors the conviction that his ancestral culture and language were diminished by the 'gringo.' The Mexican-American and Indian live upon land their ancestors named but which they no longer inherit, except in unrefracted memory." While other Californians worry about mundane problems, he says, "Mexican-Americans weigh metaphors. There is a search for some alternative to the metaphor of the American melting pot, some new metaphor for American life with a connotation that is not oblivion. In a recent magazine article, a Mexican-American actor suggests the metaphor of a salad; America is a tossed salad. One has also heard: America is a mosaic. A rainbow. What is sought is some image of social union that won't melt down." He ended by saying that "Proposition 63 is a balding, pot-bellied, frightened, third- or fourth-generation proposition. It is the Mexican immigrant, running under cover of night, that middle-aged California now fears. The Mexican has become the future. Proposition 63 seeks to withdraw the horizon."[104]

Three days later appeared an editorial penned by Hayakawa that traced his roots to 1938 and a meeting with Alfred Korzybski, founder of the Institute of General Semantics in Chicago, who "taught us that communication is the fundamental survival mechanism for all human life." So it became clear why Hayakawa was devoting his retirement years to "the cause of safeguarding and protecting the English language in California."[105] He wrote,

> The answer lies in the fact that a common language between people is the critical element that enables us to resolve differences, cooperate with each other, understand and respect other points of view and work toward realizing our individual social, cultural and economic goals.
>
> Failure to communicate—whether between individuals or nations—makes for distrust, discord, fistfights and even wars.

> One of the primary sources of our strength as a nation has been our past willingness to recognize and accept the primacy of English and to make it our unofficial language. Generations of immigrants have applied themselves to the task of learning English in a worthy effort to "become Americans" and "get ahead."
>
> While the vast majority of immigrants still enter the American mainstream through the time-proven "melting pot" process, some special-interest groups are mounting a challenge to it in a misguided effort to promote cultural pluralism. They would raise other languages to equal status with English, and promote a bilingual and bicultural state and nation.[106]

That, he said, "is a recipe for disaster." Hayakawa pointed to "Canada, Belgium, South Africa, Sri Lanka and other areas of the world. The results have ranged from disharmony to bloody strife. Their sad experience should be object lessons to us, rather than models."[107]

There was never much doubt that Proposition 63 would pass. Not only did it have popular support, but the *Los Angeles Times* reported that the opposition had raised less than one hundred thousand dollars for radio advertising.[108] The vote was 5,138,597 (73.25 percent) in favor and 1,876,639 (26.75 percent) against; the measure carried every county in the state. Among the highly urbanized counties, its margin was lowest in San Francisco County (53.1 percent), seventeen points higher in Los Angeles County (70.6 percent), and above the statewide percentage in San Diego and Orange Counties (76.9 percent and 78.0 percent respectively). With one exception—the 69.6 percent voting yes in Imperial County—majorities that exceeded the statewide percentage were recorded in the ten counties that qualified for bilingual ballots, ranging from a low of 73.9 percent in Fresno County to a high of 83.8 percent in Yuba County.[109]

Aftermath

Controversy did follow in the wake of the referendum, though only in a few places. In February 1987 the Bellflower Planning Commission held a public hearing on an ordinance to require 75 percent of all sign space to be written in English. After opposing testimony from local merchants and representatives of LULAC and the ACLU, the matter was referred to the city attorney for study.[110]

In April, at a community meeting held in Garden Grove to discuss revitalizing a downtown boulevard, longtime businessman John Perrot told the gathering that he was "up in arms over Garden Grove being turned into a Koreatown" and urged that English be required on all business signs. "Nobody can understand these signs but Koreans. The use of English is what has kept us together. These are selfish immigrants who want to stay separate." To assist him, Perrot recruited Frank J. Arcuri, a leader of past English Only drives in Monterey Park. "The real racists are the foreigners who come over here and segregate us. A segregated city is something we gave up on a long time ago in this country," Arcuri said. "Put these signs in a language we can understand."[111]

In Monterey Park, which approved Proposition 63 by a 56–44 percent margin, Councilman Barry Hatch renewed his attack on business signs written in Chinese. "We're going to return Monterey Park as an English-speaking city," he vowed. Mayor G. Monty Manibog, however, said that he doubted the city could go beyond the sign ordinance adopted in March 1986, to require all establishments to have at least one English sign describing the nature of their businesses.[112]

But the English Only forces chose another line of attack. Their slate of candidates, elected to the Monterey Park City Council in 1987, with former councilman Barry Hatch as the new mayor, pledged to implement the new official English law. Concerned about the number of Chinese-language books in the Bruggemeyer Memorial Library, in October 1987 the council dissolved the library's Board of Trustees and instituted an advisory commission to give input to the city council. A lawsuit was filed in superior court by the Friends of the Library and People for the American Way—a liberal advocacy group founded by television producer Norman Lear—to reinstate the library board. Mary D. Nichols of People for the American Way charged that since its takeover the city council had "virtually eliminated the budget for non-English-language reading materials."[113] Elsewhere she stated that the 1988–89 budget for foreign-language materials had been slashed from more than eleven thousand dollars to around three thousand. But the city librarian denied the allegation: "If the council had adopted a policy restricting the library to purchasing only English-language books and subscriptions my professional ethics would have required that I work to get the policy rescinded immediately or resign my position in protest."[114]

In a legal development with implications for all California, a rule mandating that municipal court employees in Huntington Park only speak English during working hours was overturned by the U.S. Ninth Circuit Court in *Gutierrez v. Municipal Court of the Southeast Judicial District* after a court interpreter filed suit. District court judge Richard A. Gadbois Jr., a Reagan appointee, issued a preliminary injunction in May 1985 against the Municipal Court of the Southeast Judicial District of Los Angeles County on the grounds that the work rule likely violated Title VII of the 1964 Civil Rights Act.

The opinion for the Ninth Circuit Court of Appeals, which had the reputation of being a liberal court, was authored by Judge Stephen Roy Reinhardt, a Carter appointee. He rejected the appellants' arguments that the United States and California were English-speaking jurisdictions, that the rule was needed to prevent the workplace from becoming a "Tower of Babel," that it promoted racial harmony, and that supervisors who were not bilingual could not oversee their subordinates. The final defense, that the English Only rule "is required by [Article III, section 6, of] the California Constitution," was rejected on three grounds. First, the provision did not extend to the workplace: "While section 6 may conceivably have some concrete application to official government communications, if and when the measure is appropriately implemented by the state legislature, it appears otherwise to be primarily a symbolic statement concerning the importance of preserving, protecting, and strengthening the English language." Second, the court drew a distinction between official and private uses of language: "Although the precise question of private conversations among public employees was not addressed in the ballot arguments, it appears that the distinction the proponents attempted to draw was between official communications and private affairs. While the initiative addressed . . . the former subject, most if not all of the speech barred here would fall in the latter category." Third, the adoption of a constitutional amendment does not "*ipso facto* create a business necessity. A state enactment cannot constitute the business justification for the adoption of a discriminatory rule unless the state measure itself meets the business necessity test; otherwise employers could justify discriminatory regulations by relying on state laws that encourage or require discriminatory conduct."[115]

When the defendants requested a rehearing of the case by the Ninth Circuit en banc, the refusal by the majority provoked a sharp dissent by circuit judge J. Alex Kozinski, who was joined by David R. Thompson and Diarmuid O'Scannlain. Kozinski charged that, "by giving employees the nearly absolute right to speak a language other than English, the panel's opinion will exacerbate ethnic tensions and force employers to establish separate supervisory tracks for employees who choose to speak another language during working hours."[116]

Official English advocates anticipated far-reaching changes: Assemblyman Frank Hill had promised to introduce new legislation requiring that drivers' tests, applications for welfare, university student aid forms, and materials for other state services be provided only in English. "We're going to have a whole lot of bills" along those lines, he said. "If we're not successful—and we might not be because the Legislature is still controlled by liberals—then we'll package them all together, go back to our network of 60,000 volunteers, put it on the ballot and pass it over the heads of the Legislature."[117]

Hill's legislative agenda was not forthcoming during the 1987–88 session, but legislation was proposed by anti-63 Democrats to restrict implementation of the official English law. One measure by Senator Torres, Senate Bill 930, was approved by two committees before the third reading, when it was passed by the senate on a 21–6 vote. In the Assembly the measure was cleared by four standing committees but was placed on the inactive file.[118] The bill was sidetracked because a legislative fight was brewing over an even more controversial measure, Assembly Bill 183, sponsored by Elihu M. Harris (D-Oakland), one of the chamber's six black members.

Harris's bill, entitled the Proposition 63 Implementation Act of 1987, stipulated that the only legal remedy could be a civil action brought against the state in superior court: "No action may be brought pursuant to this division against any state agency, against any state officer or employee in an individual capacity, against any local government agency or any officer or employee of any local government agency, or against any private corporation, association, or individual." The act would require written notice to the attorney general at least 90 days before such action was filed and "within 120 days of the effective date of the statute which the action challenges." Failure to so comply would result "in the dismissal of any action." Legal relief would be "limited to an order enjoining the enforcement of any statute enacted after November 4, 1986," meaning that any legislation enacted before the date Proposition 63 was approved would be immune from enforcement. The act continued, "Neither monetary damages, attorneys' fees, nor costs shall be assessed any party in any action" under this provision.[119]

Assembly Bill 183 had been cleared for floor action by four standing committees of the Assembly, but the Democrats could not muster the votes for final passage. On third reading, the bill was defeated 35–37, and after Harris's motion for reconsideration, it was defeated even more handily (3–27).[120] All thirty-five yea votes on the first roll call were cast by Democrats, all but three no votes by Republicans; only three Democrats voted for its reconsideration, however, whereas Republicans accounted for all but one of the votes against that motion. By all appearances the Democrats backed away from the anti-63 legislation when, given the outcome of the 1986 referendum, they were threatened with political retribution. Harris had advised his Democratic colleagues to abstain on reconsideration, because Assemblyman Frank Hill threatened to mail out two hundred thousand leaflets statewide informing voters of the Democratic ploy. "I don't like threats, and I don't like blackmail," said Harris. "This bill would avoid frivolous lawsuits and wasting taxpayers' money." But Hill charged that Assembly Bill 183 was an "attempt to overturn Proposition 63 and thwart the will of the people."[121]

Though Assemblyman Hill was able to block this legislation, the Republicans had no more luck in gaining rigorous enforcement of Proposition 63. In the 1989–90 session, Assembly Bill 2090, with nine Republican Assembly members as the co-sponsors, noted that "state agencies have continued to operate, at times, in languages other than English"—it cited the Department of Motor Vehicles' September 1988 revised driver's license application form in Spanish—and mandated a broad coverage of the law. The bill would include the "legislative, executive, and judicial branches . . . [a]ll political subdivisions, departments, agencies, organizations, and instrumentalities of this state, including local governments and municipalities . . . [a]ll statutes, ordinances, rules, orders, programs, and policies," and "all government officials and employees during the performance of government business." It further mandated that "this state and all political subdivisions of this state shall act in English and in no other language," that "no entity to which this article applies shall make or enforce a law, order, decree, or policy which requires the use of a language other than English," and that "no governmental document shall be valid, effective, or enforceable unless it is in the English language."[122] Only five exceptions were included under Assembly Bill 2090:

> (1) To assist students who are not proficient in the English language, to the extent necessary to comply with federal law, by giving educational instruction in a language other than English to provide as rapid as possible a transition to English.
>
> (2) To comply with other federal laws.
>
> (3) To teach a student a foreign language as part of a required or voluntary educational curriculum.
>
> (4) To protect public health or safety.
>
> (5) To protect the rights of criminal defendants or victims of crime.[123]

The bill was referred to the Committee on Governmental Efficiency and Consumer Protection, which refused to report it to the full Assembly.

Three days after the November 4, 1986 vote on Proposition 63, a *Los Angeles Times* editorial cautioned against any overreaction: "The legal-aid groups that opposed the initiative should not panic now and try to have it declared unconstitutional. The sponsors of Proposition 63 would only come back with another initiative that could be worse and would certainly be more divisive.

It would be wiser for the groups to challenge, on a case-by-case basis, any extreme or fallacious efforts to dictate English as the language of the land."[124]

That advice was probably well taken. Two years later, according to one opponent of the proposition, there was hardly any noticeable impact from the law. "As far as the person on the street [is concerned], I don't think anything has changed," said John Huerta, formerly a lawyer with MALDEF. As of June 1990, only six lawsuits had been filed in California following the enactment; five of them concerned English Only work rules.[125] Proposition 63 mandated no policy changes but rather left implementation to the state legislature, and the legislature has remained stalemated.

First Lessons

What is noteworthy about the Florida and California episodes is that both occurred in areas with large concentrations of linguistic minorities and both focused on issues that, though they may not have directly affected many in the Anglo population, were real and not simply imaginary ills. Institutionalizing bilingualism, whether in Dade County, San Francisco, or anywhere else, raises questions on which reasonable people can disagree. Indeed, today there is debate among intellectuals about how much multiculturalism is too much and concern about how it can be abused by devotees of political correctness.

The public debate, as framed by the proponents of official English legislation, was cast in language that emphasized desired *social* values. Analysis of the rhetoric used by those who favored San Francisco's Proposition O identifies eight rationales for its approval.

1. Contain costs: "Bilingual ballots waste scarce tax dollars."
2. Recognize logic: "Knowledge of English is already required for citizenship, which is a prerequisite to vote."
3. Redress unfairness: "Immigrants in the past felt it a duty and a privilege to learn English."
4. Encourage national unity: "A common language is the basis of American nationhood."

5. Promote full life: "The individual who fails to learn English is condemned to semi-citizenship, condemned to low pay, condemned to remain in the ghetto."
6. Encourage English acquisition: "The provisions [bilingual ballots] prolong English illiteracy."
7. Reduce number of uninformed voters: "It is questionable whether a non-English-speaking voter can form an opinion and cast an intelligent vote."
8. Discourage ethnic bossism: "Multi-lingual ballots encourage political bossism."[126]

Only the first of those arguments remotely implies that an economic self-interest, even narrowly construed, motivated the promoters of the English Only policy or presumably the vast number of voters who supported the agenda. But since minorities cannot understand how their use of bilingual ballots or their cultural pride can so deeply hurt the majority, they can easy fall into a us-versus-them mentality and attribute the entire problem to racism, latent if not overt. What happened in San Francisco, however, ought to urge us to be cautious before jumping to that conclusion. In the opinion of Kathryn Woolard, "While there is little doubt that xenophobia plays an important role in these referendums, this explanation alone does not seem entirely adequate to account for the high approval rates, particularly in areas like San Francisco which are generally known for liberal voting patterns. Perhaps what needs to be questioned is San Francisco's mythic liberalism, but many people are taken by surprise when they learn that the voters of that city were the first to approve one of the new generation of anti-bilingual measures."[127]

The local discontents quickly spread throughout Florida and California, even though most counties in those states were far removed from the agitation. Only seven of sixty-seven Florida counties and ten of fifty-eight California counties are officially designated as bilingual pursuant to the amended Voting Rights Act of 1965. The racist hypothesis might seem to be a good candidate for explaining the initial outbursts in these states, but can that account for why so many citizens, who seemingly were not touched by the controversy, voted for Amendment 11 and Proposition 63?

Trying to explain mass behavior may involve intangible anxieties, not real-life policy problems, and it is for this reason that the nativist hypothesis, among the alternatives, makes intuitive sense. Before any firm conclusions can be drawn, however, let us proceed to the battles over English Only in Arizona, Colorado, and Texas.

5

ARIZONA, COLORADO,
AND TEXAS:
THE AGITATION FOR
OFFICIAL ENGLISH SPREADS

Arizona and Colorado also had constitutional amendments on the November 1988 ballot to establish English as their official languages. In this chapter I will discuss the political dynamics affecting the controversy in these states and then chronicle the failed attempt in Texas. Next I will summarize all five cases—Arizona, California, Colorado, Florida, and Texas—in order to draw some conclusions about the origin and evolution of each dispute, the key actors, the roles played by political elites, public opinion and organized interests, and the nature of the debate triggered by these ballot propositions.

ARIZONA

"Encouraging people not to learn English encourages people to have jobs that are menial and low-paying," said Arizona state representative Dave Carson (R-Prescott), the key legislative sponsor of an official English bill in 1987. But what further inflamed the issue in Arizona was that the question arose just after Republican governor Evan Mecham had canceled a January 19 holiday to honor the Reverend Dr. Martin Luther King Jr. "There is a sense in the Hispanic and black communities and among Anglos who fought for civil rights the last 20 years that there is a major thrust toward turning the clock back," said Tom Espinoza, a Phoenix developer and leader of the emerging opposition. Almost immediately the charge of racism surfaced. Declared senate minority whip Peter Rios (D-Hayden): "Let us not send out messages to the world that we have to be white to be all right in Arizona." But Carson was undeterred by the denunciations. "If we form language ghettos, we also are forming economic ghettos. And that doesn't benefit anybody," he said, suggesting that the Hispanic leadership had a vested interest in keeping the community segregated.[1]

Tucson Unified School District deputy superintendent Stan Paz, a member of the board of the National Association for Bilingual Education, when interviewed in February, agreed with the allegation of racism, saying that official English advocates feared "the browning of America. . . . People are using this as a facade for the real issue—the fear they have of the increase of minority people in the Southwest and the urban centers of the country." State senator Jesús Higuera (D-Tucson), a leading opponent of English Only legislation, added that U.S. English believed "the melting pot got dirty, so we're going to clean it and paint it white."[2]

Legislative Initiatives

Three official language bills were introduced in the thirty-eighth session of the Arizona legislature, which convened on January 12, 1987. The two authored by Representative Carson, House Bill 2031 and House Concurrent Resolution 2002, were co-sponsored by the same fourteen House members and two senators, and a companion measure in the upper chamber was Senate Concurrent Resolution 1005. The wording of House Bill 2031 and Senate Concurrent Resolution 1005 was identical:

> A. English is the official language of the state.
>
> B. This state or a political subdivision of this state shall not make or enforce a law which requires the use of a language other than English.
>
> C. A court of this state shall not issue an order or decree requiring that proceedings or matters to which this chapter applies be conducted in a language other than English.

D. The provisions of this chapter apply to statutes, ordinances, rules, orders, programs and policies.

E. This chapter does not prohibit educational instruction in a language other than English if the instruction is used to make students proficient in English or to teach students a foreign language.

F. The legislature may enforce this article by appropriate legislation.[3]

House Concurrent Resolution 2002 was brief, stating:

A. English is the official language of this state. The legislature shall enforce this section by appropriate legislation. The legislature shall not make any law which diminishes the role of English as the common and official language of this state.

B. A person who is a resident or doing business in this state may commence a civil action in superior court to enforce this section.[4]

But the measure stalled in the Senate Judiciary Committee, as 250 people packed the public hearing rooms during the three hours of testimony. "This was one little battle, but we're still at war," said Tom Espinoza.[5] Judiciary chair Peter Kay (R-Phoenix), the key senate sponsor, was joined by fellow Republicans S.H. Runyan (Litchfield Park), Pete Corpstein (Paradise Valley), and John T. Mawhinney (Tucson) but lacked one vote to report the measure to the full senate; the next day Kay announced he was holding Senate Concurrent Resolution 1005 indefinitely.

On the nine-member committee, Republicans Tony West (Phoenix) and Jacque Steiner (Phoenix) joined Democrats Jaime Gutierrez (Tucson), Jones Osborn (Yuma), and Peter Rios to block the bill. Senate Concurrent Resolution 1005 was formally sponsored by a majority of the Judiciary Committee, and committee reports indicate that it was Senator West who reversed his position and refused to send the measure to the floor. "I don't think this Legislature needs to deal with issues that polarize the community," commented West later.[6]

After the 1986 California referendum, U.S. English mailed letters to six thousand legislators around the country to urge the

134   NATIVISM REBORN?

enactment of similar laws. Its state coordinator in Arizona was Robert D. Park, a retired criminal investigator with the Immigration and Naturalization Service, who viewed the problem in these terms: "We're talking about enormous, increasing amounts of money to serve this group of people who, despite 200 years of successfully integrating people, have to have biculturalism and bilingualism." His concerns were reflected in a 1986 poll by Arizona State University in which 65 percent of respondents expressed opposition to using any language other than English for instructional purposes.[7]

Stanley Diamond, then West Coast director for U.S. English, and Robert Park threatened to go public if the official English legislation failed. "There's so much broad support for this thing in Arizona, I have to hold them off," said Park, noting that his group already had forty-four hundred members statewide. A spring 1986 poll of voters in Maricopa and Pima Counties by the Phoenix-based Behavior Research Institute found that 54 percent favored and 38 percent opposed such a law.[8]

In March it became known that Governor Mecham was against the legislation even though the state GOP had adopted a resolution in January supporting a constitutional amendment. "That's the governor's opinion, and he's entitled to it," said state GOP chairman Burt Kruglick. "The state committee voted to have English as the state's official language." But Robert Park believed that Mecham's stand would help the official English initiative drive. "The general public feels very strongly about this," he stated. "I feel when somebody like that takes a stand against it, it makes people think about it. And the more people think about it, the more people come to our camp."[9]

Just days later, Senator Peter Kay, who earlier had decided not to pursue his legislative agenda, chose to move ahead because he had received sixty-five letters favoring the measure and only two opposing it. "The overwhelming majority of people seem to favor it, so I think everyone should have the opportunity to go on record," he stated, meaning that the Judiciary Committee should take a vote. Then Kay offered a comment about the governor: "I told him he made a lot of people happy who never voted for him and never will and made a lot of people unhappy who voted for him."[10]

Of the two senate Republicans who blocked sending the bill to the floor, Jacque Steiner was reportedly still opposed, whereas Tony West was noncommittal. But eventually Kay prevailed, and the Judiciary Committee voted 5–4 to send the bill to the senate, but with the suggestion from Steiner that no recommendation be made. "Frankly," said Steiner, who then changed her mind and voted yes, "there's been heavy, heavy lobbying on both sides. I had to ask myself, 'Do I oppose it enough as an individual (to vote no) despite the very strong and sincere support of many constituents I represent?' I vote 'aye.'" Tony West joined Democrats Rios, Gutierrez, and Osborn in voting no. "It's not popular for me to vote (no) in my district," West stated, "but I take that risk because I have to live with my conscience. We, as leaders and elected officials, have a responsibility to try to be cohesive, to bring the community together, not to polarize and divide people."[11]

Later in March, however, Senator Kay retreated again. His bill was scheduled for debate, but the opposition Democrats were ready to filibuster. Kay requested that the bill be stricken from the calendar. "I think, quite frankly, with some effort, we might have gotten this through the Senate," he declared. On the other hand, "we cannot avoid tying the English-language bill with other items of great controversy," namely Governor Mecham's cancellation of the King holiday and his recently publicized use of the term *pickaninnies* to refer to black children. The GOP legislative caucus discussed the bill in closed session, and according to reports, Kay apparently had the sixteen votes needed to win. Senator Gutierrez was "shocked" at the turn of events but expressed relief: "I think he realized that the atmosphere is not the best right now for that type of thing."[12]

In early April more than two thousand Spanish-speaking Arizonans marched on the Capitol carrying posters that read "Yes to English Excellence, No to English Only." The demonstration was organized by the English Excellence Committee, led by José A. Ronstadt, director of editorial policy at the Spanish-language radio station KPHX. "This type of legislation is really very divisive," he said. "You cannot separate language from culture, and our culture is something we want to keep." Later that day he declared: "This peaceful demonstration is not against the use of the English language. It is against legalizing discrimination—legalizing what's already in our environment." At the Capitol, senate minority leader Alan Stephens (D-Phoenix) told the group: "Because many of you spoke up, Senator Peter Kay withdrew the bill . . . but we need to hear from you on other issues, too."[13]

A concerted attack on the English bill was planned in May 1987, at the thirty-sixth annual state convention of the League of United Latin American Citizens. Representative Armando Ruiz (D-Phoenix) proposed an alternative initiative drive to put a measure on the ballot that would accept English as the official language but also recognize the importance of other languages and bilingual education. "We feel insulted" by English Only legislation, Ruiz said. "It's a very, very racist bill."[14]

Arizonans for Official English

Kay's retreat had prompted Robert Park to announce the start of an initiative to force a referendum vote. In late May Park's group Arizonans for Official English filed a statement of organization with the secretary of state. For an initiative to qualify for the November 1988 ballot, 130,048 valid signatures had to be collected by July 7, 1988. By August 1987 it was announced that former U.S. senator Barry Goldwater (R-Ariz.) had agreed to serve as honorary chair of Arizonans for Official English. "I guess I'm a little disappointed, because Senator Goldwater has shared quite a history with Arizona, and he certainly has seen the cultural impact of different groups in Arizona's development," said Senator Gutierrez upon hearing the news.[15]

Goldwater said he was asked by his former Senate colleague S.I. Hayakawa, honorary chair of U.S. English, to accept the ceremonial post. "You live in this country, you speak English, you live in Mexico, you speak Spanish, and if you live in France, you speak French," remarked Goldwater. Arizonans for Official English received direct funding from the U.S. English Legislative Task Force, acknowledged Kathy Bricker, treasurer for the national organization. "Arizona . . . is a state close to the Mexican border that is impacted heavily by the immigration of non-English speakers, one where the issue is well-known and where there's great pressure because of the change in population," she observed.[16]

Not until October 1987 was the counterorganization Arizona English formed to get its alternative referendum on the ballot. The initiative it proposed stipulated that "the state of Arizona shall provide the opportunity to learn and be proficient in the English language and guarantee the right and freedom to learn and use other languages." The organization's leader, Armando Ruiz, said his group wanted to "recognize Arizona's unique history, languages and diversity," as well as oppose any official language law.[17]

In January 1988 U.S. English president Linda Chavez came to Arizona to assist the petition drive and agreed to a debate with former Democratic congressman Jim McNulty. "It is the single will of the United States to have a common bond of language," she declared. "U.S. English does not support English only. We are not restricting private rights of individuals in private discourse. Our concern is the use of English by government, not by individuals." McNulty said official English would wipe out bilingual education programs that had been helpful. "It will not help Hispanics learn English but will build up resentment among Hispanics," retorted McNulty. "This land with its enormous diversity does not need that kind of divisiveness."[18]

Arizona English

After the legislature reconvened in January, the advocates of English Plus nearly won a decisive battle. In the House their measure, House Concurrent Resolution 2012, was formally introduced by Armando Ruiz and seven other representatives and co-sponsored by another thirty-one members, while its senate counterpart, Senate Concurrent Resolution 1007, was authored by Gutierrez and Rios with the backing of eight co-sponsors. All ten senators were Democrats, but in the lower house almost as many Republicans as Democrats (18:21) backed Resolution 2012. Since the GOP held a lopsided majority in both chambers (19:11 in the senate and 36:24 in the House), a unified Republican Party could have defeated this threat to official English.

Of the Republicans who endorsed the Arizona English option, one represented Flagstaff, where Northern Arizona University is located, and two came from the Phoenix suburb of Tempe, home of Arizona State University. Two others lived in Tucson, five came from Mesa, and six came from Phoenix; all those cities have Hispanic concentrations. The remaining two representatives were from the towns of Glendale and Casa Grande. These Republicans likely felt some pressure from their constituents not to follow the party line. By backing this legislation they could make the argument that they did, in fact, support English through efforts to increase language proficiency. The constitutional amendments proposed in both houses had identical texts:

1. *Purpose of English literacy*
Section 1. This state recognizes that limited English literacy is a barrier to full participation in the political and economic mainstream of this state and this nation.

2. *Arizona's official policy of English literacy*
Section 2. The official policy of this state is to promote proficiency in English, the common language of the United States, while recognizing this state's unique history and diversity.

3. *Guarantee of rights*
Section 3. This state shall provide its citizens with the opportunity to learn and be proficient in the English language and shall guarantee the right and freedom to learn and use other languages.

4. *Enforcement*
Section 4. The legislature shall take the steps necessary to provide the opportunity for the citizens of this state to learn and be proficient in the English language.

5. *Private cause of action*
Section 5. A person does not have a private cause of action under this article unless the legislature explicitly and expressly provides persons with this private cause of action.[19]

House Concurrent Resolution 2012 was referred to the Rules and Judiciary Committees but was reassigned to the Education Committee, which recommended its approval. The Rules Committee also acted favorably, as did the House Committee of the Whole. Then Resolution 2012 was amended and approved on the third reading by a 47–8 vote (with five members not voting). All eight opposing votes were cast by Republicans, including Dave Carson, who authored the official English bill in the previous session; twenty-seven Republicans and twenty Democrats forged a bipartisan coalition on the winning side. When House Concurrent Resolution 2012 arrived in the senate, it was referred to the Judiciary Committee, chaired by Senator Peter Kay. Kay threatened not to consider the measure unless the House also passed a resolution to declare English the official language of the state. "Political hardball is what they're playing," said Representative Ruiz.[20]

Senate Concurrent Resolution 1007 was referred to the Senate Education Committee, where Jacque Steiner, the chair, canceled a scheduled hearing after talking with Senator Kay. However, House Concurrent Resolution 2012, after being forwarded to the senate, was nearly approved. It was sent to the Judiciary Committee (it was later withdrawn) and the Rules Committee, thus bypassing Education, and Rules recommended passage after its consideration by all members as a Committee of the Whole. The senate Committee of the Whole also favored approval, but on the third reading, the resolution failed enactment on a 14–15–1 roll-call vote. Unlike the bipartisan voting in the House, this senate roll call showed a partisan cleavage. All eleven Democratic senators voted in favor, joined by three Republicans, and all fifteen votes against the resolution were cast by the GOP (the nonvoter was also a Republican).

Senate refusal to put the Arizona English proposition directly on the ballot was a serious defeat, given that U.S. English, as early as May, had collected one hundred thousand names, compared with about seventy thousand for Arizona English. The U.S. English proponents hired American Petition Consultants of Sacramento, California, to gather names on petitions. So when the July 7 deadline arrived, Arizonans for Official English submitted 209,154 signatures to secretary of state Jim Shumway, well above the necessary 130,048 valid names. "With a combined effort, we turned in the largest number (of signatures) for any ballot issue for the state of Arizona," declared Robert Park. "People who understand what our issue is about support us wholeheartedly. By declaring English the official language of Arizona, we are underscoring one of the fundamental common bonds shared by all Arizona citizens— language."[21]

Financial statements filed with the secretary of state show that, by mid-August, Arizonans for Official English had outspent the opposition five to one. The group reported expenditures of

$159,638.22, compared with $28,889.09 for Arizona English. The U.S. English Task Force alone contributed $154,864.47 to the movement, while the major backers of Arizona English were the Arizona Education Association ($10,000), the Arizona Association of Bi-Lingual Educators ($500), and the Arkansas Social Justice Committee ($8,170).[22] Arizona English, having failed in its petition drive to qualify for the November ballot, regrouped as Arizonans against Constitutional Tampering and still later became The No on 106 Committee. Senator Jesús Higuera and Representative Armando Ruiz continued as leaders of the fledgling counterorganization.

In August news stories about harassment of non-English speakers placed the blame on official English agitation. The Payless Cashway store in Yuma issued a memo banning employees from speaking Spanish unless the use of the language was necessary to complete a sale, but a complaint was filed by the Arizona Civil Liberties Union and the company rescinded its policy. "All of a sudden we are starting to hear about these kinds of cases," said Louis Rhodes, director of the Arizona Civil Liberties Union. "I believe the English-only movement has to be fueling it." Two incidents the year before occurred in Tucson. First, the Tucson Ramada Inn had issued a memo prohibiting employees from speaking any language other than English. The second incident involved Rafael Lugo, an employee of the Tucson Pepsi-Cola bottling company. Though he spoke little English, Lugo had worked sixteen years at the plant. In May 1987 he was fired, ostensibly because his job now required a better command of English. The bad publicity led to talk of an organized boycott against Pepsi. The reaction by Arizonans for Official English was articulated by Robert Park: "Our measure," he said, "would affect only government, not business."[23]

The Tanton Memo

The political bombshell that affected the Arizona petition drive came one month before election day, when the contents of an October 10, 1986, memo written by Dr. John Tanton, chairman and founder of U.S. English, were publicized. Since U.S. English accounted for 97 percent of all contributions to Arizonans for Official English, this revelation gave new credibility to the allegations that the movement was racist. Perry Baker and William Meek, Phoenix political consultants with the anti–Proposition 106 coalition, provided a copy of the seven-page memo to the *Arizona Republic.* Said Meek, "I think it's clear he's a racist. He's a racist in the pure sense, because he's sitting there looking at demographic information and simply assuming that because there's going to be more of them (minorities) than there are of us, that there's going to be a conflict."[24]

According to Tanton, the memo's purpose was to stimulate thinking at the WITAN IV conference on the consequences of immigration to California and the United States, though he was aware of its controversial nature. With respect to politics, he wrote:

> Is apartheid in southern California's future? The demographic picture in South Africa now is startlingly similar to what we'll see in California in 2030. In southern Africa, a white minority owns the property, has the best jobs and education and speaks one language. A non-white majority has poor education, jobs and income, owns little property, is on its way to political power and speaks a different language.
>
> In the California of 2030, the non-Hispanic whites and Asians will own the property, have the good jobs and education, speak one language and be mostly Protestant and "other." The blacks and Hispanics will have the poor jobs, will lack education, own little property, speak another language and will be mainly Catholic. Will there be strength in this diversity? Or will this prove a social and political San Andreas Fault?[25]

Given the possibility of higher reproductive rates among the immigrants, he added: "Perhaps this is the first instance in which those with their pants up are going to get caught by those with their pants down!" Then Tanton broached "the theory of a moratorium: the pause in immigration between 1930–1950, combined with the assimilating experience of fighting side by side in the trenches of World War II, gave us a needed pause so that we could assimilate the mass of people who came in the early years of the century. Do we again need such a pause?"[26]

Because of the memo flap—anti-106 forces labeled it "the Nazi memo"—leaders of Arizonans for Official English distanced themselves from U.S. English. Until the end of 1987, U.S. English and its campaign-financing arm, the U.S. English Legislative Task Force, were located in Washington, D.C., along with another group—U.S.—that Tanton led. Officials of U.S. English contended that their organization was transformed into a nonprofit group separate from U.S. during the first six months of 1988. Linda Chavez, president of U.S. English, also defended the group's contributions to Arizonans for Official English, which totaled $160,603 (through September 23, compared with only $2,635 raised by the anti-106 campaign). "We have given them financial assistance, as other national organizations do to local efforts that they support," Chavez said. "There's nothing un-American about that." Arizonans for Official English replied that the racist charges would only add to the controversy. Declared Robert Park: "There's no question it's an escalation. And if they want to polarize the people of Arizona, all they have to do is keep it up."[27]

Within days of the revelation, Walter Cronkite, who for more than a decade had anchored the CBS-TV evening news, made known his resignation from the advisory board of U.S. English. In a letter to Linda Chavez, he wrote that "because I cannot agree with all details of every campaign and do not have the time to explain my personal position, the use of my name at times has proved embarrassing." Therefore, he asked that his name be removed from letterhead and other materials. "This letter, in fact, is prompted by just such a situation in your current effort to achieve legislation in Arizona." Cronkite had mixed emotions about his support for the official language movement: "For your information, I remain firmly opposed to bilingualism in the Canadian pattern, but I also cannot favor legislation that could even remotely be interpreted to restrict the civil rights or the educational opportunities of our minority population."[28]

A few days later Chavez announced her departure, whereupon John Tanton decided to resign from U.S. English. Chavez viewed Tanton's memo as "anti-Catholic" and "anti-Hispanic" and had been contemplating her resignation, but the decision was prompted by information she obtained from a freelance journalist about certain financial contributors to U.S. English and other groups like the Federation for American Immigration Reform and

Population Environment Balance. Chavez was told that these financial backers advocated forced sterilization and that they had subsidized the reprinting of *Camp of the Saints*, which Chavez labeled "a paranoid, racist fantasy" about "Third World people sort of taking over the world. In a certain point in political life, you realize that perceptions are reality. I just didn't want to be in a position to defend those actions."[29]

Chavez's departure caused Tanton to rethink his affiliation. "I looked at the whole situation and realized that I was becoming the point of a lot of this business, and I thought it would be best if I stepped down as well," he commented. "First of all, I'm going to defend myself against such charges that come along, and I think I can do that better on my own than I can as a member of the organization. Second and third, I think the organization can pursue its mission and the people who are working on the initiatives in the various states can do so better if whatever controversy is swirling around me is removed from the scene."[30]

Tanton was succeeded by retired Air Force colonel Stanley Diamond, a founding board member of U.S. English who chaired the state group in California. Diamond tried to recover the high ground by challenging his opponents to debate the issue. Saying that "we have been called traitors . . . bigots . . . Nazis," he asserted: "There's been little or no attempt to deal with the issue of English as the official language of Arizona. This is a formal challenge to our opponents to debate us on statewide television to get this issue out of the gutter, out of the big lies, out of the character assassinations . . . and move it to a debate where both sides can be heard with their arguments in depth. And we will assist in the payment and in the sponsorship."[31]

The debate never materialized. Arizonans for Official English was now on the defensive, and moreover, the political establishment was lined up against Proposition 106. Among the opponents were former Democratic governor Bruce Babbitt, former Republican governor Evan Mecham (who was recalled from office), incumbent Democratic governor Rose Mofford (who took office after Mecham was recalled), former Democratic attorney general Jack LaSota, U.S. senators Dennis DeConcini (D) and John McCain (R), Congressman Morris Udall (D), and nonpartisan Phoenix mayor

Terry Goddard. The Arizona Judges Association and the Council on Judicial Administration were opposed for obvious reasons. "If I allow an interpreter in court, I can be sued," opined Pima County superior court judge Linda Rodriguez. The League of Arizona Cities and Towns, the Arizona Education Association, the Arizona School Board Association, and the Tohono O'Odham Nation were also named among the opposition.[32]

One politician who showed caution in resisting the measure was Republican attorney general Robert K. Corbin, who was not entirely forthcoming about his position: "I know how I'm going to vote on it, but I'm not going to say publicly because I might be involved in a lawsuit having to defend the state on it."[33]

In a major public relations defeat for the proposition, the Arizona Ecumenical Council (AEC), a coalition of eleven Christian denominations with about eight hundred thousand members, joined with Jewish leaders to denounce it. "We are opposed to Proposition 106 because we see it as divisive to the community, as discriminatory, as unnecessarily coercive and, in some situations, even punitive," said Arlo Nau for the AEC. "On that basis, we feel a fundamental Christian commitment to encourage people to vote against Proposition 106." Among the church leaders who spoke against Proposition 106 were Bishop Howard Wennes of the Arizona–Southern Nevada Synod of the Evangelical Lutheran Church in America, Bishop Thomas O'Brien of the Catholic diocese of Phoenix, and Bishop Joseph Heistand of the Episcopal diocese of Arizona. Heistand offered this rationale for the popularity of the proposition: "It's wrapped in the American flag. It's wrapped in patriotism, God and mother and apple pie and Chevrolet and Ford or whatever you drive."[34]

Leaders of Arizonans for Official English countered that any pro-106 religious leaders would be afraid to speak out given the campaign being waged against them. "The level of intimidation and rhetoric of our opponents have made a large effort to stifle debate," said Robert Park. The fact that church leaders who support Proposition 106 "don't come out and say something," he added, "I believe is indicative of the levels of intimidation. No one likes to be called a racist or a bigot."[35]

The intense controversy following the renewed charges of racism chipped away at popular support for the referendum. A midsummer survey by the Behavior Research Institute found that 66 percent of Maricopa County voters favored Proposition 106, and in early September a poll by Lawrence Research of Santa Ana, California, found 61 percent approval. But an October poll by the Behavior Research Institute found that approval had fallen to the 57 percent level, and a U.S. West survey the same month revealed that the proposition barely had majority support. "I am concerned there's been some slippage," said Robert Park. "It's the lies the opposition has been putting out that has caused the erosion. We want to get the truth out."[36]

Proposition 106 worried the Native Americans of Arizona. In Apache County, which had a majority Navajo population, as well as in Navajo, Coconino, Gila, and Graham Counties, residents were concerned about whether official business with Native Americans lacking English proficiency could be conducted in the Navajo language. Upward of twenty thousand posters had been circulated on reservations, and public forums had been held, urging a no vote on the referendum. "We face a situation where our language already is dying, and now these white men are trying to stack this on top," said Edgar Perry, director of the White Mountain Apaches cultural center.[37]

A Narrow Win

Proposition 106 did pass, but with only 50.5 percent of the votes cast; the margin of victory was only 11,659 of 1,157,259 votes. In nine of Arizona's fifteen counties the majority voted against the referendum, with support ranging from 25.2 percent in Apache County to 49.7 percent in Pima County, which includes Tucson. The winning percentage in Maricopa County (Phoenix) reflected the statewide average. The greatest margin for 106 occurred in the sparsely populated counties of Yuma (65.0 percent), La Paz (63.5 percent), and Mohave (67.8 percent).[38] All Arizona counties are officially bilingual for Spanish speakers, and nine are also designated as bilingual for Native American tongues—Apache, Coconino, Gila, Graham, Maricopa, Navajo, Pima, Pinal, and Yuma.

So in comparing the Arizona results with the landslides won by the referenda in Florida and California, there seems little doubt that the Tanton revelations and the highly restrictive language of the Arizona amendment caused many non-Hispanic whites to vote against the proposition. During the final weeks before election day, voters were also confronted with a flood of television ads from opponents of the measure. One ad was criticized for using pictures of Adolf Hitler and Nazi death-camp prisoners to heighten fears about Proposition 106. Reports to the secretary of state indicate that Arizonans for Official English spent $307,773.04 through the end of 1988 on the referendum campaign and related legal expenses, of which $304,343.75 was contributed by the U.S. English Legislative Task Force.[39]

During the election postmortem, critics raised the specter of economic harm to Arizona, and other opponents threatened to go to court. Lottery officials promised to continue using Spanish in their advertisements. "We're going to continue to carry on as we have in the past, until somebody tells us different," said Marie Chapple Camacho. Governor Rose Mofford said that the amendment "could hamper our state's ability to expand our economic development and tourism." A legal challenge also came two days after the election, when Maria-Kelly Yniguez, a bilingual employee of the Risk Management Division of the Arizona Department of Administration, filed the first lawsuit, asking U.S. district court judge Paul Rosenblatt to declare official English unconstitutional and block its implementation. "I am afraid to speak Spanish at my work place. And I will not do so until I have a court order," said Yniguez, who had actively opposed Proposition 106.[40]

Without an authoritative opinion on the impact of the new law, educators and government officials showed passive refusal to comply. Superintendent Paul Houston of the Tucson Unified School District issued a memo, stating: "Until TUSD receives explicit guidance from recognized legal authority, every employee and child should remain secure that there will be no change in district approved practices and procedures." City attorney Fred Dean of Tucson authored an opinion that employees should speak whatever language was necessary to do their jobs and that a strict interpretation of official English would invite lawsuits. On November 15 the city manager of El Mirage, near Phoenix, also told municipal employees to disregard the measure.[41]

Responding to inquiries from state agencies, attorney general Robert Corbin appointed a seven-member task force to deal with the legal uncertainties. On December 5, 1988, the governor reluctantly signed the canvass of the general election to put the law into effect, though the previous week she had threatened not to do so: "I may be breaking the law, but if it's grounds for removal from office, then I'm breaking the law." When asked by a reporter why she did not refuse to sign the enabling legislation pending legal challenges, Mofford responded: "The people have spoken in no uncertain terms, and I feel very comfortable about signing it because I think it will be resolved [in the courts]."[42]

The attorney general continued his tactful approach, putting distance between himself and the governor: "I know Rose said ignore it, but I don't know if the agencies feel that way or not." It was also reported that senate Judiciary Committee chair Peter Kay (who was defeated in his bid for reelection) made a formal request to Corbin to explain the meaning of Proposition 106. Kay asked nine specific questions, including whether the law applied to state lottery officials, drivers' license information, a trade office in Taiwan operated by the Commerce Department, and non-English names for highways, bridges, or towns.[43]

The attorney general's advisory opinion was forthcoming in a letter dated January 24, 1989, to Senator Robert B. Usdane, who presided over the upper chamber of the legislature. Corbin gave a narrow reading of Proposition 106 that, in retrospect, may have averted needless litigation and moderated the controversy. The interpretation he gave to the key wording of subsection 3(a)—"This State and all political subdivisions of this State shall act in English and in no other language"—limited the scope of official English to governmental documents, excluding personal interactions. None of the items raised in Senator Kay's questions were prohibited given Corbin's understanding: "In summary, we conclude that Proposition 106 requires official acts of government to be in English. It does not prohibit the use of languages other than English that are reasonably necessary to facilitate the day-to-day operation of government. Proposition 106, therefore, is constitutional, under both the Arizona and United States Constitutions, and compatible with applicable federal law."[44]

The opposition, however, wanted the law repealed. "Confusion, uncertainty and stress as well as anger are the only clear consequences of Proposition 106," said Democratic senator Jesús Higuera of Tucson. "This divisive law must be removed from our (state) Constitution. Either the courts declare Proposition 106 unconstitutional or a state-wide committee will be formed to repeal 106."[45] Higuera was joined by Representative Armando Ruiz, who announced that the existing organization The No on 106 Committee would meet to form citizens' awareness groups to monitor violations of individual rights caused by the new enactment.

Repeal Efforts

Repeal efforts failed. When the thirty-ninth legislature convened in January 1989, Senate Concurrent Resolution 1022 and House Concurrent Resolution 2020 were introduced to repeal the official English amendment to the constitution. On both measures a total of nine senators and nineteen representatives were listed as cosponsors, many fewer than the ten senators and thirty-nine representatives who in 1988 had co-sponsored an English Plus alternative (H.C.R. 2012; S.C.R. 1007). Whereas that previous legislation had strong bipartisan support, in 1989 all the senators and representatives but one—James A. Hartdegen (R–Casa Grande)—sponsoring Senate Concurrent Resolution 1022 and House Concurrent Resolution 2020 were Democrats. The GOP stood united on this question, and thirteen other Democrats in both houses refrained from endorsing the repeal resolutions. The measures were referred to the Judiciary Committees of each chamber, where they died from lack of action.[46]

The repeal effort was not necessary, as things turned out. In early 1990 U.S. district judge Rosenblatt, a Reagan appointee, ruled on the lawsuit brought by Yniguez, invalidating the law on free speech grounds. Governor Mofford, the only person with legal standing to appeal his decision, said she would not do so. "I am happy the courts ruled it unconstitutional," she said, noting that the law was "flawed from the beginning."[47]

Because the law "is a prohibition on the use of any language other than English by all officers and employees of all political subdivisions in Arizona while performing their official duties," Rosenblatt argued that it could prevent legislators from talking to their constituents or judges from carrying out official duties, such as performing marriages in a language other than English.[48] Arguably Rosenblatt could have dismissed the case against the defendants on the grounds that "no actual case or controversy" existed to justify an injunction or declaratory judgment. Rosenblatt summarized their point of view:

> The defendants' assertion that a case or controversy is lacking is derived primarily from what they perceive as the conjectural and hypothetical and self-imposed nature of the injury Yniguez alleges she has suffered and is continuing to suffer from as a result of the enactment of Article XXVIII. It is the defendants' position that the existence of Article XXVIII does not constitute a justiciable threat because Attorney General Corbin has formally interpreted Article XXVIII as not imposing any restrictions on Yniguez's continued use of Spanish during the course of her official duties and the defendants have stated on the record that Yniguez may continue to speak Spanish without fear of official retribution, and because the possibility of her being sued by a private citizen under the private right of action provision of Article XXVIII is too remote and speculative to constitute an actual injury.[49]

In the absence of any attempt at enforcement, the judge refused to grant injunctive relief; he also ruled that the Fourteenth Amendment was not violated. Nonetheless, Rosenblatt agreed with the plaintiffs respecting "Article XXVIII's potential for chilling First Amendment rights" and also agreed that "Yniguez's self-imposed decision to refrain from speaking Spanish while performing her job . . . is but a product of her legitimate sensitivity to the perils posed by the Article's language and her desire to restrict her conduct to that which is unquestionably safe." Such a law is "substantially overbroad," he wrote. Then he took issue with the attorney general's advisory opinion, which Rosenblatt referred to as a "remarkable job of plastic surgery upon the face of the ordinance" but one that he would not accept. He threw aside the attorney general's narrow construction of the word *acts* (to mean "sovereign acts") and noted that the language applied to "all government officials and employees during the performance of government business."[50] In sum, Article XXVIII violated the First Amendment of the U.S. Constitution.

COLORADO

On January 7, 1987, a one-sentence bill, House Resolution 1038, declaring English "the official language of the state of Colorado" was introduced in the Colorado General Assembly. Its chief sponsor was Republican representative Barbara Philips of Colorado Springs, a sixty-one-year-old mother of five children and a former elementary schoolteacher, who was joined by nine others in the House and eight senators—all Republicans—as co-sponsors. The bill was referred to the Committee on State Affairs, and almost immediately public outcry arose against the measure.

The *Denver Post* editorialized that the bill's supporters "aren't really concerned about English per se. They're worried about the flood of immigration from Latin America, and the threat this may pose to the nation's cultural integrity." Specifically, "they fear that the growth of Hispanic ghettoes in cities like Los Angeles and Miami—where Spanish-speaking aliens may live for years without ever learning English—eventually may fracture the body politic in the same way that French-speakers in Quebec have weakened the sense of national unity in Canada." But "even if today's immigrants don't turn out to realize" that to "get ahead, you simply have to be fluent in English," the *Post* opposed the bill because "the strident rhetoric of the 'official language' folks conveys a discouraging air of cultural arrogance that can easily be interpreted as racism by those for whom English is a second language."[51]

The next month an angry exchange occurred when Philips and co-sponsor Representative Ed Carpenter (R-Grand Junction) appeared before the State Board of Education to explain the legislation. Board member Richard Kraft said the bill exemplified "xenophobic ethnocentrism" because it "sends a message that other languages are second-class, less important." He added, "It has been very divisive and adds nothing to the discussion of how children learn English." But Philips was opposed to bilingual programs designed to "maintain" a child's native language. "I would hope that parents whose children must participate in such programs would have a remedy to file suit under my bill," she said. The purpose was to "protect" English and "put into statute what is already true in custom." Kraft countered: "I don't think we need to protect English. If we were in danger of English being wiped out, that might be different. But I just don't feel a threat to the English language, and the message your bill is sending is dangerous to minority communities." To the contrary, responded Philips, the "commonality of English is what holds people from diverse groups, languages and cultures together. We don't want divisiveness among our people."[52]

Colorado Official English Committee

Although the GOP had a twenty-five to ten advantage over the Democrats in the senate and held forty-one of sixty-five seats in the House, Governor Roy Romer was a Democrat. Philips, who understood that Romer had promised to veto the bill, on March 5 withdrew it from consideration. At the same time, she vowed to get the proposal on the ballot in 1988. She announced the formation of an Official English Committee to begin collecting the signatures of 50,688 registered voters. "I've heard from my constituents—81 percent support it," she said. "I've heard from all over the state. . . . I think it's going to pass."[53]

By the November 1, 1987, deadline, Glen Philips, Representative Philips's husband, and his allies in the Colorado Official English Committee had collected more than 102,000 signatures—double the necessary number to put the proposition on the ballot. One of the early statements against adoption came from the Roman Catholic Church, from Bishop Richard Hanifen of Colorado Springs and Archbishop J. Francis Stafford of Denver. The proposition is a "pointlessly provocative initiative that has the potential of creating an atmosphere of hostility and resentment," said Stafford, while Hanifen followed with a statement in the *Catholic Harold*, the diocesan newspaper. "I cannot support a bill which has the appearance of excluding other languages from the dignity they deserve." Furthermore, he added, "I personally dislike, even resent, any actions taken officially which could be construed as showing prejudice against (Hispanics), or fear of these beautiful citizens of our state."[54]

Opposition Forces

The opposition was led by Richard Castro, executive director of the Denver Human Rights and Community Relations Agency. Besides Coloradans for Language Freedom, which had already been formed, Castro indicated that Representatives Phil Hernandez and Tony Hernandez as well as Ken Salazar, chief counsel to Governor Romer, were forming another organization—Colorado Unity—which attorney general Duane Woodard, a Republican, had agreed to chair. Castro was "disappointed but not surprised" about the large number of people who signed the petitions and added that "a lot of the public doesn't really understand the hidden agenda." But Glen Philips countered that the Official English Committee would begin "dispelling the rumors and false information" about the proposition. He stated: "This is a unifying measure. It puts onto the record what has unified our nation over the past 200 years. We've had people from every country in the globe to become a part of the American society. What has enabled them to do that has been the commonality of one language."[55]

The Democratic mayor of Denver, Federico Peña, issued a prepared statement: "I believe [voters] will recognize that a simplistic change of this sort in the constitution will be divisive and do absolutely nothing to serve as a constructive solution that will ensure English language proficiency on the part of American citizens." Jewish leaders also condemned the proposal. Marilyn Braveman, national director of education for the American Jewish Committee, told a public gathering that "opposing a group's language is the first step to suppressing a people," and she recounted that her own mother would not allow her children to speak any language but English in order to assimilate them. Braveman asserted that such thinking caused Jews to lose much of their culture by "giving up their languages, changing their names and literally cutting off their noses." Thus many Jews face an identity crisis, she said, "and we hope it's an experience no one else has to go through." The English Only movement does not represent "just subtle forms of racism, it is racism," Braveman contended. "It connotes some type of superiority of people who want to speak English only."[56]

A Hispanic veterans group, the Colorado GI Forum, declared that enactment of the measure "may give rise to prejudice and loss of freedom of speech of minorities who speak other languages in conducting official business and may be interpreted as anti-Hispanic." Richard Castro, also a member of the Forum, was the organizer of the broad-based Coalition against the English-Only Bill. Both Castro and Forum president John Soto said they supported the view of English as the primary language of the United States but they also supported the concept of pluralism. Castro said the bill "brings up old stereotypes" and implies that "if you don't support it, you're unpatriotic." Soto added: "It has created a lot of unnecessary fear of what it might mean in the future."[57]

Governor Romer offered alternative language to declare English the "predominant" language of Colorado with the intent that the state would endeavor to "ensure that all of its citizens are fully proficient in the English language."[58] Another attempt to moderate the conflict was made by Senator Terry Considine (R-Englewood), who unveiled a proposal before the Hispanic Republican Assembly that voters should be allowed in 1988 to approve a statement opposing discrimination based on language, religion, or ethnic origin, indicating that Hispanics should tone down their opposition because most people who signed the petition were not bigots. His plan was to introduce such a bill when the legislature reconvened in January 1988. Richard Castro was reported as saying that Republicans should oppose the Philips measure outright, though Senator Bob Martinez (D–Commerce City) was agreeable to Considine's plan. "It's a good idea," he said. "I would support it. Anything we could do to take the edge off (the Philips proposal) I would support." And senate president Ted Strickland (R-Westminister) agreed that the GOP could be hurt by an extraordinary Hispanic voter turnout. "I think there is a real potential for that injury," he noted. But Representative Philips retorted, "Coloradans don't want two languages, side by side, with equal status."[59]

Early signs that the proposition would pass were reflected in a January 1988 *Denver Post*/NewsCenter 4 poll showing 63 percent favoring and 28 percent opposing the initiative. There was a partisan differential, with 78 percent of Republicans but only 48 percent of Democrats in favor, though the greatest support was found among older Coloradans, people with annual incomes between twenty and fifty thousand dollars, and people with less than a college education. Another survey taken five months later found the division to be 64 to 28 percent, with 8 percent undecided.[60]

The opponents of English Only raised the specter of racism and linguistic repression. One speaker at the Language Liberty and Dignity symposium at the University of Southern Colorado recalled that McDonald's Restaurants were being sued for displaying bilingual signs, and others equated the movement with racist agitation. According to Ed Montour, an organizer of this event, "English-only is based on racism. It's ugly and aimed at destroying our people." David Sandoval, a professor of Chicano Studies at USC, said the threat of a Hispanic majority fueled a racist hysteria he termed a "brown scare."[61]

Then U.S. senator Bill Armstrong (R-Colo.) announced his opposition to the constitutional amendment, calling it "ill-timed and ill-advised" and "not only controversial, but also patently offensive to many people, including Hispanics." But he warned Coloradans not to "portray this amendment as a test of racial tolerance in this state" because "it's going to pass, in my opinion, [and] I don't think we should escalate the stakes." But clearly the senator was thinking politically in his address to a luncheon of Hispanic Republicans, when he noted that Hispanics constituted a "terribly important political force in this country" and were crucial to the election hopes of Vice President George Bush.[62]

Tempers flared at a public debate held at the Gold Acres Senior Citizens Center in Colorado Springs between José Barrera, a community representative with the Colorado Springs Human Relations Department, and Barbara Philips. When Barrera began his remarks in Spanish, members of the audience shouted, "We can't understand you," before he had the chance to translate his opening statements in English. "The right-wing fanatics leading this effort see bilingualism as a threat and as un-American," Barrera continued, but Philips retorted: "The amendment says the official language of government will be English." Furthermore, "The business of the state Legislature, the courts and school instruction will be in English. The Legislature is not going to become a little United Nations."[63] Her remarks and the reception given to Barrera upset many Hispanics in the audience, and Philips, after others denounced her, called an abrupt halt to the proceedings.

What apparently inspired Philips's opposition to bilingualism was her firsthand experience as a teacher at Lowell Elementary School in Colorado Springs. Although only a third of the students were Hispanic, the school was designated bilingual, and some programs were taught in Spanish even though every child in the school spoke English. "There was no need for teaching in a foreign language, but that's what they said we had to do," Philips recalled. "The children didn't want it, the teachers didn't want it and the program was a failure. The students' scores fell dramatically."[64]

The often-heard charges of racism had no foundation, she asserted: "It's absurd—absolutely absurd. That's the most desperate argument of all." The opponents were not appeased. "Whether she admits it or not, it has racial implications," declared Richard Castro. "If it does pass, it opens the door for the zealots in our society who want to use a measure like this to do harm. . . . There already have been statements about Hispanic patriotism, Hispanic loyalty to country and charges of Hispanic separatism. None is well founded," he said. "They can't name one responsible Hispanic national leader who is trying to force a national Hispanic language. While a lot of it has to do with language, unquestionably a lot more concern deals with racial implications and interpretations."[65]

Additional charges surfaced when it was alleged that the official English movement might have violated state law by using taxpayer-supported telephones and state workers as an answering service. Philips listed her state capitol office telephone number for citizens wanting a speaker who advocated passage of the referendum, but she denied any wrongdoing, saying that "not a penny" of taxpayer funds was used. But attorney general Duane Woodard, an opponent, said that state law prohibited using "any state money or resources" for a political campaign and that "the switchboard at the state Capitol is no place to be handling calls for the English-only movement."[66]

Among the prominent Democrats opposed to Amendment 1 were Governor Romer, Lieutenant Governor Mike Callihan, and Denver mayor Peña. The Democratic Party of Colorado officially opposed the constitutional change; the Republican Party took no formal stand, despite the opposition of some statewide GOP officials, including attorney general Woodard and U.S. senator Bill Armstrong. Official English was unable to obtain Republican endorsement, so "the opposition was never solidly bi-partisan." The Adams County Board of Commissioners also registered opposition.[67]

Charges and Countercharges

The level of conflict rose in August 1988, after S.I. Hayakawa alleged that Denver attorneys Barry Roseman, Henry Feldman, and Kenneth Padilla—who were seeking an injunction to block the referendum vote—were members of the National Lawyers Guild, which Hayakawa described as a Soviet front organization. "The implication of this being a Soviet front to undermine the American way of life is ridiculous and patently absurd," said Roseman, who called the allegations "red-baiting" and said they were "reckless." In a letter that Hayakawa had mailed inadvertently to the federal district court the previous month, he linked the National Lawyers Guild to the International Association of Democratic Lawyers. "The IADL has been one of the most useful Communist front organizations at the service of the Soviet Communist Party," then-senator Hayakawa had declared during a 1978 congressional hearing, and he again repeated the allegation when interviewed by the press: "It's obvious to me why a Soviet front group would want to undermine our effort to maintain national unity."[68]

The lawyers sued on behalf of Rita Montero, a bilingual resident of Denver who was contesting the fact that the petitions were written only in English. U.S. district judge Jim Carrigan, a Carter appointee, ruled in her favor. "I feel vindicated on our position that the Spanish-speaking population was disenfranchised in the initiative process," said Padilla. "People ought to be advised of their (voter) rights in Spanish."[69] Failure to print the petitions also in Spanish in twelve bilingual counties—Alamosa, Archuleta, Bent, Conejos, Costilla, El Paso, Huerfano, Las Animas, Otero, Pueblo,

Rio Grande, and Saguache—according to Judge Carrigan, had violated the Voting Rights Act of 1965, inasmuch as a 1976 amendment requires that minority citizens in areas where another language is predominant be given election materials in their own language. Thus Carrigan invalidated at least sixty-one thousand signatures collected in those bilingual counties as well as in English-speaking counties where the signatures came from residents of the twelve bilingual counties.

Secretary of state Natalie Meyer, a Republican, however, indicated that no state had been required to print initiative petitions in any language other than English and promised to get an expedited appeal from the Tenth U.S. Circuit Court of Appeals. Representative Philips agreed with those sentiments: "We're shocked that the judge would keep Colorado voters from voting on this initiative. . . . We had 102,000 Coloradans sign our petition. Judge Carrigan is trying to disenfranchise those people. . . . All we did was follow the law." The sweeping interpretation by the district judge even alarmed some referendum opponents, like the attorney general, who feared "negative ramifications" on all statewide initiatives since passage of the 1965 act. "I haven't researched it, but there's no reason to believe they might not have a good shot" to contest them, Woodard noted. "Just because a law has been on the books five years does not make it sacrosanct when it comes to constitutionality."[70]

While lawyers for the secretary of state doubted that the district court ruling would be upheld on appeal, U.S. English moved to salvage the ballot proposition by hiring American Petition Consultants of Sacramento, California, to collect at least fifteen thousand signatures by the October 3 deadline, which Carrigan set to redress the deficiency in legal signatures. The expenditure of one hundred thousand dollars by U.S. English represented the first use of paid petition circulators for a Colorado initiative, according to secretary of state officials, and some of those funds were diverted to filing the appeal of Carrigan's decision. When first approached for assistance, however, U.S. English refused to help fund Representative Philips's campaign. "They turned me down," she said. "They said a volunteer effort is very difficult and they felt it would be more productive to help the campaign in Florida."[71]

Later U.S. English made a strategic reversal and gave direct and indirect assistance.

The September 16 ruling by Carrigan was set aside by a three-judge panel of the Tenth Circuit Court of Appeals in mid-October; it ruled that petitions are not election materials and need not be bilingual. The majority opinion by appellate judge John Moore, whom Reagan had appointed, likened the process of distributing petitions to a candidate seeking a party nomination. "Until there's something to vote on, there's no election process," Moore said. Outside the courthouse, protesters surrounded Glen Philips and secretary of state Meyer, calling them "racists" and "pigs." Now scheduled for a November 8 vote, Amendment 1 would alter the Colorado constitution to "declare that the English language is the official language of the State of Colorado."[72]

As election day approached, the rhetorical battle heated up. "No one likes being called a racist, but it doesn't bother me, because those accusations come from a few people who have no basic logic to their arguments," said Glen Philips. At this moment in the campaign, however, the controversial anti-Hispanic memo by John Tanton, chairman of U.S. English, surfaced during the battle over the Arizona official language referendum. In a media blitz, the opponents under the banner of Colorado Unity used radio commercials, including one in which civil rights leader Jesse Jackson urged the defeat of Amendment 1 and another that compared an official English language to an official newspaper—the Soviet Union's *Pravda*.[73]

For its part, U.S. English reportedly spent $120,000 in Colorado. In direct aid, the Official English Committee obtained at least $2,962 from U.S. English and $1,000 from English First, another single-issue group located in Springfield, Virginia. The president of English First, Larry Pratt, was also secretary of the Council on Inter-American Security, whose controversial 1985 report *On Creating a Hispanic America: A Nation within a Nation* hinted that Hispanics represented a threat to national security and that bilingualism caused cultural apartheid.[74]

The Majority Speaks

The referendum passed with 64 percent of the vote statewide, but it won more narrowly in highly urbanized counties, getting 50.1 percent in Denver County, 51.4 percent in Pueblo County, and 52.7 percent in Boulder County. It did better in Arapahoe and Jefferson Counties (63.8 percent and 65.4 percent respectively), where some of the Denver suburbs are located, and in El Paso County (69.2 percent), which includes the city of Colorado Springs (Philips's legislative district). Amendment 1 got majority approval in all but eight counties. Of those, seven—Alamosa, Bent, Conejos, Costilla, Huerfano, Las Animas, and Saguache—were bilingual counties based on the amended 1965 Voting Rights Act (the other county showing less than majority support was La Plata). With the exception of El Paso County, the twelve bilingual counties—most of which hug the Colorado border with New Mexico—cast votes below the statewide percentage for the referendum.[75]

The end of voting did not end the controversy, and almost immediately rumors surfaced that non-English speakers were being harassed.[76] The attorneys for Rita Montero went back to court, this time asking Denver district court judge John N. McMullen to rule that the secretary of state illegally allowed the referendum vote. Just days before the balloting, Montero had charged that the petition drive was fraught with "tampering, fraud and misrepresentation," but secretary of state Meyer had dismissed her complaint, saying it should have been filed within ten days of December 15, 1987, when Meyer had rejected her original complaint. McMullen upheld Meyer's decision. If she had not certified the ballot, the secretary of state "would have taken a ballot proposal away from the people by default," he declared. "That's hardly consistent with the notion that people should have the right to vote on ballot issues."[77]

Heartened by victory, the proponents of the referendum measure announced formation of the Colorado English Language Political Action Committee (CELPAC) to establish English courses in workplaces and to supplement adult education programs in public schools but also to channel funds to political candidates, specifically the opponents of Democratic governor Roy Romer and GOP senator Bill Armstrong in the 1990 elections.[78] For its part, the opposition tried to minimize the short-term impact of the amendment.

As a "preventive action," Denver mayor Federico Peña signed an executive order barring city officials from discriminating against citizens or employees for speaking a language other than English, and a similar action was taken by Governor Romer. Romer's executive order stated that Amendment 1 "shall not be used to deny any person who speaks a language other than English the right to due process including interpreters in the courts, voting rights, bilingual or English as a second language educational instruction, or assistance in languages other than English." It also encouraged Coloradans "to obtain proficiency in the English language and to maintain and enhance their ability to speak languages other than English." In reaction, Representative Philips stated: "I hope they're not trying to circumvent the amendment." She added: "We want to avoid official bilingualism. The people of Colorado have spoken, and overwhelmingly so."[79] Two years after the referendum vote, according to news reports, the constitutional amendment had had little policy impact in Colorado.[80] Beyond that, Representative Philips, who was narrowly reelected to the House in 1988, was defeated in November 1990.

TEXAS

Texas was a logical target for the English Only advocates. Hispanics comprised 22.8 percent of its population in 1985, and updated projections show that Texas will become a majority minority state around the year 2015. But attempts during the 1980s to enact official English legislation failed. By focusing on Texas as an outlier among states with concentrations of Spanish speakers, we can identify the critical variables differentiating it from Arizona, California, Colorado, and Florida and also investigate whether common experiences affected the entire group of states.

The Texas story began in 1985, when state representative Kae T. Patrick (R–San Antonio) was the lone sponsor of House Concurrent Resolution 13, which died in the Committee on State Affairs. Having an official language was more important than having an official bird, Patrick reportedly said, and his bill was to be "a statement" that Texans have a common language that is a "binding force," regardless of their different heritages.[81] House Concurrent Resolution 13 read:

> WHEREAS, Language is the vehicle of communication between people, used for expressing ideas and feelings and

recording history, and the reliance of a society on a single language facilities the exchange of information and beliefs and the full integration of all its members; and

WHEREAS, Effective communication among the citizens of Texas gains importance with the increasing diversity and complexity of our state; and

WHEREAS, In Texas, the English language has become the basic language of commerce, education, and official business; now, therefore, be it

RESOLVED, That the 69th Legislature of the State of Texas recognize English as the official language of Texas.[82]

Two years later, Representative L.P. "Pete" Patterson (D-Brookston) sponsored House Joint Resolution 55 along with co-sponsors Billy Clemons (D-Pollok), Jim Horn (R-Denton), Jerry Yost (R-Longview), Foster Whaley (D-Pampa), M.A. Taylor (R-Waco), Tom Waldrop (D-Corsicana), and Talmadge Heflin (R-Houston). (Two others, Ben Campbell [R–Flower Mound] and Jim McWilliams [D-Hallsville] originally were listed but later withdrew as co-sponsors.) An equal number of Republicans and Democrats authored this legislation. Their proposal would have amended Article XVI of the Texas constitution by adding a section 70:

Sec. 70. (a) English is the official language of the State of Texas.

(b) The Legislature shall enforce this section by appropriate legislation. The Legislature and officials of this State shall take all steps necessary to ensure that the role of English as the common language of the State is preserved and enhanced. The Legislature may not enact a law that diminishes or ignores the role of English as the common language of the State.

(c) Any person who is a resident of or doing business in this State has standing to sue the State to enforce this section, and the district courts have jurisdiction to hear cases brought to enforce this section. The Legislature may provide reasonable and appropriate limitations on the time and manner of suits brought under this section.[83]

The resolution's chief sponsor claimed that minorities in Texas "cannot receive the full benefit of our society and cannot reach their full life's potential" without knowing English. His measure, filed on Texas Independence Day, was viewed as "a gesture which provides [as] important [a] symbol as the flag." The proposed constitutional amendment was to be submitted to the voters in the November 8, 1988, election. That never happened. As Representative Al Luna (D-Houston) predicted, "One-half hour after this amendment was born, it's dead." Leading the fight against the bill was the Mexican American Legislative Caucus, chaired by Luna, who held a news conference after Patterson's announcement to report that he and his allies had collected signatures from sixty-one representatives on a petition against the bill, enough to kill the proposal. Two-thirds of the 150-member House and two-thirds of the 31-member senate were required to place a proposed constitutional amendment on the ballot (Resolution 55 had no sponsor in the upper chamber). "The English-only movement does nothing more than raise anxieties and cause divisiveness," said Representative Hugo Berlanga (D–Corpus Christi), House Speaker pro tem. "It's unfortunate that this legislation has been filed, and I'm just as glad we've given it an early funeral." But Patterson disputed those allegations, saying: "I think that's just a bunch of hogwash. As far as I'm concerned, it's an educational issue. It's a job issue." He declared, "If we have to spend additional dollars in order to allow every student in our public schools in this state to speak English, then we should do it. We need to make that conversion."[84]

House Joint Resolution 55 was referred to the House Committee of State Affairs, where it died, but not before hearings were held. According to one observer, "The committee majority appeared to have made up its mind in advance that it wasn't going to recommend the amendment to the House and simply was yielding to demands for the hearing." Mark Sanders of the *Houston Post* reported that there "was standing room only during the evening hearing, which was marked by applause for speakers advocating the plan and grumbles from the audience when lawmakers grilled the idea's supporters."[85]

"My first language was Spanish," stated Representative Lena Guerrero (D-Austin). "I learned English, and I didn't need a constitutional amendment to do that." Then she asked Patterson if he "was opposed to bilingual education? Is that why you proposed this?" He replied that bilingual education "has its usefulness" but that it should be improved so that everyone is fluent in English. According to news reports, Dagoberto Barrera, a vocational counselor from Brownsville, favored the plan because, he said, non-English speakers are "segregated" and are thus vulnerable to "communist infiltration."[86]

Minutes of that April 20, 1987 committee hearing show that House Joint Resolution 55 was endorsed by twenty individuals, some of whom represented the American Ethnic Coalition, English First, Pro America, the Parents Union of Texas, and the National Association of Retired Federal Employees. Ten others spoke against the bill, including representatives of Bilingual Classroom Teachers at Allan Elementary School, the Texas Association for Bilingual Education, the Texas Baptist Christian Life Commission, the Hispanic Chamber of Commerce, the Texas Association of Mexican-American Chambers of Commerce, the Austin Area Association for Bilingual Education, and the Texas Civil Liberties Union.[87]

This measure caused Vice President George Bush to become involved in the controversy. "I don't know that we need to have some formal statement," he said in an interview with the *Dallas Morning News.* "I want to see everybody learn to speak English, but I don't see what good an amendment does in that regard." Bush also talked about bilingual education and said that its purpose was "not to have two tracks, it is to have one track: English." That sentiment was echoed by the vice president in his commencement address at the University of Texas at El Paso. "I believe that every child, while treasuring his cultural heritage, should early on be fluent in English," he said. "To that end I have long supported bilingual education."[88]

Bush went to Texas to bolster his standing in anticipation of the 1988 presidential primary. He would win the support of Texas Republicans, notwithstanding his views on official English or his difference of opinion with the GOP rank and file. A Texas poll found that three-fourths of voters supported the 1987 legislation, but the vice president reiterated, "I'm not in favor of legislation," and then shifted focus: "I think we ought to get together behind having every kid learn to speak English in our bilingual programs."[89]

A poll conducted by researchers at Texas A&M University found that 74 percent of respondents favored the Patterson measure, with 20 percent opposed and 6 percent having no opinion. The resolution was backed by 80 percent of whites and 69 percent of blacks but only 40 percent of Hispanics—56 percent of them expressed opposition. The majority in all areas of Texas were supportive, though the proportion ranged from 60 percent in south Texas (which includes San Antonio, a city with a huge Hispanic presence) to over 80 percent in north Texas (where smaller numbers of Spanish speakers are found). Even though the issue polarized the state Democratic and Republican party leadership, the poll found no partisanship among the rank and file. Eighty percent of Republicans favored the measure, as did 70 percent of Democrats.[90]

Governor Bill Clements was one Republican who wished the issue would go away. When asked if official English legislation would be on the agenda for a special session of the legislature, Clements's press secretary, Reggie Bashur, said it was unlikely. "The governor considers a lot more issues are more important at this point in time. He has not even considered the idea of putting it on the call if there is a special session," said Bashur. It was reported that the governor repeatedly refused to take a stand on the question, even before the state Republican Executive Committee. Some feared that English Only would divide the GOP. "It has introduced an issue in the party that is not needed," opined GOP activist Bob Bailon. "It's going to become another litmus test for candidates like abortion."[91]

On the other hand, there appeared to be little chance that the issue would divide organizational Democrats in Texas. The chairman of Mexican-American Democrats, Ruben Bonilla, called the movement "patriotically misunderstood. It wraps itself in the American flag, motherhood and apple pie and it is difficult for some to establish a position against it." But his group was taking no chances. He believed that Mexican American Democrats ought to ensure that "assurances are received from any candidates with state-wide aspirations that they soundly reject the proposition."[92]

Though Representative Patterson had garnered only eighty-seven promises of support, short of the required one hundred votes, he remained committed to the cause. "We're going to continue to push for it," he said. "We're going to try to put enough pressure on the governor to put it on the call of the special session." The reason the measure died in committee, he believed, was that legislative leaders did not "want the full House to have to vote on it because of the politics involved."[93] Leading the fight against the bill was the Mexican American Legislative Caucus, chaired by Representative Luna, who declared that he was "sorry the movement went as far as it did." He said, "It's racist and a backward step," and added that it was a "kick in the pants and slap in the face" to Hispanics across Texas. "We're not a monolingual state," said Luna. "We're sort of a bilingual state and that is not bad." The Mexican American Legislative Caucus targeted Pete Patterson for electoral defeat, but Patterson was undeterred: "If [English Only] ever got on the ballot, you would see at least two-thirds of the people support this," he said.[94]

According to reports, virtually all state Democratic leaders were opposed to official English, including Mayor Henry Cisneros of San Antonio, but the concept was embraced by the state Republican Executive Committee. The sixty-four-member body approved putting the proposition on the March 8, 1988, GOP primary ballot "on a voice vote and with little debate," though state chairman George Strake, noting "the sensitivity of the issue," said it was not meant as a slap at any ethnic group.[95]

The nonbinding referendum asked whether "English should be established as the official language of the state of Texas and the United States of America." The GOP committee resolution that initiated the process stated that "segregation by language is just as divisive and destructive of human rights and equality as segregation by race, religion or sex." The week before, Governor Clements finally had expressed his opposition by calling official English a "non-issue" that "brings on a racial overtone." He recommended: "Just forget it." The ballot question was championed by the American Ethnic Coalition (AEC), whose chairman, Lou Zaeske of Bryan, countered that Clements's opposition was based on a "misunderstanding" that resulted from the English Only label given to the movement. Instead, it should be called the official English movement.[96]

GOP state chairman George Strake rejected the argument that the movement was "racist" and said that, rather, the Republicans supported it "for national unity" and to "encourage English proficiency." About the same time, however, Willie Vellasquez, director of the Southwest Voter Registration and Education Project, charged that "English Only is clearly anti-Hispanic." He warned, "Republicans have an excellent opportunity to make inroads in the Chicano community, but if they keep this up, those voters will go back to their traditional margins of supporting Democrats by as much as 85 percent."[97]

The purpose of Zaeske's nonbinding ballot question was to put pressure on the state legislature; Texas has no initiative process by which the voters can directly put such a policy on the ballot in a referendum. A nonscientific telephone call-in "Sound-Off Survey" conducted by the *Dallas Times Herald* in late February 1988 recorded 83 percent responding yes to the question "Should Texas pass a law making English the official language of the state?"[98] Whether or not this poll was a valid measure, a similar tide of partisan opinion was registered in March, when 92 percent of voting Republicans supported the official English ballot proposition in the GOP primary. That lopsided result had no effect on lawmakers, however, though new efforts would be made in the next session of the legislature.

Following the English Only referenda victories in Florida, Colorado, and Arizona, Lou Zaeske of the AEC announced that twenty-three newly elected members of the legislature had promised to sponsor legislation making English the official language of Texas. Beyond that, Zaeske threatened to run in 1990 as a Republican for the senate seat held by Kent Caperton, a Democrat from Bryan, Zaeske's hometown. At least 70 percent of that district favored official English, said Zaeske, yet Caperton "refuses to even support, let alone sponsor, Official English legislation." Zaeske's opponents also played a political gambit when state senators Carlos Truan (D–Corpus Christi) and Chet Edwards (D-Duncanville) announced that they and eleven other senators had signed a letter to

Lieutenant Governor Bill Hobby saying that they were against such legislation. "The issue here is not whether English should be the primary language of Texas," said Edwards. "It already is. The fact is, English is the language of common usage from birth certificate to coffee shops to death certificates."[99]

When the seventy-first session of the legislature convened on January 10, 1989, two measures were introduced, House Joint Resolution 48 and House Bill 2467. Joint Resolution 48 was sponsored by Representative Patterson and his allies from 1987— Heflin and Horn—along with Representatives Jeff Wentworth (R–San Antonio), Bill Hollowell (D–Grand Saline), Bill Thomas (R-Greenville), Glenn Repp (R-Duncanville), John Willy (R-Angleton), and Randy Pennington (R-Houston). This time the sponsorship of official English had a decidedly partisan cast, as seven of the nine were Republicans. Pennington was the lone author of House Bill 2467. House Joint Resolution 48 was identical to the constitutional amendment proposed in 1987, whereas House Bill 2467 attempted an end run around the problem of the two-thirds requirement to change the constitution. It was designed to allow the voters on November 6, 1990, to "be permitted to vote in a non-binding referendum. The ballot shall be printed to permit voting for or against the proposition: 'English shall be the official language in which the business and affairs of government are conducted in Texas."[100]

Again public testimony was received by the Committee on State Affairs, with the same outcome. Two groups that had opposed the 1987 amendment reappeared—the Texas Baptist Christian Life Commission and the Texas Civil Liberties Union—but this time some national organizations joined the opposition, which included the Texas State Teachers Association, the National Association of Latino Elected Officials, the Mexican American Legal Defense and Education Fund, the Texas Catholic Conference, the Hispanic Women's Network of Texas, the League of United Latin American Citizens of Texas, and the liberal advocacy group People for the American Way. The ranks of the proponents were limited to advocates from the AEC and English First. The committee heard a balanced presentation of views: nine persons testified against the measure, and nine others spoke in favor, including Lou Zaeske.[101]

Zaeske said that the AEC had forty thousand members in Texas and that "Texans likewise deserve a referendum vote on the official English question." This is why he preferred a binding referendum, but he would accept House Bill 2467. The citizens of Texas, he added, are "growing increasingly impatient waiting for the opportunity to vote on official English." Then a member of the committee who was undecided noted that he had "not had one letter that I can recall or one constituent from my district call me and express a sincere concern about this." At that point the testimony shifted to the topic of bilingual education. Zaeske said that "what passes these days for bilingual education many times is really monolingual education in Spanish in many parts of the state." He believed that such activity was "diminishing" the status of English. Going further, the AEC chairman responded to a question about the bilingual ballot, saying that "it would be a violation of the constitutional amendment" and also was a violation of the Fourteenth Amendment to the U.S. Constitution, which provides for equal protection. Although he could speak Czech, there were no ballots in Czech.[102] The committee adjourned with both measures still pending, ending the first—and perhaps only—chapter in the debate over English Only for Texas. When the seventy-second session of the legislature convened in 1991, no one sponsored a bill to pursue that policy agenda.

CONCLUSIONS

What lessons can be learned from the states of Arizona, California, Colorado, and Florida, where referenda were successfully used, and the failed effort in Texas? First, in each case the popular initiative was organized by a single-issue group with the direct or indirect assistance of U.S. English: Arizonans for Official English, the California English Committee, the Colorado Official English Committee, Florida English, Dade Americans United to Protect the English Language, and the American Ethnic Coalition in Texas. The opponents also mobilized through single-issue forums and ad hoc coalitions: Arizona English, Californians United Committee against Proposition 63, Colorado Unity, and Speak Up Now for Florida.

Across these states only a limited number of other interests felt obliged to become involved in the antireferendum movements. These included associations of bilingual educators as well as religious groups—always the Roman Catholic Church, given that Hispanics are predominantly Catholic, and often representatives of Protestant denominations and Jewish organizations. Invariably advocates for the ACLU or its local chapters denounced the proposals and gave assistance in litigation. Since the laws were perceived as anti-Spanish, Hispanic community leaders and political elites were prominent (the Mexican American Legislative Caucus won pledges from enough legislators to block consideration of the proposed constitutional amendment in Texas), though groups of Asians and other ethnic minorities joined the alliance in California, and in Arizona, Native American leaders made known their opposition. The Cuban community of Florida, however, kept a relatively low profile, to the chagrin of many bilingual activists.

The ad hoc coalitions opposing English Only formed relatively late in each state, thus giving advocates the time to define the issues. These coalitions seemed ill-organized, lacked an effective public relations strategy to reach voters (especially in Florida), and failed to raise adequate funds or, in the case of Arizona, even the necessary signatures to get an alternative referendum on the ballot. For the most part, businesses, trade associations, and unions were not involved in these disputes, nor were civil rights groups like the Urban League or the NAACP in the vanguard of the opposition.

Second, the ranks of the opposition included the political establishment; Democratic politicians in Arizona, Colorado, and California were generally unified against the referenda, while the Republican Party was divided. State GOP organizations endorsed official English in Arizona and Texas, and the leading promoters in Arizona and Colorado were Republicans, as was the large contingent of legislative sponsors in California and most backers of the ill-fated effort in Texas. Those attempts were blocked by Democratic majorities in the California, Florida, and Texas legislatures and by a threatened veto by Colorado's Democratic governor. The Republicans who held statewide offices and thus might be reluctant to offend Hispanic voters, like California governor Deukmejian and Governor Mecham of Arizona or U.S. senators Armstrong of Colorado and McCain of Arizona, were opposed.

The one glaring exception to these trends is Florida, where most sponsors of the previous official English bills were Democrats. This pattern was more typical of southern states (see chapter 8) than of the western states that held referenda. Unique to Florida is the fact that the large Cuban population of Dade County is loyal to the Republican Party, whereas Hispanics in Arizona, California, and Colorado tend to vote Democratic.[103] Florida Republicans would have fewer incentives to push this agenda than Democrats, who could appeal to non-Hispanic white and black voters, but the reverse political logic could encourage the GOP to promote English Only in western and southwestern states.

Third, invariably the charge was made that English Only was racist and that those who advocated that policy were bigots. For psychological reasons, this was a natural reflex action by a minority that felt deeply aggrieved. On political grounds, it could hardly have been an effective counterstrategy given the fact that opinion polls showed, in each state, that official English had substantial public support from the very beginning. Describing what went wrong in trying to defeat those ballot propositions, the former director of the English Plus Information Clearinghouse opined that "an alternative to English Only, whether a policy stressing the value of multiple language skills or preservation of linguistic rights, must *make sense* to a public based on its own experience, which is still limited with respect to language as a political issue."[104]

In Arizona, the Tanton memo was so unsettling that many more people decided to vote against official English, though elsewhere it did not have that effect. But then, having won the moral high ground, the opponents lowered themselves to running television ads that tried to make an association between English Only and Nazi death camps. The proponents also engaged in name-calling—the Red-baiting by S.I. Hayakawa toward the end of the Colorado campaign also comes to mind—so overall the intellectual content of the public debate on English Only versus English Plus was not encouraging. While each side had its arsenal of arguments, they became irrelevant once charges led to counter-charges and personal accusations eclipsed reasoned discourse.

Fourth, being out-financed and out-organized, the opposition forces turned to the judiciary to try to derail the referendum process by raising procedural issues about the petition drives or constitutional objections against the implementation of the laws. Efforts to stop the popular vote in Colorado and Florida failed, though ultimately that strategy may prevail on constitutional grounds if recent California and Arizona decisions are upheld by the U.S. Supreme Court. The attack on English Only on free speech grounds is a potent legal tool given the preferred position of the Bill of Rights in our constitutional system, though the specific question of official English statutes remains an area of unsettled law. It is noteworthy, however, that federal district court judges Richard A. Gadbois Jr., who issued the temporary injunction against an English Only rule by the Municipal Court of the Southeast Judicial District of Los Angeles County, and Paul Rosenblatt, who nullified the Arizona official English constitutional amendment on free speech grounds, were both appointed by President Reagan. If two Reagan appointees had serious reservations about English Only—notwithstanding the fact that the Reagan Administration was especially sensitive to the ideological leanings of its judicial nominees—then the early signs cast doubt on whether this kind of legislation will have any more than a purely symbolic impact.

But then symbolism always has been the driving force behind these measures, and also behind their opposition. While the Cubans of south Florida had refused to expend their political capital in a losing battle to defeat Amendment 11—the state official English law—and disparaged its real effects on the growing Spanish-speaking population there, once they became the majority and markedly increased their representation on the Metro–Dade County Board of County Commissioners, they moved quickly to gain repeal of the Dade County official English law.

Finally, most of the referenda were passed by overwhelming margins, despite all the accusations. Only in Arizona, where tangible evidence surfaced giving credibility to racist allegations, did the voters barely pass the initiative. During the course of these referenda campaigns, and also during the failed effort in Texas, opinion polls correctly gauged the breadth of support for official English. What we do not know from the surveys is the intensity of feelings among population subgroups and what socioeconomic and political characteristics yielded the greatest approval for those proposals. Nor was there any attempt to determine how salient English Only was among the electorates of those states, which is relevant to the long-term staying power of this issue.

The dynamics of public opinion are given closer scrutiny in the next chapter. Analysis of survey data and voting behavior may determine whether the organizational activists on both sides represent well-defined constituencies in the general population. Or the controversy over English Only and English Plus may well pit two "intense minorities" against a huge "apathetic majority." If true, this situation would indicate that, while most Americans are supportive of official English legislation, ordinary citizens do little more than express opinions to pollsters or cast ballots in referenda when the opportunity arises.

6

MAJORITY OPINION
AND THE OFFICIAL
ENGLISH CONTROVERSY

In this chapter I will review the few existing studies of public opinion on official English, examine the 1990 and 1992 National Election Studies, and then analyze voting statistics in five referenda in order to draw conclusions about public attitudes. Although polling data and voting outcomes show widespread support for establishing English as the official language, raw totals do not indicate which Americans are most disposed to supporting that cause and what groups, if any, constitute that distinct minority that is opposed to this kind of legislation. Determining which socio-economic and political factors affect support and opposition will add to our understanding of what kind of backlash is being manifested by this political movement. Moreover, by comparing these attributes of the public with those of legislators who promoted an official English policy agenda in the states, we can begin to address the more critical question of whether this agitation reflects an elitist (top-down) political agenda or a genuine mass (bottom-up) movement.

EXISTING RESEARCH

The limited research on public attitudes toward official English legislation has focused on two general questions: How salient is this issue? and What socioeconomic and political attributes are correlated with support (or opposition) to the laws? All the polling during the Alabama, Arizona, California, Colorado, Florida, and Texas campaigns showed lopsided majority support for codifying the English language. Even in Connecticut, by many standards a liberal state, a 1987 statewide poll showed that 91 percent agreed that English should be the official language of the United States.[1]

While there is no doubt that the American people favor an official English declaration, scholars disagree about whether this issue, once we proceed from generalities to public policy, has any salience for the average citizen. One who thinks it does is David F. Marshall. He claims that "the issue of an official language is fraught with potential hostility and is conducive even to possibilities for violence, a potential powder keg needing only the proverbial match to ignite a political fire storm." A counterargument is made by Selma K. Sonntag. In her view, "language issues are not particularly salient in the United States, as they are in such countries as Belgium where they do indeed function as a powder keg. This low political saliency in the United States is at least partially attributable . . . to past language legislation such as bilingual education and bilingual balloting which identifies target populations primarily according to socioeconomic criteria rather than linguistic criteria." The criteria used for allocating federal funds for language assistance, according to Sonntag, "reinforce socioeconomic identity, and competition based on that identity, rather than linguistic identity."[2]

As validation, Sonntag included questions in the July 1989 California Poll to evaluate salience by determining whether respondents made public their views on this issue. In her analysis, more than four times as many respondents favored as opposed the English Only proposal (73.9 percent versus 17.1 percent), but almost equal proportions of proponents (75 percent) and opponents (74 percent) had expressed no opinion on the subject even though the poll was taken about three months before the referendum vote. Nor was the pattern much different when only minorities were considered. Almost two-thirds of blacks (66.7 percent) and Hispanics (63.9 percent) and more than two-thirds of Asians (67.3 percent) favored Proposition 63. Among those who had expressed an opinion on the subject, Hispanics (24.9 percent) were more likely to have done so than Asians (18.2 percent) or blacks (13.8 percent).

But income, ethnicity, and education had no effect, though Sonntag did find that political ideology affected salience. Respondents who were "strong conservatives" were more likely to express an opinion, but they represented only about a third of the sample (32.2 percent). Sonntag concluded that "the official English issue is not dividing the population along language lines; indeed, there is broad consensus *for* official English legislation."[3]

Carol Schmid examined exit polls in California and Texas in 1988 and observed that "the most striking finding is the marked difference in support for this legislation between Hispanics and Anglos at all educational and income categories in both California and Texas." Ethnic division cut across both population groups without much differentiation, leading Schmid to conclude: "The high levels of support from Anglos of all socioeconomic and educational levels—rather than mainly from groups that are falling in status—appear related to generalized fears and anxieties about the monumental economic, social, and political problems facing Americans. In contrast, Hispanics see the English Only movement as a new means to justify discrimination, a phenomenon driven by prejudice and fear, and a threat to their ethnic community." The analysis also showed an influence of party and ideology. In both Texas and California, more than three-fourths of Republicans and conservatives favored an official English law, whereas the "only Anglo group [in California] where the majority consistently opposed Official English was among self-reported liberals." (In Texas, 50 percent of the liberals favored the law.) Thus, Schmid speculated that "unlike traditional right-wing causes, it has been successful in portraying language restrictionism as a patriotic movement whose purpose is to 'protect the only common bond which holds our diverse society together.'"[4]

Connie Dyste examined various survey data, including an August 1986 California Poll showing that "the strongest supporters of Proposition 63 were Whites, conservatives, and less educated . . . [while the] strongest opponents were Hispanics and Asians, the highly educated . . . and liberals." The findings also suggested that "although many people were aware of the measure, few understood its context or purpose. Proposition 63 was also symbolic on a more ideological plane. To many people it represented a basic social norm of American society—Americans speak English—and in that sense it was very hard to be against it."[5] The California referendum, in other words, affirmed the obvious.

The lack of salience of English Only as a political issue coupled with the abstract questions used to probe attitudes may produce artificially high levels of approval. This position is argued by Ana Celia Zentella based on a comparison of different questions asked by *New York Times*/CBS News surveys in 1986 and 1987. From June 19 to June 23, 1986, pollsters asked: "In parts of this country where many people speak a language other than English, should state and local governments conduct business in that language, as well as in English, or should they only use English?" The following year, from May 11 to May 14, 1987, the question was "Would you favor or oppose an amendment to the Constitution that requires federal, state, and local governments to conduct business in English and not use other languages, even in places where many people don't speak English?" Sixty percent chose English Only in the first round, but the second question split the sample: 47 percent favored an amendment, and 47 percent opposed it. Thirty subclassifications were used to differentiate respondents in these polls. Of those, majorities (ranging from 51 to 82 percent) in twenty-eight categories favored using only English in 1986. For the second question, however, support dropped in every case; a majority (ranging from 51 to 56 percent) of only seven groups favored a constitutional amendment. Zentella attributes the decline in approval to wording differences and the punitive overtones of the second question. She writes, "Too many voters separate the proclamation of official English from its repercussions, i.e., they believe that declaring English the official language is merely a long overdue rectification of an oversight, a symbolic gesture that will ensure the primacy of English as a *lingua franca*, but one that in no way will jeopardize the rights of speakers of other languages." During the successful 1988 English Only campaigns in Arizona, Florida, and Colorado, she recalls, voters "were encouraged to separate the law from its repercussions by the vague or exemption-riddled wording of the propositions," so warnings about the potential impact of those laws on non-English speakers did not register with the electorate.[6]

One deficiency in these studies was their failure to use multivariate analysis to identify which variables, among those tested, were the strongest predictors of support for official English. Such an analysis of exit polling during the 1986 California referenda was done by Jack Citrin and his associates. They argued that "for most citizens English proficiency is a highly resonant symbol of American nationality. The evidence strongly suggests that an important reason for the popularity of 'official English' is the pervasive public desire to reaffirm an attachment to a traditional image of Americanism that now seems vulnerable." In other words, the appeal of English Only for most Americans is symbolic, not grounded in self-interest. Nearly three-fourths of Californians approved Proposition 63 in 1986, but the degree of support varied according to political factors. Contrary to what Schmid found six months earlier, the results on election day indicated "widespread support for the English Language Amendment in almost every segment of the electorate. To be sure, Hispanic and Asian voters [at 39 percent and 58 percent approval respectively] were less likely to approve Proposition 63 than the other two ethnic groups, but blacks and whites [at 67 and 72 percent] did not differ significantly in their support."[7]

These researchers also concluded that "the cracks in the general consensus about the desirability of 'official English' also were strongly related to party and ideology. Registered Republicans were more likely than registered Democrats to vote for Proposition 63. . . . And this divergence in outlook grows even larger when we compare voters grouped by their evaluation of President Reagan's job performance . . . or other indicators of 'social' liberalism-conservatism." Beyond the specific issue of official English legislation, elsewhere Citrin, Beth Reingold, and Donald P. Green show that the symbolic power of "Americanism" as a value orientation yields a generalized antipathy toward newcomers, which also is related to party and ideology. They point out that "the apparent connection between a Republican party identification and negative attitudes toward cultural minorities can be attributed to the tendency for Republicans to be conservative and Democrats to be liberal."[8]

NATIONAL ELECTION STUDY

In 1990 and 1992, the National Election Study asked nationwide panels this question: "Do you favor a law making English the official language of the United States, meaning government business would be conducted in English only, or do you oppose such a law?" In two respects this question differs from those asked in most other surveys. First, the respondents had to judge the propriety of an official language for the entire country, not just one state; second, the middle phrase may have forced them to give more consideration to the impact of this kind of policy. In 1990, 54.4 percent favored an official English law; this proportion increased by ten percentage points by 1992 (table 6.1).

Table 6.1   National Election Studies on Support for an Official English Law, 1990 and 1992 (Percentage Favoring)

Variable	1990		1992	
	(N)	%[a]	(N)	%[a]
National Sample	(463)	54.4%	(2,200)	64.5%
State Groups[b]				
Referenda states (4)	(72)	66.7	(394)	69.0
Statutory states (11)	(94)	43.6	(496)	64.1
Other states (35)	(297)	53.1	(1,310)	63.3
Party Affiliation				
Republican	(190)	62.6	(836)	72.0
Independent	(32)	53.1	(244)	57.8
Democratic	(227)	48.5	(1,091)	60.1
Ideology				
Conservative	(124)	66.9	(1,156)	69.2
Moderate	(81)	46.9	(157)	66.2
Liberal	(61)	47.5	(729)	56.4
1988/1992 Presidential Vote				
Bush	(170)	62.9	(555)	74.6
Dukakis/Clinton	(143)	48.3	(783)	59.6
Perot	—	—	(300)	69.7

Personal Income				
High income	(164)	57.3	(389)	66.8
Middle income	(99)	57.6	(293)	63.1
Low income	(179)	49.7	(1,367)	63.4
Educational Level				
College degree and above	(113)	53.1	(514)	60.1
Some college	(109)	57.8	(513)	64.5
High school diploma	(153)	54.9	(722)	70.4
Less than high school	(87)	50.6	(395)	58.5
Race/Ethnicity				
Non-Hispanic whites	(374)	57.2	(1,688)	68.4
Non-Hispanic nonwhites	(56)	46.4	(319)	57.1
Hispanic	(4)	25.0	(20)	60.0
Hometown Population				
Under 50,000	(331)	55.6	(933)	65.8
50,000 to 249,999	(81)	54.3	(370)	59.7
250,000 and above	(51)	47.1	(307)	61.9

[a]For the five-point scale in 1990, the percentages choosing "strongly favor" and "not so strongly favor" are combined, whereas for the three-point scale in 1992, the percentage choosing "favor" is reported.

[b]The four referenda states are Arizona, California, Colorado, and Florida; the eleven statutory states are Alabama, Arkansas, Georgia, Indiana, Kentucky, Mississippi, North Carolina, North Dakota, South Carolina, Tennessee, and Virginia; the thirty-five other states include Hawaii, Illinois, and Nebraska.

Sources: American National Election Study, 1991: "1990–91 Panel Study of the Political Consequences of War / 1991 Pilot Study"; American National Election Study, 1992: "Pre- and Post-Election Survey," both from the Center for Political Studies, Institute for Social Research, University of Michigan.

The sample for the 1990 "pilot" study was about one-fifth as large as the 1992 survey, so the early findings are more tentative compared with the reanalysis. Overall, however, the findings are parallel and consistent with what previous literature showed. The poll is subdivided according to the same political, socio-economic, and racial variables used throughout this book, with the one exception that respondents were asked whom they voted for in 1988 or 1992, not whether they voted for Reagan in 1984.

In both NES surveys, Republicans, conservatives, Bush voters, non-Hispanic whites, and residents of cities and towns with populations less than fifty thousand were most supportive of English Only. Majorities of every demographic grouping in 1992 favored the law, though the smallest approval margins were recorded among independents, liberals, and non-Hispanic nonwhites. The 60 percent support ranking among Hispanics in 1992 may be an artifact of the small sample size ($N = 20$), although some state polls indicate that a sizable minority, if not the majority, of Hispanics give approval to official English. There is no obvious relationship in these frequencies between income or educational level and support for English Only.

Especially important is the division of opinion according to groups of states. As expected, people who live in the four states that held referenda are most likely to approve: 66.7 percent in 1990 and 69.0 percent in 1992. One would think that people living in the thirty-five states without such legislation would be less supportive when compared with respondents from eleven states with official English statutes; they were, but barely, in 1992, and they were more supportive in 1990.[9] These results give credence to what other information indicates, namely that the agitation to pass English Only laws—almost entirely in the South—was driven by elites and was not the consequence of grass-roots pressures from the citizenry.

MULTIVARIATE ANALYSIS

To evaluate which variables are the most important in explaining support for official English, I subjected eight predictors to a logistical regression analysis (see Appendix C, table C.2). The variables IDEOLOGY, PARTY, BUSH, and CLINTON test the political hypothesis. That racist hypothesis is evaluated with WHITE, the economic hypothesis with EDUCATION and INCOME, and the cultural hypothesis uses POPULATION, based on the assumption that nativism is a small-town or rural phenomenon.

The model predicts no better than by chance, though three variables do reach high levels of statistical significance. The strongest predictors are WHITE, then EDUCATION (with a negative value), and finally PARTY. Thus, non-Hispanic whites, people with lower educational achievement, and Republicans are more likely to be supporters of official English laws.[10] These findings are consistent with the existing literature and indicate that, as the controversy over English Only becomes politicized at the national level, racial and political overtones may come to dominate the public debate, as was the case in the four states with referenda campaigns.

Jack Citrin and his associates also analyzed the 1992 National Election Study to evaluate whether the ethos of American nationalism suffers from an identity crisis. They identify "cosmopolitan liberalism" as dominant but now challenged by the rival ideologies "nativism" and "multiculturalism." One of their findings, which was not expected, was that "neither blacks nor even Hispanics were more likely than whites to reject the idea that speaking English is a defining element of being American. Whatever the position of ethnic activists, among the general public the symbolic meaning of learning English as a rite of initiation to full citizenship is equally powerful among all three racial-ethnic groups." These researchers derived two aggregate measures to determine the appeal of the competing ideologies; they found that "both indices were related to partisan and ideological leanings, with Republicans and conservatives predictably scoring higher on the Nativism Index and significantly lower on the Multiculturalism Index than Democrats and liberals."[11]

Public opinion, especially in places where the issue is not a salient one, may not necessarily translate into political action. While exit polls are the ideal method to correlate voting behavior with individual attributes and attitudes in order to infer motivation, exit polling was done only in California and Texas. Since demographic projections indicate that Anglos will become a minority of the California population sometime in the next century, the pattern of support for English Only may be unique to California and not representative of other states, especially those with very small Hispanic populations, such as Alabama.

Aggregate voting statistics take us a step beyond opinion to behavior, and county-level data allow for analysis across many states, given the array of readily available demographic information on U.S. counties. The "ecological fallacy" means that one cannot use aggregate (voting) data to specify individual behavior.[12] Despite the limitations of aggregate measures, in the absence of better data, this analysis offers yet another clue to the socioeconomic underpinnings of anti-Hispanic sentiments in the mass electorate. Was voter support greatest in counties with sizable pockets of poverty? Was it greatest in counties dominated by other racial minorities or by affluent whites?

This statistical analysis of referenda voting in Arizona, California, Colorado, and Florida will complement their case histories; here, in addition, the referendum in Alabama will be included. Because the Alabama constitutional amendment was co-sponsored by sixty-three members of the lower house, where a roll-call vote was also taken on final passage, it affords the only opportunity to evaluate the political behavior of the electorate as it relates to the legislative behavior of their representatives. Some background on the Alabama case will first be necessary.

ALABAMA

On June 5, 1990, the voters of Alabama approved an official English amendment to the state constitution by 88.5 percent, the largest proportion to pass such an amendment to date. The measure carried overwhelmingly in all sixty-seven counties of the state. Credit for its overwhelming approval was taken by the Alabama English Committee, working with U.S. English; a U.S. English newsletter stated that the organization "worked tirelessly to discuss the importance of the Official English measure with the public, media, and legislators."[13] The referendum process was required to ratify the constitutional amendment proposed by the state legislature; this amendment passed the House on April 26, 1989, and the senate on May 3. As enacted, the measure read:

> English is the official language of the state of Alabama. The legislature shall enforce this amendment by appropriate legislation. The legislature and officials of the state of Alabama shall take all steps necessary to insure that the role of English as the common language of the state of Alabama is preserved and enhanced. The legislature shall make no law

which diminishes or ignores the role of English as the common language of the state of Alabama.

Any person who is a resident of or doing business in the state of Alabama shall have standing to sue the state of Alabama to enforce this amendment, and the courts of record of the state of Alabama shall have jurisdiction to hear cases brought to enforce this provision. The legislature may provide reasonable and appropriate limitations on the time and manner of suits brought under this amendment.

The amendment began its way through the legislative process as House Bill 401, co-sponsored by 63 of the 105-member lower house. The primary sponsor was Representative T. Euclid Rains (D–26th Dist.), of Guntersville, whose district included De Kalb and Marshall Counties in northeastern Alabama. "We are long overdue in having a common language," said Rains the day after the 69–4 roll call on his bill in the House. He added that the measure would protect the state from demands to produce election ballots in a foreign language.[14] One week later the senate agreed, voting 29–0, and the measure was forwarded to the secretary of state.

There was never much doubt that the electorate would approve the referendum, and a modest campaign was orchestrated by the Alabama English Committee. In May 1990 an editorial in the *Montgomery Advertiser* endorsed the amendment even though "only relatively small concentrations of non-English-speaking citizens are found [and] concern that some language other than English will eventually become the language of government seems at first glance foolish." But the writer viewed the proposition as "a serious effort to address an issue of serious concern."[15] The editorial continued:

> The United States always has had large number of immigrants to whom English was a second language. But until recently, it was always assumed that it was desirable for the U.S. immigrant population to learn English. That is no longer always the case in many areas of the nation.
>
> A common language for a nation services the same purpose as a common currency or system of measurement. To get an idea of the problems of having more than one official language, voters need look no farther than Canada, which

> designates both French and English as official languages. The
> cost in time and money in duplicating such things as forms,
> government documents, and signs is tremendous.
>   But monetary costs may be the least troubling problem
> of dual languages. Of much more concern is the potential for
> divisiveness that not having a common language would
> create.[16]

So while "keeping alive ethnic traditions" is desirable, "a common language provides a bond which ties the nation together, a bond which gives each of the nation's ethnic populations even greater strength as a part of the whole." Although the amendment would not prohibit bilingual education nor the teaching of foreign languages, the "point is not so much that English should be the official language, but that the nation needs a common tongue. The official language should be the language historically and presently written and spoken by the overwhelming majority of Americans. If that were Spanish or German or even Urdu, then the official language should correspond. But the language written and spoken by all but a relative handful of U.S. citizens has been, and for the foreseeable future will be, English."[17]

After the referendum vote, the many proponents and few opponents of the measure reacted as expected. Tom Doron, chair of the Alabama English Committee, said its approval would "send a signal to the federal government that Alabama wants a one-language country," whereas Martin McCaffery, vice president of the Civil Liberties Union of Alabama, reportedly said that the purpose of the amendment was to keep non-English-speaking people out of state government. David Schoen, another Civil Liberties Union of Alabama board member, speculated: "It sounds absurd, but it's not out of the realm of possibility for a parent to file suit if a child has to take a mandatory foreign language." He continued, "It's a potential nightmare. . . . I think it really conflicts with federal law." Not surprised by the magnitude of support for the amendment, Schoen believed that "it appeals to patriotism . . . the gut feeling that this country is going to foreigners"; voters in Alabama, he said, are especially responsive to issues with a patriotic flavor.[18]

But Doron disputed the civil libertarians by pointing out that his group supported the teaching of second languages and that he did not expect any lawsuits that might cost taxpayer dollars. "That's not necessary in Alabama," he stated. "English is already the customary language in the state." Doron added that the Vietnamese who settled in the Bayou La Batre area of coastal Alabama might be the only people who spoke a foreign language as often as English, but he said that "these people quickly assimilated themselves into American society by learning English."[19]

Immediately following the landslide victory, both U.S. senators from Alabama signed on with the official English movement. Democratic senator Richard Shelby authored a bill toward the end of the 101st Congress, co-sponsored by fellow Democratic senator Howell Heflin, that would be the first *statute* to designate English as the language of government. "Rarely does an issue win approval by 89 percent of an electorate," observed Senator Shelby of the referendum victory, which clearly motivated his action.[20]

REFERENDA VOTING

In evaluating the referenda voting that established English as the official language of Alabama, Arizona, California, Colorado, and Florida, I used the vote by county as the unit of analysis. Three multiple regression models were derived for each state. The first includes eight socioeconomic and political variables. Based on those results, two other models were generated that include only the four most important predictors of English Only voting. Since these laws date from the early 1980s, the demographic attributes of counties reflect the 1980 U.S. census. The dependent variable is the percentage of the county vote in the referendum that favored establishing English as the official language (ENGLISH). The independent variables are the same as those used to analyze which states among the fifty adopted official English laws (see chapter 3).

The five states under consideration here are sufficiently diverse for a researcher to investigate the five hypotheses that drive the analysis. Alabama had a sizable black population (25.6 percent)—blacks constituted the majority in ten counties—but very few Spanish-speaking residents (.4 percent). Colorado and California ranked among the top five nationally in numbers of Spanish speakers, but only 3.5 percent of the residents of Colorado and 7.7

percent of the residents of California were black, both figures below the national average. In California and especially Colorado, Spanish speakers were concentrated in a few counties. In 1980, two-thirds of Colorado counties had a population that was less than 10 percent Spanish, while 44 percent of the counties had a population less than 5 percent Spanish. The Spanish minority of California grew to 22.1 percent by 1985, though in 1980 a majority of counties (52 percent) had less than 10 percent Spanish, and nearly one-fourth (24 percent) had less than 5 percent.

Whereas the Spanish-speaking residents of Arizona, Colorado, and California are largely Hispanics who generally vote Democratic, a large share of Floridians of Spanish descent are Cubans loyal to the Republican Party. The proportion of blacks in Florida (13.8 percent) was barely higher than the national average, but these residents represented one-fifth to three-fifths of the population in thirteen counties of that state. The Spanish-speaking minority is very concentrated. In 1980 Spanish speakers comprised 35.7 percent of the population of Dade County (where the English Only agitation began) but more than 10 percent of the total population in only three other Florida counties (Hardee, Hendry, and Monroe). Counties with percentages of black residents above the state average were located in north Florida, whereas Spanish speakers were concentrated in the south.

The Arizona population in 1980 was only 2.7 percent black. Santa Cruz County was three-fourths Spanish; Greenlee County was nearly one-half Spanish; six other counties had a Spanish population exceeding 20 percent; and Native Americans were the majority in Navajo County. Arizona poses difficulties for statistical verification, as it has only fifteen counties. One county, La Paz, for which there are data on the 1984 presidential vote and the 1988 referendum, did not exist in 1980, so no census statistics are available. I dropped La Paz County from this analysis, leaving a universe of fourteen counties for Arizona.

THE EIGHT-VARIABLE MODEL

The eight-variable regression model shows highly significant predictors of voting for official English laws (Appendix C, table C.3).

The results give mixed support to the class hypothesis, that counties with more people in groups of lower socioeconomic status would vote more heavily for English Only laws. INCOME has the least impact, and its positive, significant relationship to voting in California is contrary to the hypothesis. COLLEGE shows the expected negative, significant relationship to voting patterns in California, Colorado, and Florida. The negative values for POVERTY in Florida and Colorado imply that areas with more people below the federal poverty line gave fewer votes for official English.

If nativism was originally a small-town and rural phenomenon, that pattern does not extend to the official English movement today. Though RURAL was found to be a significant, positive predictor only for California voting, in Alabama, Arizona, and Florida the negative relationships (none being significant) imply that non-rural areas tended to vote more for establishing English as the official language. POPULATION was irrelevant except in Florida, where counties with smaller total populations tended to vote for the referendum.

Most consistent among the five states, but contrary to the racial hypothesis, is the finding that counties with higher percentages of Spanish speakers tended to vote against official English. This relationship was statistically significant in all the states except Alabama, and the Alabama Beta Weight for SPANISH was likewise negative, though very weak due to the fact that so few Spanish speakers live in any of Alabama's counties. Wilcox County, with 2.4 percent of its population being Spanish speaking in 1980, had the largest concentration in the state.

Given that Spanish speakers represented a distinct minority even in counties where they were concentrated, it is unlikely that the negative Beta Weights for SPANISH can be attributed solely to Spanish speakers who voted against official English. It seems plausible that Anglos who reside in these multicultural counties and who regularly interact with Spanish speakers might become more tolerant and accommodating than those Anglos who live in all-white enclaves. For whatever reason, voting for official English is not correlated with areas having higher percentages of Hispanics, which casts some doubt on the racist hypothesis.

For Alabama, BLACK strongly correlates with voting for the ballot proposition, but for the other states BLACK had no effect. There seems little doubt that African Americans in Alabama voted alongside whites for that constitutional amendment. The vote supporting official English exceeded 80 percent in all but five Alabama counties, and in the ten counties with black majorities the percentage ranged from 71.2 percent (Greene County) to 93.8 percent (Lowndes County), even though the number of Spanish speakers did not exceed 2.4 percent in any black-majority county.

The intercorrelation matrices for Arizona, California, Colorado, and Florida indicate that Spanish speakers tended not to reside in counties with black populations. Alabama was unique for the contrary tendency of Spanish speakers to settle in counties populated by blacks.[21] Ethnic rivalry may explain why Alabama blacks voted for official English, but the impact on Alabama whites may result from politics or ideology.

The political hypothesis is also validated. A vote for Reagan in 1984 was statistically related to a vote for the official English referenda in Alabama, California, and Colorado, with Alabama showing an especially strong relationship. The intercorrelation matrix for Alabama shows a modest relationship between REAGAN and ENGLISH (.445) but a stronger and negative relationship between BLACK and REAGAN (-.719). In the eight-variable regression, the Beta Weight for REAGAN in Alabama (.895) represents the strongest of any relationship, while the Beta Weight for BLACK in Alabama (.661) is the second strongest. In sum, white-majority counties in Alabama tended to vote both for Ronald Reagan and official English, whereas black-majority counties did not vote for Reagan but nonetheless favored the referendum.

FOUR-VARIABLE MODELS

The four-variable regression models (see Appendix C, table C.4) permit us to examine the important variables SPANISH, BLACK, COLLEGE, and REAGAN in the first model and SPANISH, BLACK, POVERTY, and REAGAN in the second. Here our purpose is to specify more carefully the workings of the class hypothesis. Is the anti-Spanish backlash tied to economic deprivation, as historians would imply, or to low levels of education, as studies of intolerance would suggest? The latter is given more support by these findings. Not only is the total explainable variance higher in three models with COLLEGE, compared to those with POVERTY, but POVERTY—deemed a significant predictor in one alternative regression (Florida)—operates contrary to our expectations. However in California and Colorado, COLLEGE is a significant and negative predictor of voting behavior, though less important a factor than SPANISH or REAGAN in California or SPANISH in Colorado.

SPANISH carries a negative, statistically significant value for California, Colorado, and Florida. REAGAN, which was not a significant predictor of voting patterns in Arizona or Florida in the eight-variable model, rises to the level of statistical significance for all states in the four-variable models. In Alabama, Arizona, and California, voting for Reagan in 1984 was the strongest predictor of which counties cast votes for English Only legislation.

SUMMARY

Thus, this analysis offers no support for the nativist hypothesis, but the class dynamics suggest that areas of low education rather than low income or abject poverty foster an intolerance of non-English speakers. Nor do the findings validate the racist hypothesis, since in the areas where Spanish speakers reside, fewer votes tended to be cast for official language laws. Only in Alabama is support for official English possibly related to ethnic rivalry between blacks and Spanish-speaking residents (despite the fact that very few Hispanics live in Alabama). BLACK did not surface as even marginally important anywhere else. It would seem that REAGAN is consistently the single most important predictor of voting for official English across all five states. So while the backlash against Spanish speakers may be broad-based, the cutting edge of support for English Only may reflect a modern conservative ideology more than simply the reemergence of historical forces.

In Alabama the hypothesis of ethnic rivalry can be directly evaluated at the elite and mass level, given the existence of counties with large black majorities. Of the eighteen blacks in the lower house of the state legislature in 1989, only five voted for the proposed constitutional amendment. Four voted no, and nine abstained. Yet the referendum easily won in all the black-majority counties of Alabama. To what degree did the state representatives, both blacks and whites, whose districts included the black-majority counties represent the popular preference in their legislative behavior? This issue is less compelling for whites since the referendum was approved by all the white-majority counties in Alabama and white representatives voted 64–0 in favor (with twenty-three not voting).

Six districts of the Alabama House of Representatives encompassed the ten black-majority counties (table 6.2). All six representatives were Democrats, but their behavior varied according to their race. Of the black members, Lucius Black Sr. voted no, Jenkins Bryant Jr. voted yes, and James L. Thomas abstained. Of the white representatives, Harrell Blakeney and W.F. Cosby Jr. not only voted for the bill but also signed on as co-sponsors, whereas George H. Clay abstained. From these data we cannot be sure about the racial mix of the voters who participated in the referendum, but the overwhelming majority in all these counties supported official English. The data are more conclusive for Black, Blakeney, and Clay because these legislators solely represented five of the black-majority counties, whereas the other legislators represented districts among which Dallas County was divided. Assuming that white representatives were elected from districts gerrymandered to be white dominant within black-majority counties, which means that the black representatives whose districts include those same counties also would be guaranteed black dominance, then unless there was a huge disparity between how blacks and whites voted in the 1990 referendum, these patterns would indicate that two of the black representatives (Black and Thomas) acted contrary to the wishes of the black citizens in their districts.

Thus, the evidence from previous research coupled with these findings validates the political hypothesis. Although most citizens favor official English, among the most reliable supporters are Republicans and conservatives. The PARTY variable was statistically significant in the National Election Study, indicating that more Republicans than Democrats endorsed the English Only law,

Table 6.2 Voting Behavior of Alabama Legislators Representing Black-Majority Counties, 1989

District	County	% Black	% Pro-English	Representative (Race)	Vote
66	Marengo	53.3	87.5	Harrell Blakeney (W)	Yes
67	Greene	78.0	71.2	Lucius Black Sr. (B)	No
	Sumter	69.3	89.2		
68	Hale	62.8	89.7	Jenkins Bryant Jr. (B)	Yes
	Perry	60.1	88.5		
	Dallas	54.6	79.0		
69	Dallas	54.6	79.0	James L. Thomas (B)	Abstain
	Wilcox	68.8	83.3		
	Lowndes	75.0	93.8		
70	Dallas	54.6	79.0	W.F. Crosby Jr. (W)	Yes
82	Bullock	67.6	82.3	George H. Clay (W)	Abstain
	Macon	84.2	82.0		

Sources: the roll call vote from State of Alabama, 1989 regular session, *House Journal*, vol. 7, p. 1743; information on members from *In the Legislature of the State of Alabama, 1989*; both located at the State Department of Archives and History, Montgomery. Racial composition of counties from 1980 U.S. Census; vote by county on Amendment no. 1 from the Elections and Registration Division, secretary of state, Montgomery.

and referenda voting in all five states was related to whether counties had cast a disproportionate number of ballots for Ronald Reagan in 1984.

WHITE was the strongest predictor of attitudes in the 1992 NES database, a finding consistent with virtually all the existing research: more Anglos favor English Only than African Americans, Asians, or Hispanics. It is curious, however, that SPANISH carried a negative value in the analysis of referenda voting, indicating that counties with larger numbers of Hispanics cast more votes against those propositions. Aggregate data cannot tell us who those voters are. Assuming that voter turnout is higher among whites than Hispanics and since the percentage of Spanish-speaking residents is relatively low in the majority of counties in those five states, then that result may be attributed more to Anglos who voted against the referenda than to a highly mobilized Hispanic electorate.[22] It has already been noted that 48 percent of the officially designated bilingual counties in Arizona, California, Colorado, and Florida returned votes favoring the referenda in proportions *above* the statewide percentages.

The data on educational and income levels from California and Texas exit polls, as reported by Schmid, cast some doubt on the class explanation, but the 1992 NES analysis reported that people with less education (but not necessarily low income) were more supportive of official English laws. The level of education in counties was negatively related to voting for English Only referenda in California and Colorado, and overall, the COLLEGE variable outperformed the POVERTY variable. These findings are tentative but point to the reverse class hypothesis as being grounded in intolerance owing to a lack of formal education rather than to economic competition among less-skilled workers.

One cannot say with perfect certainty that Hispanics are uniformly opposed to official English, even though they may be the target of this backlash. A firm conclusion on this question is handicapped by the small samples in national surveys, like the NES of 1992, which found most Hispanics favoring English Only. Exit polls indicated to Citrin and his associates that 39 percent of Hispanics voted for the California referendum. Schmid's analysis of 1988 exit polls showed much less support for official English among Hispanics in California, as well as Texas, yet Sonntag reported that 64 percent of Hispanics told a California pollster in July 1989 that they favored Proposition 63. At the very least, the polls indicate that a sizable minority of Spanish speakers approve of those laws.

The majority of blacks support official English, according to the California Polls examined by Dyste, Sonntag, and Citrin and his associates, and this finding was confirmed in the 1992 National Election Study. But these data—like other statewide polls—also show that blacks are less supportive of official English than are whites.

If blacks, because of their generally lower socioeconomic status, have unique reasons for disliking new immigrant groups, then they should be more opposed to Spanish speakers than Anglos. But they are not, and for that reason the racial hypothesis carries more empirical weight than the alternative of ethnic conflict. Evidence indicates possible exceptions to that generalization, though: the pattern of referendum voting in black-majority counties of Alabama is one example. Also recall that, whereas 56 percent of blacks voted against the 1980 Dade County official English ordinance, by 1988 upward of two-thirds of blacks in Florida, some polls showed, favored the statewide referendum on English Only. Black opinion may be shifting on this issue.

The national organizations of Latinos are unified against official English, and Hispanic politicians and community leaders were instrumental in derailing the bills introduced in the Texas and Colorado legislatures. Hispanics were also prominently involved in coalitions to defeat the California and Arizona referenda. Proponents of English Only argue that the Hispanic leaders do not represent their constituents on this issue. While that is not exactly true, Hispanic citizens are less solidly opposed to official English than the strident rhetoric of the Hispanic leadership would imply.

Another possible instance of elite-mass divergence on the issue involves African Americans. This came to light in Alabama, where the official English referendum was handily approved in black-majority counties despite the fact that black members of the state legislature who represented those areas largely voted against the measure or they did not vote. African American politicians in

California, notably House Speaker Willie Brown, were against Proposition 63, although the polls showed its popularity among black voters.[23] Since more blacks hold legislative office in the South and blacks constitute a sizable bloc in the legislatures of Mississippi, Georgia, and North Carolina, those states may offer researchers the opportunity to answer in a more definite manner the question of whether black leaders and their black constituents disagree.

The behavior of political elites is the subject of the next two chapters. In chapter 7, I will use a series of case studies of the laws enacted in southern and midwestern states to outline the policy-making process and to explain the purpose behind the legislation. Then in chapter 8 I will offer a statistical portrait of the legislators who sponsored those bills, the areas they represented, and how members voted on the measures.

7

LEGISLATIVE INTENT: WHY STATES PASSED OFFICIAL ENGLISH LAWS

In this chapter I evaluate the legislative process by which official English bills were enacted in nine states—Arkansas, Indiana, Kentucky, Mississippi, North Carolina, North Dakota, South Carolina, Tennessee, and Virginia—to assess why the issue was brought before those state legislatures. The cases are discussed in chronological order, beginning with Virginia. Archival records varied greatly among the states. Legislative histories were available for all the cases, and seven states recorded how members voted on the final roll call, but the only states that retained complete files of committee reports and hearing statements were North Carolina and North Dakota. While perfect information is not available for most of the enactments, using a parallel approach to comparative research on the entire group of states may yield a few important insights on how these bills were addressed by these state legislatures.

VIRGINIA

In 1981 Virginia became the first state in the late twentieth century to codify English as the official language of the state. Its decision deserves close attention, because that action, predating the establishment of U.S. English, provides an early warning sign of the concerns that prompted this departure in language policy. The law began as House Bill 1770 in 1981 and then was amended in 1986 by House Bill 403: "English shall be designated as the official language of the Commonwealth of Virginia. School boards shall have no obligation to teach the standard curriculum, *except courses in foreign languages*, in a language other than English. *School boards shall endeavor to provide instruction in the English language which shall be designed to promote the education of students for whom English is a second language*" (1986 amendment in italics). The original wording thus made no allowance for teaching "the standard curriculum" in any language other than English, and the measure precluded bilingual education programs. Opposition to bilingual education was clearly the motivation behind this statute. Unlike laws in other states, which are located in state codes along with statutes designating a state bird, flower, song, and the like, this official English law is found in the Virginia code that deals with educational policy. Its purpose was to influence education, not just to be symbolic.

House Bill 1770 was introduced to the House of Delegates by members Raymond R. Guest Jr. (R–Front Royal) and John D. Gray (D-Hampton).1 Front Royal is located in Warren County in the area of northern Virginia lying near the West Virginia border, and Hampton is an independent city on the Atlantic seaboard. Reported favorably by the Committee on Education on a 12–0–0 vote, the bill then passed the House of Delegates on a 96–0 vote (with four members not voting). The senate, following approval by its Committee on Education and Health, approved House Bill 1770 en bloc (with forty-nine other measures) on a 39–0 vote (with one nonvoter), which suggests that the official English bill was not remotely controversial at the time. (L. Douglas Wilder, then the only black state senator, who was elected governor in 1990 and briefly ran as a 1992 Democratic presidential nominee, voted yes on the bill.)

At that time the Virginia legislature was also sending a message about bilingual education to federal authorities concerning controversial regulations being applied to Fairfax County.2 The county, adjacent to Washington, D.C., is home to thousands of federal employees. The legislature's declaration, House Joint Resolution 236, was also referred to the Education Committee, and its sponsors included twenty-two members of the House of Delegates, though the chief "patron" was Howard E. Copeland (D–Virginia Beach). The Education Committee voted 10–0–0 to report Resolution 236 with no amendments, and the House approved it by voice vote.

The Virginia senate approved House Joint Resolution 236 after the Rules Committee amended it by adding four clauses:

> WHEREAS, the United States Department of Education has proposed regulations that would require public schools to teach children with limited command of English in their native language while they learn English and that would preclude other methods of instruction such as intensive instruction in English alone; and

> WHEREAS, such regulations approach the mandating of curriculum by the federal government and usurp the powers and functions of the states and local school boards; and

> WHEREAS, the costs of changing to bilingual instruction from intensive English instruction or other methods of instruction and the greater expense of bilingual instructional programs will strain already hard-pressed state and local budgets; and

> WHEREAS, there is no evidence that bilingual instruction is a superior method; rather, it may merely delay assimilation of the children into regular classrooms; and

> WHEREAS, English is the national and unifying language of the many peoples who have become known simply as Americans and who speak with one tongue; and

> WHEREAS, there is empirical experience to demonstrate that non-English speaking students learn English most rapidly when they are not instructed in their native language; and

> *WHEREAS, the United States Secretary of Education has expressed his intentions to rescind the proposed regulations and adopt more flexible regulations; and*

> *WHEREAS, the United States Secretary of Education recently waived the proposed regulations as to the program instituted by the County of Fairfax for teaching English as a second language;*

> RESOLVED by the House of Delegates, the Senate concurring, That the General Assembly of Virginia expresses its

total and adamant opposition to the regulations proposed by
the United States Department of Education relating to bilingual instruction; and, be it

*RESOLVED FURTHER, that the General Assembly of Vir-
ginia commends the United States Secretary of Education for
his stated intention to rescind the proposed regulations and
for his action with regard to the Fairfax County Public
Schools; and be it*

*RESOLVED FURTHER, that the General Assembly of Vir-
ginia encourages the United States Secretary of Education to
develop new regulations for instruction of foreign language
students in consultation with the states; and be it*

RESOLVED FINALLY, That the Clerk of the House of Delegates send a copy of this resolution to each member of the Virginia delegation to the Congress of the United States, to the
President of the United States, and to the United States Secretary of Education.[3] [Rules Committee emendations in italics]

That wording was accepted, and House Joint Resolution 236 was
approved en bloc, with eleven other resolutions, on a voice vote.

Not only did the Delegates take issue with "transitional"
bilingual educational programs—favoring the immersion approach—but the senate amendments were designed to appeal for a
change in policy by the incoming Reagan Administration. President Reagan eventually named two Secretaries of Education. T.H.
Bell served during Reagan's entire first term, and then William J.
Bennett was appointed to the office. Bennett advocated "transitional" rather than "maintenance" bilingual education programs
and was quickly personified as an enemy of multiculturalism.

The resentment against federal authority seemed not to be
appeased, although the Virginia legislature managed to make some
accommodation for bilingual education in its 1986 amendments to
the official English law.[4] Those changes were proposed in House
Bill 403, co-sponsored by Frederick H. Creekmore (D-Chesapeake), Thomas V. Forehand Jr. (D-Chesapeake), and N. Leslie
Saunders (D-Chesterfield). The Education Committee of the
House of Delegates, which reviewed the bill, voted 11–1–0 to offered a substitute that would amend and reenact section 22.1-212.1

of the Code of Virginia. It passed the House on a 95–2 vote.
In the senate, the Education and Health Committee reported
the bill with amendments, adding the phrase "except courses in
foreign languages" and inserting the sentence "School boards shall
provide instruction designed to facilitate the mainstreaming of students for whom English is a second language." Both were
approved by voice vote; then House Bill 403 was approved en
bloc (with nine other measures), the senate voting 40–0.
When the senate version of House Bill 403 was returned to
the House of Delegates, the changes were rejected. Presumably to
show his contempt for language that more or less endorsed bilingual educational programs, Theodore V. Morrison Jr. (D–Newport
News) moved that the bill be referred to the Committee on Chesa-
peake and Its Tributaries. Though his motion was ruled out of order,
the senate amendments were defeated 35–62. Morrison and Guest,
who had authored the official English bill in 1981 (his co-sponsor,
Gray, was not a member in 1986), voted with the opposition. Nine
of twenty-two delegates who sponsored the 1981 antibilingual resolution were still members, and they split 6–3 on the amendments.
Back in the upper chamber, Senator William T. Parker
(D-Chesapeake) moved that the senate request a conference committee but insist on its amendments to the bill, and the senators
agreed to that on a 40–0 vote. In the House of Delegates, a motion
by Creekmore that the house accede to the senate request for a
conference on House Bill 403 was accepted, whereupon three
members from each chamber were named to negotiate the differences. The Speaker, though he had voted against the senate
amendments to the bill, appointed Creekmore and Saunders—the
two co-sponsors of House Bill 403 who voted for the amendments—and one member who voted against them, George W.
Grayson (D-Williamsburg), as conferees for the lower chamber.
Both sides ultimately retained the phrase "except courses in
foreign languages" but revised the last sentence to read: "School
boards shall endeavor to provide instruction in the English language which shall be designed to promote the education of students
for whom English is a second language." The report was adopted
by the senate, which voted 38–0, but the 82–11–1 tally in the House

showed residual opposition: all but one of the eleven votes against the conference report were from delegates who had rejected the original senate wording. But Guest shifted, voting in favor of the compromise, as did the majority of those opposed to the senate language. Creekmore, Forehand, and Saunders also voted in favor.

Adverse experience with federal mandates concerning bilingual educational programs motivated Virginia to pass its English language law. Similar problems did not inspire the English Only enactments by the states of Indiana, Tennessee, and Kentucky, all of which occurred in 1984.

INDIANA

The process in Indiana began when Senate Bill 243 was introduced.[5] The key sponsor, Senator Joseph Corcoran (R-Seymour), recalled his experiences living in Canada from 1965 to 1968: "I saw what happens when you wind up with two languages. In order to function in business, to work in government, to achieve anything at all you have to be bilingual . . . capable of speaking both English and French."[6] In a lengthy editorial, the *Indianapolis Star* expressed a hope for an "early passage" of the Corcoran bill:

> A common tongue for communication is essential to any society, whether tribal group or large industrial state. This is almost universally recognized. Nigeria, the most populous African nation, has 380 different languages, none of them mutually intelligible. So that the 77 million citizens can understand each other, Nigeria's official language is notably enough, English. So is Ghana's.
>
> For similar reasons French is the official language of the Ivory Coast, which has several tribal languages.
>
> This month the USSR announced it was overhauling its school system to improve the quality of education in primary and secondary schools. The plan calls for all children, regardless of their mother tongue, to master Russian by the time they leave high school. Many children in the Soviet Union's 15 constituent areas speak Russian poorly and study in their native language.

It's not a matter of narrow chauvinism, for example, that Spanish is the official language of Argentina, which has a heavy Italian ethnic presence, but simply that its constitution, laws, official documents, road signs, etc. are in Spanish. An official language does not mean, nor does Corcoran contend it does, that other tongues shouldn't be spoken. Knowledge of different languages is a mark of culture. But a society needs one language in which everybody is functionally literate.[7]

A later news account stated that Corcoran believed the bill would put Indiana in the vanguard of efforts to end bilingualism as governmental and educational policy. He was quoted as saying: "Yes, I hope it would. I hope it would get those kids out of that crutch treatment and into learning English." According to the report, Corcoran had learned that "certain elements" in East Chicago, home to a sizable Hispanic population, wanted to use Spanish in the schools there.[8] Another legislator who co-sponsored this legislation agreed that the bill was meant to be an "attention-getter" for educators.[9] Corcoran was joined in sponsoring the legislation by three other senators and three House members (a total of five Republicans and two Democrats). After a recommendation to pass the measure by the senate Committee on Public Policy, the bill was adopted by the senate on a 36–13 roll-call vote. The Committee on Public Policy and Veterans Affairs of the House also reported the bill to the floor, again without any amendments, whereupon it was approved by a more than two-to-one margin (65–30). All but one of the opposition votes in the senate were cast by Democrats, who also accounted for twenty-six of thirty no votes in the lower chamber. This division of opinion resulted, as one sponsor recollected, because the Indiana Civil Liberties Union came out against the bill and the black caucus of the General Assembly was also opposed.[10]

Nikolai Burlakoff, director of the International Center of Indianapolis, responded that the bill was "not helping our image as a progressive state." He noted that Indianapolis International Airport had no bilingual signs and added: "The danger of another language's becoming dominant here is minimal. However, by stressing

English so strongly, we may alienate some groups who feel another language is important to them. It's sad."[11]

The Indiana Department of Instruction (DPI) took no position on the pending legislation and continued to implement a federally funded bilingual-bicultural educational project targeted at about five thousand students needing help in learning English as a second language. "The law's vagueness is puzzling," said Joseph P. Di-Laura of the DPI. "It's going to need clarification." While Senator Corcoran agreed that federal law and court rulings took precedence over the Indiana statute, he had a longer-term perspective: "Conceivably, in a few years we'll see some changes in federal legislation, and Indiana may be one of the contributing factors causing that change."[12]

A senate sponsor of the Indiana law explained that the measure was his "own cause" and resulted from an awareness of population changes elsewhere in the country. He acted "in anticipation" of future problems, and his objective was to "set the position" in law that English was the official language. Some constituents became aware of the legislation "in the latter days of the session," and all comments to him about the law since then, he added, had been "complimentary" and "supportive." Two of the House co-sponsors made similar observations. They were not aware of any local problems and were invited to assist with the bill. When asked if their action would help them politically, one said, "I don't think so." The other declared, "Not to any extent," since his constituents probably "didn't particularly care."[13]

TENNESSEE

The debate in the Tennessee General Assembly on House Bill 2119 and Senate Bill 2065 was brief and tinged with levity.[14] Eight members from both houses co-sponsored these bills. House Bill 2119 was endorsed by the Committee on State and Local Government and was considered first by the lower chamber, where, on the floor, Representative C. Ray Davis (D-Milan) called the legislation a "housekeeping" bill designed to establish a "legal basis" for local school boards to conduct classes in English and local governments to do business in English, to keep down the expenses of local government, and to establish a method for denying requests to post signs in other languages and or to use other languages in schools and businesses. When Representative Michael L. Kernell (D-Memphis) asked whether it prohibited teaching non-English students English so they could participate in classes, Davis answered, "No."[15] On the third reading, the bill was passed 84–1, with Representative Edward H. Moody (R-Morristown) being the only dissenter.

A newswriter observed that Senate Bill 2065 was reported by a "good-humored" State and Local Government Committee with seven affirmative votes and two abstentions. Senator Frank Lashlee (D-Camden) was reportedly asked by Senator Jim Lewis (D–South Pittsburg): "We don't know anyone who speaks another language, do you?" Lashlee responded: "Where I come from, it's a language all its own." Nonetheless, he reportedly said that the time might come when a second language, like Spanish, would become equally well used.[16]

This kind of lighthearted exchange continued on the senate floor as discussions focused on the bill's purpose and the meaning of American English. In the senate there was a motion to make Senate Bill 2065 conform with House Bill 2119 and another to substitute House Bill 2119 for Senate Bill 2065. Both were adopted. During floor debate Senator Lashlee commented that the wording "American English" sounded funny to Senator Douglas Henry Jr. (D-Nashville) but proceeded to refer to the "bilingual situation" facing local governments, noting that local governments needed something legal to say that English "will be our standard language" insofar as "all the states" will be faced with many other languages being introduced into the United States.[17]

Two amendments were offered. First, Senator Henry proposed to delete "American" from the phrase "American English"; in debate, he said that he wanted a "definite" language and questioned what American English was. Senator Lashlee indicated that he was an American and liked "American English" but had no problem with Henry's amendment. It was adopted. But then Senator Stephen Ira Cohen (D-Memphis) declared that Tennesseeans speak "Southern English" and not the king's English and that he was proud of being southern. (Cohen listed in his biography a membership in Irish Eyes of Memphis.[18]) Cohen made a motion to delete "American" and substitute "Southern" in the text. In what must have been a humorous moment on the floor, Senator Lashlee responded that it was "no laughing matter" and then moved that Cohen's amendment be tabled. It was, on a 25–3 vote; the three no votes were cast by Senators Cohen, Edward Davis (D-Memphis), and Carl Koella Jr. (R-Townsend). House Bill 2119 as amended was then passed 31–0.

Asked why this legislation was introduced, a House sponsor responded, "Why do we have to pay twice" for printing documents or for educating people in languages other than English? "Tax-payers," he added, "are burdened enough." While admittedly no problem existed in Tennessee "at the time," he chose to author the legislation because he had made frequent business trips to other states that had to cope with difficulties related to the Spanish language. He wanted to "avoid the problem" in Tennessee, though his bill "didn't really matter" to his constituents until what was happening elsewhere "was brought to their attention."[19] A senate sponsor agreed, recalling that the issue had "surfaced" and the legislation was intended to "head off" future problems in case the courts tried to force localities to have teachers speaking English, Spanish, German, or other languages "side by side" in classes. Asked about public opinion concerning the bill in his district, he said: "I don't think the average person on the street was aware of it."[20]

KENTUCKY

The official English legislation for Kentucky was introduced as Senate Bill 145 and referred to the Committee on State Government.[21] The one-line statute, authored solely by Senator Louis T. Peniston (D–New Castle), was reported favorably by the committee and passed by a 35–0 margin. The House Committee on State Government also endorsed the measure, which eventually cleared the floor. Before final enactment, however, an amendment to the bill was filed by Representative Thomas J. Burch (D-Louisville) that had nothing to do with the subject matter at hand. Following the statement "English is designated as the official state language of Kentucky," he proposed to add three more subsections:

(2) Denturist[s] must use the official state language to communicate with the people they make dentures for.

(3) Denturists means a person who constructs, repairs, relines, reproduces, rebases, adjusts, duplicates, supplies, alters, furnishes or fits in the human oral cavity a full or partial removable denture and who also takes impressions, bite registration, tryings, and insertion of or in any part of the human oral cavity for any of the purposes listed in this paragraph.

(4) Denturists shall be exempted from the provisions of KRS Chapter 313 and the activities under subsection 3 of Section 1 shall not constitute the practice of dentistry as defined by KRS Chapter 313.

Beyond requiring denturists to use the official language in communicating with their patients, the proposal would have exempted these technicians from the dentistry licensing requirements of the Kentucky Revised Statutes. So there was a serious purpose behind the motion, one that Burch had pursued before in his legislative career. The official English bill was a vehicle to allow laboratory technicians to do this specified kind of dental work.[22] But it was not accepted, and Senate Bill 145 was adopted on an 84–7 vote, with Burch siding with the majority. Voting no were Representatives Joe Barrows (D-Versailles), Harbert Deskins Jr. (D-Pikeville), Louie R. Guenthner Jr. (R-Louisville), Terry L. Mann (D-Newport), Raymond Overstreet (R-Liberty), Elvin E. Patrick (R-Williamsburg), and Herman W. Rattliff (R-Campbellsville).

In 1986 Georgia passed an official English resolution (see chapter 8), and five states followed with laws in 1987: Arkansas, Mississippi, North Carolina, South Carolina, and North Dakota. Another enactment came in 1989, when the Alabama legislature proposed a constitutional amendment that was ratified by the voters in 1990 (chapter 6).

ARKANSAS

The Arkansas General Assembly passed two laws in 1987.[23] What became Act 77 was Senate Bill 55, and the companion measure House Bill 1014 was adopted as Act 40. Three legislators originally sponsored these official English bills; all three came from districts in the northwestern part of the state, where the University of Arkansas is located. They were not alone for long: seventy legislators signed on as co-sponsors of the legislation. One of the House sponsors of House Bill 1014 noted that Spanish-speaking migrant workers were locating in southern Arkansas, that some Vietnamese and Cambodians had settled in the state, and that about twenty thousand Cubans were being held at a military facility near Fort Smith, though some were being helped by local sponsors to resettle in that area. While these groups were "no major concern," he wished to prevent bilingualism from "destroying good English curriculum in the schools." The Fort Smith school district was already having difficulties finding texts for bilingual programs, he said, and while he was not against bilingual programs as such, he was opposed to "implanting" a non-English language in that community. So this sponsor acted to close a "loophole." Since a 1934 state law requires English to be the instructional language in classrooms, however, a declaratory statute would be sufficient. He was "not anticipating" an enforcement problem. If one arose, the state legislature could always act at a later date.[24]

This legislator's views are consistent with the changes made to Senate Bill 55 on the senate floor. After being reported favorably by the State Agencies and Governmental Affairs Committee of the senate, one of the co-sponsors offered a floor amendment, reading, "Except that this Act shall not prohibit the public schools from performing their duty to provide equal educational opportunity to all children." The effect of this amendment would be to allow some bilingual educational instruction. The motion was adopted by voice vote, after which the bill was passed on a 30–2 roll call. The sponsor of the motion indicated that some educators in his district were concerned that the original bill might preclude the teaching of foreign languages in high school or college, and he had no intention of doing that, so the clarifying amendment was added.[25]

After the companion measure, House Bill 1014, was recommended favorably by the House Committee on Aging and Legislative Affairs, an amendment that added seventy more House co-sponsors (for a total of seventy-two in the House, plus one in the senate) was approved by the majority. Then it was formally adopted on a 94–0 vote. One House sponsor felt that his colleagues probably wanted to wait and see "how the [political] tide went." Once they began hearing positive things from their constituents, then they wished to be added as co-sponsors. Another sponsor felt that the large number of co-sponsors was a measure of the popularity of the bill but was also intended to present a unified front, since some local media commentators had "implied racism" in the matter. Having so many representatives formally endorse the bill carried more political weight than if they had only voted for it, he explained.[26]

A sponsor of House Bill 1014 said that bilingualism was "not a current problem but a potential problem" that led to this legislation, although he took note of the bilingual situations in other states, such as Louisiana, Texas, and California. Since his district mainly comprised "white Anglo-Saxon Protestants," the issue was "not an emotional thing" with his constituents. Politically, his action would neither help nor hurt him; it was basically a "neutral," though some local educators had raised questions.[27]

MISSISSIPPI

Four official English bills were introduced in the Mississippi legislature.[28] House Bill 144 was sponsored by Representatives David M. Halbrook (D-Belzoni) and Jerry E. Wilkerson (D-Daleville), House Bill 265 by Theodore J. Millette (D-Pascagoula), and House Bill 697 by H. Scott Ross (D-West Point) and Robert Warren Moak (D–Bogue Chitto). In the upper chamber, Senate Bill 2101 was introduced by Senators Aubrey M. Childre (D-Pearl) and Wayne Oliver Burkes (D-Clinton); later, Senator George E. Guerieri (D-Southaven) joined them. The four bills were referred to the Education Committees of the appropriate chamber. There were no preambles to House Bills 265 and 697—both were one-line declarations that "the English language is the official language of the State of Mississippi"—but House Bill 144, as well as Senate Bill 2101, contained an identical preface that gives a clue to the motivations behind this legislation:

> WHEREAS, new immigrants have historically been welcomed and quickly assimilated into our national fabric

adding their talents, industry and zeal to the strength and unity of our nation; and

WHEREAS, this assimilation was fostered by the bonding cement of a common language; and

WHEREAS, this common language has been responsible to a great extent for the United States evolving into a nation with a strong national identity while still preserving the richness of ethnic and cultural diversity; and

WHEREAS, in a pluralistic society such as ours, government should foster the similarities that unite us; and

WHEREAS, we recognize the principle that a common language is necessary to preserve the basic internal unity required for political stability and national cohesion, but we also encourage the study of foreign languages in the schools of the State of Mississippi and recognize the right of individuals and groups to use other languages; and

WHEREAS, it is not the intent of this act to prohibit or discourage the use of foreign languages and cultures in private contexts, such as homes, community groups, churches or private organizations; and

WHEREAS, it is not the intent of the Legislature to prohibit the teaching of foreign languages in the public schools or colleges, nor to prohibit foreign language requirements in academic institutions:

NOW, THEREFORE, BE IT ENACTED BY THE LEGISLATURE OF THE STATE OF MISSISSIPPI:

SECTION 1. English is designated the official language of the State of Mississippi. There is no obligation for any public school to teach the standard curriculum in a language other than English.

SECTION 2. This act shall take effect and be in force from and after July 1, 1987.

Two of the House Bills died in the House Education Committee, though on February 3 the committee did recommend passage of House Bill 265. But on the twelfth of February Representative Thomas H. Walman (D-McComb) moved to recommit House Bill 265, perhaps being alert to the fact that the senate six days earlier had passed Senate Bill 2101. Whatever the reason,

House Bill 265 was recommitted on a 94–22 vote to the Education Committee, where it died along with House Bills 144 and 697. In the senate, Senate Bill 2101 was reported by the Education Committee and approved on a 50–1 roll-call vote; the negative vote was cast by Wendell H. Bryan II (D-Amory). The preamble argues that while pluralism should be allowed in "private contexts," the state of Mississippi ought to foster a common language in order to achieve social unity. A legislator who authored one of the official English bills noted that people from Maine to California to Florida speak the same language. Therefore he strongly believed that a "common language is the strength of the country" and essential for "the economy and commerce" and "national cohesiveness." Another sponsor expressed a similar opinion that, while he supported foreign language study, he also felt that people "need to learn English as soon as possible to become part of the American citizenry."[29]

When Senate Bill 2101 was forwarded to the House, the Education Committee recommended its approval, but on the floor Representative Halbrook offered an amendment. He proposed stripping away the second line of the original: "There is no obligation for any public school to teach the standard curriculum in a language other than English." The change allowed the possibility of bilingual education programs. But other legislators then proposed three more amendments to Halbrook's; according to one sponsor, these proposals were made "in jest and seriousness."[30]

The first amendment poked some fun at the General Assembly by declaring that "this act shall take effect and be in force on such date that each member of the Mississippi Legislature shall have completed a course of remedial English and passed an English proficiency test developed and administered by the State Department of Education." The second amendment provided for a local option (and probably a good bit of humor); each county could hold a referendum on "approving the use of a language other than English as the official language of the county." It elaborated:

> that any county wherein there exists a substantial interest in a language other than English; or any county in which there is

a substantial number of persons who speak a language other than English; or any county in which there is a city named for a Polish war hero [the county seat of Attala County is Kosciusko]; or any county names for an Indian Chief [Itawamba County] or any county named for an Indian tribe [Chickasaw and Choctaw Counties] may adopt as the official language of such county any language other than English if approved by a majority of the electors of such county voting in an election held on such proposition. It is further provided that any three (3) continuous coast counties housing a significant number of inhabitants named Dubaz and Vecchio [both were state representatives] may elect to adopt the Yugoslav language as their official language as provided for herein.

The final section of this amendment also mandated that "the following words and terms will be no longer recognized in this state since said words and terms are either incomprehensible or are not of pure English extraction: Y'all; Hominy; canoe; up-air; downnair; and yonder."

The third amendment required that "all official symbols and insignia of the State of Mississippi and any of its agencies, institutions or subdivisions shall be in English." This would mean that the Mississippi motto, *Virtute et armis*, would have to be changed to "By valor and arms."

These three amendments were handily defeated on 85–31, 77–41, and 78–38 roll-call votes. Final passage of the bill in the lower chamber came on a 93–27 vote. The amendments were not merely attempts at humor, because, of the twenty-seven representatives who voted against the official English bill, most stuck together to vote against the motions to table them (representing twenty-five, twenty-four, and twenty-two of the votes cast against tabling the three amendments).

One who authored the Mississippi legislation said that no problem existed in Mississippi but that "in other states there were court rulings to require teaching in the language of the students." That concern prompted him to introduce a bill. When asked whether the measure would have a political impact, his candid response was "I don't think so, not significantly." His action on the measure "did not help or hurt politically" with his constituents, he believed.[31]

Those sentiments were echoed by another sponsor, who could not recollect that any apparent problem was addressed by the bill. His action was of "no help" politically in his district, and no bilingual publications or educational programs were available in Mississippi, he said, "that I know of." A third co-sponsor agreed, saying that the bill "was to rectify a problem that did not even exist," and so "I don't think it was even noticed" by the public. Nor was he aware of any non-English publications by the state government.[32]

NORTH CAROLINA

Though the outcome of the dispute was not much in doubt, the opponents of official English put up some resistance in North Carolina.[33] Ultimately they achieved a partial victory, since only a symbolic statute emerged from the lawmaking process. While Senate Bill 115, making English the official language of the state, was enacted, it was substantively weakened by an amendment offered in committee. As introduced by Senators Franklin L. Block (D-Wilmington) and Marshall A. Rauch (D-Gastonia) on March 5, 1987, the bill proposed that a new section be added to chapter 145 of the General Statutes. The original statement, including the language deleted by amendment, reads as follows:

(a) Purpose. English is the common language of the people of the United States of America and the State of North Carolina. This section is intended to preserve, protect and strengthen the English language, and not to supersede any of the rights guaranteed to the people by the Constitution of the United States or the Constitution of North Carolina.

(b) English as the Official Language of North Carolina. English is the official language of the State of North Carolina.

(c) *Enforcement. The General Assembly shall enforce this section by appropriate legislation. The General Assembly and officials of the State of North Carolina shall take all steps necessary to insure that the role of English as the*

common language of the State of North Carolina is pre-
served and enhanced. The General Assembly shall make no
law which diminishes or ignores the role of English as the
common language of the State of North Carolina.

(d) *Personal Right of Action and Jurisdiction of Courts. Any*
person who is a resident of or doing business in the State of
North Carolina shall have standing to sue the State of North
Carolina to enforce this section. The courts of record of the
State of North Carolina shall have jurisdiction to hear cases
brought to enforce this section. The General Assembly may
provide reasonable and appropriate limitations on the time
and manner of suits brought under this section.[34] [portions
deleted by amendment in italics]

The bill was assigned to the Committee on Judiciary-IV of the
senate. A motion by Senator Dennis Jay Winner (D-Asheville)—
who would support the bill on the floor vote—to delete sections c
and d was adopted. Then the legislation was reported to the floor,
where Senator Block moved for adoption of Committee Amendment 1. As amended, Senate Bill 115 was passed 42–0 on the
second reading on April 3, but William N. Martin (D-Greensboro),
a black senator, objected to a third reading, thus forcing the bill to
remain on the calendar until April 7. It was then passed 47–1
following a third reading. Nine Republicans in the North Carolina
senate and all Democrats but one (with two abstentions) supported
the bill. The lone dissenter was Martin, though he did vote for
Committee Amendment 1 on the second reading. Three other black
legislators, Senators Ralph A. Hunt (D-Durham), Wanda H. Hunt
(D-Moore), and James F. Richardson (D-Charlotte), voted for
Committee Amendment 1 and for final enactment.

Though the bill was now reduced to a symbolic gesture, attempts were made to defeat even this legislation in the House,
where Senate Bill 115 was assigned to the Judiciary-I Committee.
It heard testimony from Norman E. Jarrard, a professor of English
at North Carolina Agricultural and Technical State University, who
also submitted a memorandum from the national leadership of
Teachers of English to Speakers of Other Languages (TESOL) to
its local affiliates and resolutions adopted by the Linguistic Society
of America, the Modern Language Association of America, and

the National Council of Teachers of English, all opposing official English legislation.

In his prepared statement, Professor Jarrard declared that "such laws have been obtaining overwhelming public support in spite of the fact that most language professionals, including English teachers, are very much opposed to them. Although the laws seem to be innocent on the surface, the sponsors make no bones about their desire to do away with tax-supported bilingual education programs, to stop printing multilingual ballots, to stop giving driver's license tests in any language other than English, and so forth." Asserting that "the prejudice against new citizens is very close to the surface" and that such laws "are designed to discourage immigration because of the myth that foreigners take jobs from white Anglo-Saxon Americans who, of course, speak English without an 'accent,'" he concluded that "such laws are linguistically naive (compare the California law mandating one particular dialect of English) and mean-spirited and unbecoming a fair-minded, democratic pluralistic society. The stated purpose to unify the country is not working and could not possibly work. We are better unified by understanding and accepting cultural and linguistic diversity."[35]

But Senate Bill 115 was reported favorably by the committee on June 17, though floor consideration was postponed until the twenty-fourth, when various parliamentary maneuvers necessitated that six recorded votes be taken. A motion by Representative H.M. Michaux Jr. (D-Durham), one of thirteen black House members, that the bill be withdrawn from the calendar and re-referred to the Education Committee was rejected; the House voted 63–36 for a second motion by Richard Wright (D–Tabor City) to table Michaux's motion. Wright then called the previous question, and the bill passed its second reading on a 71–29 vote. But Michaux made another attempt to block the bill, objecting to the third reading. Then Wright moved that the rules be suspended in order for the bill to be read a third time, and Wright's motion carried on a 68–32 vote. The House supported a motion from Wright to call the previous question and pass Senate Bill 115 on its third reading. The final vote on the third reading, on June 24, 1987, was 74–25. It is noteworthy that twenty-three of the negative votes were cast by

Democrats, including ten black representatives. Only one Republican voted no among the thirty-one GOP members of the House.

It was reported that Senator Block, a bill co-sponsor and a freshman Democrat, told both senate and House committees that his grandparents were Latvian immigrants who realized the importance of learning the English language despite the difficulties. During the House debate, Representative Wright, who managed the bill on the floor, called the English language "marvelous" after jokingly beginning his speech using French. But then Representative Bertha Holt (D-Alamance), who later voted no, asked Wright why the law was needed, "especially when you just finished speaking to us in some type of French." Wright responded, "We certainly have (an) obligation . . . not to become the melting pot to the extent that we all lose our identity," but he added, "For political and cultural and a wide variety of reasons, we need to have a common language." The news account indicated that Wright, when questioned further, could give no concrete reasons for the legislation.[36]

Holt called the measure "very dangerous when we do not know what this means to education." Then Representative Michaux warned that the bill was so "open-ended" that it could lead to attempts to ban teaching foreign languages in state schools and to change the state's 1893 Latin motto, *Esse quam videri*, which means "To be rather than to seem." "Is it possible to bring a suit to have the motto translated from its beautiful lilting lyric?" he asked. Michaux also contended that the bill could be used to attack bilingual education. "America is a great melting pot," Michaux told his colleagues. "Our language results from the diversity of people that we have in that melting pot."[37]

Another speaker, Representative Harry Payne (D–New Hanover), who voted in favor of the bill, responded that the measure was intended to encourage newcomers to become proficient in the English language and that it carried no ethnic or racial implications. "There is nothing anti–other culture about this bill," Payne said. Floor manager Wright agreed: "Many people have tried to make something controversial out of something that is not."[38]

Educators were uneasy about the law. Members of the National Council of State Supervisors of Foreign Languages, some forty educators responsible for state language programs, were alarmed, thinking that the official language movement might undercut student interest in foreign language. As past president L. Gerard Toussaint observed: "We don't want to regress, to fall back into isolationism and provincialism of past decades." Furthermore, "there are cultural, academic, and practical benefits to having all people maintain and develop and share their respective languages and cultures." The view of the North Carolina Department of Public Instruction was that the law was primarily an economic measure to prevent the state government from having to produce costly bilingual signs and publications. "I don't see where it will have any negative impact on the public schools," commented assistant state superintendent of instruction Joseph B. Webb.[39]

Less sanguine was the view of Jamie B. Draper, assistant director of the Joint National Committee for Languages, a agency in Washington, D.C., representing thirty language teaching associations nationwide (and an endorser of the English Plus Information Clearinghouse). "The major concern is we are finally getting to the point where learning foreign languages is considered an important thing to do," Draper declared, "and it could be that a backlash is going to come on foreign language itself."[40]

SOUTH CAROLINA

The legislation for official English in South Carolina (House Bill 2191) was introduced on January 15, 1987, with seventeen representatives (eleven Democrats and six Republicans) as sponsors. Referred to the Committee on Medical, Military, Public and Municipal Affairs, it emerged unchanged with a favorable recommendation.[41]

On the floor of the House, Representative James E. Lockemy (D-Dillon) proposed Amendment 1, which weakened the proscription against using non-English languages. The amendment was adopted. The bill, as finally enacted, read:

> SECTION 1. The English language is the official language of the State of South Carolina.
>
> SECTION 2. Neither this State nor any political subdivision thereof shall require, by law, ordinance, regulation, order,

decree, program, or policy, the use of any language other than English; *provided, that nothing in this act shall prohibit a state agency or a political subdivision of the State from requiring an applicant to have certain degrees of knowledge of a foreign language as a condition of employment where appropriate.*

SECTION 3. This act does not prohibit any law, ordinance, regulation, order, decree, program, or policy requiring educational instruction in a language other than English for the purpose of making students who use a language other than English proficient in English or making students proficient in a language in addition to English.

SECTION 4. This act takes effect upon approval by the Governor. [House amendment in italics]

The change made in section 2 coupled with the explicit wording of section 3 allowed bilingual educational programs for non-English-speaking students as well as the employment of teachers with facility in languages other than English. The amendment eliminated any suggestion that the law disallows the use of courtroom interpreters, for example, where either party to the dispute or witnesses do not speak English or speak English as a second language. The bill passed the House on February 4, 1987.

House Bill 2191 was sent to the Education Committee of the senate, which made no changes in the House language; it also reported the legislation favorably. On March 25 the senators approved the measure on the second reading after Senator Warren K. Giese (R-Columbia), a Distinguished Professor Emeritus of the University of South Carolina, moved "unanimous consent" that it be scheduled for a third reading the next day. This action, meaning that the bill would be automatically approved on its third and final reading, on March 26, implies that no substantial opposition emerged against the measure in the state senate.

Following the senate action, the *State*, a newspaper serving the capital city of Columbia, reported that the measure "ensures that, as South Carolina's non-English-speaking population grows, the state will not have to offer such things as driver's tests and elementary school classes in other languages." Some reactions   by proponents and opponents were also reported. "The ACLU and other flaming liberals are saying you are putting down minorities (with the bill) and that's not so," said House sponsor Eugene D. Foxworth Jr. (R-Charleston). "We just want to support our English-speaking heritage." But Steve Bates of the ACLU reportedly responded that most people who had come to America in the past two centuries did not speak English when they arrived. He labeled the measure "innocuous and silly" and added: "It does not show the best side of the American tradition for tolerance and openness to people throughout the world."[42] Republican governor Carroll A. Campbell Jr. signed the bill into law on April 14, though a reporter for Charleston's *News and Courier* observed that "few people outside the Capitol's walls seemed to notice or care." Concerning why the official English law was adopted, Senator Foxworth said: "Because we wanted it on the books before it became a controversy."[43]

NORTH DAKOTA

North Dakota's official English law, Senate Bill 2096, was sponsored by three state senators and two representatives.[44] Originally it read: "The English language is the official language of the state of North Dakota. School boards have no obligation to teach the standard curriculum in a language other than English."

In the upper house the bill was referred to the Education Committee, which held hearings.[45] One sponsor, Senator Harvey D. Tallackson (D-Grafton), told the committee that U.S. senator Quentin Burdick (D-N.Dak.) was supporting legislation at the federal level to make English the official language of the United States. Tallackson indicated that the language of Senate Bill 2096 did not mean that only English had to be taught in school—schools could offer as many languages as they wished—but that English would be the only language required to be taught. According to committee records, Senator Pete Naaden (R-Braddock), a co-sponsor, reiterated the view that English as an official language would keep the state united. Two representatives also testified in favor of the measure: Rosemarie Myrdal (R-Edinburg), a House co-sponsor, and Rick Berg (R-Fargo).

An assistant attorney general, Terry Adkins, reportedly said that the bill did not indicate whether or not legal transactions had to be in English, and he added that language is not part of a legal contract. Peter Gefroh, of the North Dakota Department of Instruction, indicated that he had no qualms about the bill other than a concern about the requirement that only English be taught; he believed that more than one language should be taught in the schools.

In written testimony on behalf of the North Dakota Education Association, Willis Heinrich stated that "the bill appears to be simple, with little or no impact and something which fits into our patriotic urges very nicely." But he asked rhetorically: "Why then, as we near our 100th birthday of statehood and our 200th birthday since our national Constitution, is it time to declare what we are now doing as official?" He answered, "The primary motivation behind this effort is to maintain the status quo." He was concerned "that it might downplay the importance of the native languages of many Americans" that "have contributed to a rich and dynamic English language."

Kathleen Eagle, president of the North Dakota Council of Teachers of English, an affiliate of the National Council of Teachers of English, also provided written testimony against the legislation. She read a 1986 resolution by the NCTE and explained the organization's opposition to this legislation, which "is loaded with potential for discrimination. It carries a hidden agenda to maintain social status through language, to defend the notion that when America speaks English, the rest of the world had better be prepared to listen in English, and to protect us from the growing 'Spanish menace'—the threat that by the year 2000, the majority of Americans may be Spanish-speaking people."

Eagle called upon the legislators to consider the effect of this English Only policy on Native Americans before proceeding:

> It would do North Dakota good to look into its own past at the history of Indian education and learn from our mistakes. When Native American children became part of our English-speaking education systems . . . they were told that they must speak English; they could not speak their native tongues. Talk to a Native American who was educated under that policy; let him tell you what a nightmare that was for him. Declaring English to be the "official" language implies a value judgment, and therein lies the hidden agenda of this

bill. People for whom English is not native, who think in another language, would be told that their very thoughts are not "official," somehow nonstandard, and not in keeping with the mainstream, therefore inferior.

In response to a question from the Education Committee chair, Senator Bonnie Heinrich (D-Bismarck), Eagle indicated that the Lakota language was being taught at Standing Rock College.

The concerns of these educators led to an amendment by a committee member, Senator Layton Freborg (R-Underwood), that the second sentence of the bill ("School boards have no obligation to teach the standard curriculum in a language other than English") be deleted. The amendment was passed unanimously, but then the committee voted 4–3 to recommend passage of the bill. Voting yes were Senators Freborg, Earl M. Kelly (R–Valley City), Curtis M. Peterson (R-Fargo), and E. Gene Hilken (D-Wilton), while the no votes were cast by Senators Heinrich, Jerome Kelsh (D-Fullerton), and Tim Mathern (D-Fargo). Had the one Democrat not joined three Republicans, Senate Bill 2096 would have died in committee. The party disagreement on the Education Committee tinged what seemingly was a bipartisan outcome on the senate floor. The final 38–15 roll-call vote found 88 percent of Republicans compared with 56 percent of Democrats in favor; Democrats cast twelve of the nay votes.

In opposing the bill, Heinrich said that she believed it was a rejection of the heritage of the English language, which assimilated many words from other tongues. "We are a great melting pot, and so is our language," she said. But Tallackson had reportedly decided to introduce his bill after voters in California approved an official language amendment to their state constitution. Admittedly the legislation "isn't critical to [North Dakota], but nationally I think it is," Tallackson said. Moreover, "this bill allows what we've been doing since statehood to continue," he told his critics.[46]

The House Committee on Education also had jurisdiction over Senate Bill 2096. Its favorable report on a 13–4 vote reflected the winning margin on the final enactment (78–24), but again the outcome was strained by party loyalties. In the committee, all nine Republicans voted to report the bill, whereas Democrats were evenly divided, four to four. Representative Rosemarie Myrdal floor-managed Senate Bill 2096 for the majority party. On final passage, virtually all Republicans (95 percent) voted for Senate Bill 2096, compared with a bare majority (53 percent) of Democrats. The twenty-one opposition votes were cast by the senate minority party.

Seven people gave testimony before the Education Committee of the House, including Senators Tallackson and Naaden and Representative Myrdal.[47] Myrdal said that the legislation did not oppose teaching foreign languages but that citizens need a common bond that holds them together and, also, that one condition of citizenship is the ability to use and understand a common language, which in American culture is English.

Kay Stephens, past president of the North Dakota Council of Teachers of English, testified that the National Council of Teachers of English opposed official language laws: "Our concern is that this kind of legislation, as innocuous as it may seem, is a mask to hide an anti-immigration sentiment that prevails in some states. The ability to be protected by one's State Constitution should not be dependent upon proficiency in English." Moreover, she continued, "it is important to us that our students achieve competence in the use of language. We are concerned that this bill may threaten bi-lingual programs." When Representative Archie R. Shaw (R-Mandan) asked how she felt about the bilingualism of Canada, Stephens reportedly said that each culture deserves its language. Shaw replied that a large number of immigrants who came to North Dakota were Scandinavian, but they were able to pick up the English language.

Peg Portscheller, president of the North Dakota Education Association, also spoke in opposition. She questioned whether the intent of the bill was to discriminate against the Spanish coming into North Dakota and argued that the Spanish are owed the same rights and opportunities that the Germans and Norwegians had when they came to the state. She also mentioned that the bill could threaten bilingual education. Then Representative Myrdal asked Portscheller about two differing views of bilingual education. Myrdal gave her opinion that it was better to acquire English with an emphasis on learning to speak English and then learning the curriculum in English. But Portscheller, the committee minutes indicate, disagreed with that view and repeated that students whose native tongue is not English should have the opportunity to learn in their own language.

Final testimony was given by Terry Adkins for the attorney general, whose office was trying to determine whether the bill was more a statement by the legislature than a requirement that certain services or documents be in certain languages, and by Rose Christianson, a language teacher from Cooperstown, who supported the bill on the grounds that a single language is needed for unity.

After Senate Bill 2096 was approved by both houses, Governor George A. Sinner, a Democrat, was urged to veto the bill by David Gipp, president of the United Tribes Educational Technical Center. Gipp wrote Sinner to say that "the language in this country is fundamentally 'American'" and is "strengthened" by incorporating "so many nationalities and ethnic groups." He also observed that the name Dakota itself comes from Lakota/Dakota, that is, "the name of one of the significant tribes of this region," which means friend or ally. By making English official, Gipp continued, "we may very well begin to restrict the American language, by potentially outlawing our ability to include such derivatives."[48]

Despite this opposition, the governor signed the bill into law on March 23, 1987. It thus became part of the North Dakota Century Code, which codified such designations as the state's official march ("Flickertail March"), grass (Western wheatgrass), fossil (teredo petrified wood), and beverage (milk).

PATTERNS OF LAWMAKING

The enactments of official English legislation in these nine states can be compared based on key process variables. First, in every case the official English law was approved during the regular session of the legislature when first introduced. Unlike the laws in the referenda states, none were resubmitted after having been once rejected.

Second, the laws were the product of unified party control by Democrats—who held both legislative chambers and the governorship—in Arkansas, Kentucky, and Mississippi, and unified Republican control in Indiana. The laws of North Carolina, South

Carolina, Tennessee, and Virginia were approved by Democratic majorities in both houses but were signed by Republican governors, whereas the Democratic governor of North Dakota approved legislation that had passed a Republican-controlled lower house and a Democratic-controlled senate. So five of the statutes had bipartisan support at a critical point in the lawmaking process. In the referenda states the situation differed. Democratic majorities blocked consideration of official English legislation in California, Florida, and Texas, whereas the GOP-controlled legislatures in Arizona and Colorado backed down in the face of opposition.

Of the nine enactments discussed in this chapter, five Republican and four Democratic governors signed the measures into law; two later gained national political fame. Lamar Alexander of Tennessee was named Secretary of Education under President Bush, and Bill Clinton was governor when the Arkansas bill was passed, though he came to disavow that action during the 1992 presidential campaign. In April he fielded questions via satellite from reporters attending the annual meeting of the National Association of Hispanic Journalists in Albuquerque. "I probably shouldn't have signed the one that passed, but it was passed by a veto-proof majority," Clinton said. "I agreed to sign it only after we changed the law to make it clearer that it would not affect bilingual education, something that I have always strongly supported."[49] Although Clinton takes credit for the amendment allowing bilingual education, the chief sponsor of the amendment said that he acted after hearing concerns from educators in his own district. Nor did the overwhelming support for the measure require that Clinton acquiesce in the decision. He could have taken a principled stand against the legislation and forced its enactment over his veto, which is precisely what the governor of Colorado threatened to do.

Third, when referred to a standing committee, most commonly the official English legislation of the nine states was reviewed by the committee with jurisdiction over educational matters, as occurred in Mississippi, North Dakota, Virginia, and the South Carolina senate. Otherwise, as in Tennessee, Kentucky, and the Arkansas senate, the measures were studied by committees whose purview extended to state and/or local governmental affairs. In every case the committees recommended passage, though in

North Dakota and North Carolina they tacked on amendments before sending the bills to the floor. Amendments were offered during
floor debate in Arkansas, Kentucky, Mississippi, South Carolina,
and Tennessee, and the Virginia law of 1981 was amended five
years later.

Fourth, Virginia was exceptional given the intensity of feelings and because so much time elapsed before the legislature
amended the official English law to acknowledge any need for
bilingual educational assistance. In the states that followed, the
pattern was for amendments to exempt foreign language and bilingual instruction from the general prohibition against non-English
languages. And the declarations of official English were never
strengthened by amendment; where amendments were added, they
had the effect of softening the enforcement language of the laws.

Fifth, there is evidence from two states, Mississippi and Tennessee, that legislators voted for English Only laws although they
did not take them all that seriously. If these deliberations can be
taken as a measure of intent, then seemingly the opponents of official English have exaggerated the dangers of those early and
purely symbolic statutes.

Finally, some testimony refutes the notion that official English was a policy reaction to a real problem, as was the case in
Virginia. Interviews consistently show that the sponsors of these
bills were guided by a concern for the national well-being. From
the language of the bills, public reports, and the comments from
sponsors, the compelling rationale seems to have been a desire to
defend the common English language as an essential element of
social cohesion and harmony. No situations analogous to that in
Florida, where the 1981 and 1982 bills directly focused on bilingualism and biculturalism in Dade County, existed in these states.
None of the sponsors had proposed the legislation in response to a
local problem in their districts or even within the state. Nor did
they seem aware of any state publications in a language other than
English. Rather, they were trying to head off future problems re-
sulting from bilingualism.

The sponsors of the Mississippi, Arkansas, Tennessee, and
Indiana laws had no second thoughts about their content. They believed the laws as written were sufficient. The purpose was to

provide some kind of legal cover to fend off court rulings and to resist having to teach students in a non-English language. But their intention was not to prevent bilingual instruction that might be necessary for linguistic minorities to gain proficiency in English, though the strong presumption was that such programs ought to be transitional and that English proficiency should be achieved as soon as possible. There was no need for more enforcement because there was no pressing problem.

Nor were the sponsors acting at the behest of any individual or organization in their districts. The official English bills they proposed were barely noticed by their constituents. All decision makers who were interviewed expressed the view that the political impact of their action was negligible, though what comments they had gotten from voters usually favored the legislation. Tentatively, we can conclude that those early legislative efforts (Virginia and certainly Indiana, Kentucky, and Tennessee) were not directly orchestrated by U.S. English, though some lawmakers vaguely recalled receiving materials or correspondence from "some group." The Indiana and Tennessee sponsors indicated that they were acting on their own volition, based on personal experiences with what was happening elsewhere, in the United States or Canada.

Now that we know how the English Only bills were processed and the reasons behind that legislation, the analysis can proceed to determining who, among the membership of the governmental bodies, spearheaded the efforts to codify English as the official language of the states. In the next chapter I will explore the common attributes of the sponsors and attempt to uncover the socioeconomic and political variables that best explain voting on the final roll calls approving the bills.

8

STATE LEGISLATIVE
PROCESSES AND OFFICIAL
ENGLISH

This chapter offers a portrait of the members of state legislatures who chose to lead the fight to change existing law, a battle bound to provoke much controversy in western states with sizable Spanish-speaking minority groups. What is more curious is why legislators in other states even bothered to raise this issue. Given the purely symbolic content of the legislation, how much opposition would be generated, and by whom? Did the issue provoke partisan or racial division among the political elite, and if so, where? These data are especially appropriate for evaluating, at the elite level, five alternative hypotheses about whether this backlash reflects racial, ethnic, class, political, or cultural forces.

These data were drawn from the legislative histories of fourteen states. The laws of Nebraska, Illinois, and Hawaii predate the current movement to codify the English language and thus are excluded from this examination. Florida is also omitted, because the last attempt to pass a statute occurred two years before the 1988 referendum. For three other states—Arizona, California, and Colorado—only those sponsors who introduced bills in the year the referendum occurred or in the prior year are included here.

In the eleven other states, the primary legislative sponsors were those who introduced official English bills in the session that enacted a law. All sponsors are included, not just those who co-authored the specific bill enacted, because some legislators sponsored more than one measure while sometimes multiple bills with different sponsors were reconciled or consolidated by a committee before floor action. The objective here is to determine who brought the policy question before the legislatures and what attributes they share. It should be noted that all 122 primary sponsors of official English legislation were white; two black legislators in Alabama and one in Arkansas were part of large groups who co-sponsored bills in those states.

The tables that follow categorize the 122 key sponsors by party affiliation and the political, economic, and demographic makeup of their home counties, defined as the counties where they reside.[1] Home counties always fall within the boundaries of the sponsors' legislative districts. Where a district includes many counties, I have assumed for the purposes of this study that legislators are likely to reside in the most populous county, given the exigencies of electoral politics.

To extrapolate the exact statistics for 122 districts would pose an array of serious methodological problems. Highly urbanized counties include several districts, just as very rural districts span many counties. Census tract data would be needed to align the demographic statistics with the boundaries of each legislative district, while precinct- or township-level voting data would be needed to derive the percentage of votes cast for Ronald Reagan in the 1984 presidential election. On the other hand, a variety of socioeconomic and political indicators are readily available for all U.S. counties; thus, home counties are used as a proxy to reflect the makeup of the legislators' electoral constituencies. Throughout this discussion, the eleven mainly southern and midwestern states with official English statutes are differentiated from the three southwestern and mountain states where referenda were held.

These data suggest that Democrats were more likely than Republicans to initiate legislative proposals to codify English as the official language of a state. While bipartisan sponsorship characterized the progress of the bills in five states—Arkansas, Indiana, North Dakota, South Carolina, and Virginia—only Democrats were key sponsors in Alabama, Georgia, Kentucky, Mississippi, North Carolina, and Tennessee.

Overall, most legislative sponsors in the statutory states were Democrats, because all these states except Indiana and North

Table 8.1. Party Affiliation of Legislative Sponsors of Official English Laws and Their Home County Vote for Ronald Reagan in 1984

	Party Affiliation			
	Senate		House	
	Democrats	*Republicans*	*Democrats*	*Republicans*
Statutory States	11 (65%)	6 (35%)	32 (73%)	12 (27%)
Referenda States	1 (7%)	13 (93%)	2 (4%)	45 (96%)
Total	12 (39%)	19 (61%)	34 (37%)	57 (63%)

	Home County Vote for Ronald Reagan in 1984[a]			
	Democrats		Republicans	
	State Average		*State Average*	
	Vote % for Reagan		Vote % for Reagan	
	Over	*Under*	*Over*	*Under*
Statutory States	23 (53%)	20 (47%)	14 (78%)	4 (22%)
Referenda States	2 (67%)	1 (33%)	45 (78%)	13 (22%)
Total	25 (54%)	21 (46%)	59 (78%)	17 (22%)

[a]Number of counties over and under statewide vote percentages for Reagan in 1984:
Arizona 66%, Arkansas 61%, Alabama 61%, California 58%, Colorado 63%, Georgia 60%, Indiana 62%, Kentucky 60%, Mississippi 62%, North Dakota 65%, North Carolina 62%, South Carolina 64%, Tennessee 58%, Virginia 62%.
Note: Only the primary sponsors are considered here, since a large number of representatives signed on as co-sponsors in Alabama, Arkansas, and Georgia.

Dakota are southern, where historically the Democratic Party has dominated (table 8.1).

The majority of sponsors were GOP legislators in Indiana, where Republicans had control of both houses, and in North Dakota, where Republicans held the majority in the lower chamber. Whereas a degree of bipartisanship typified the eleven statutory states, however, extreme partisanship characterized the pattern of sponsorship in Arizona, California, and Colorado. Seventy percent of the sponsors in the group of eleven states were Democrats, as were 72 percent in the nine southern states only, though Republicans constituted three-fourths of the sponsors in Indiana and North Dakota. But in Arizona and Colorado all sponsors were Republicans, and all but three of the twenty-six California sponsors of official English proposals also had GOP credentials.

Since Hispanics generally tend to vote Democratic, possibly the language controversy was designed to strengthen the Republican hold over Anglos in the referenda states with sizable Spanish-speaking minorities. Where no large Hispanic concentrations are found—across the South—the purely symbolic appeal of English language laws clearly encourages both Republicans and Democrats to promote official language legislation. Southern Democrats traditionally have voted conservatively on various social issues, although additional political incentives may encourage them to promote official language legislation. I have assessed this dynamic by examining the percentage of votes given to Reagan in 1984, in an election that ranks as the fifth largest landslide in U.S. history, in the key sponsors' home counties.

Key sponsors from both parties represented home counties that cast more votes for Reagan than he received statewide; this trend was especially noticeable among Republicans. Overall, 78 percent of Republicans and 54 percent of Democrats resided in counties where Ronald Reagan was exceptionally popular. This pattern holds for the majority of legislative sponsors regardless of party in Arkansas, Georgia, Indiana, Mississippi, North Carolina, and South Carolina, as well as Arizona, California, and Colorado. In the other states, all the Democratic sponsors promoted official English legislation even though a smaller proportion of voters in their home counties voted for Reagan than did voters statewide.

So while Republicans were defending a conservative position in the debate over bilingualism, consistent with the political realities of their constituency base, similar ideological considerations may have influenced some southern Democrats as well. Perhaps the socioeconomic makeup of their constituencies will provide more clues to help explain their legislative behavior.

One can assume that city residents would be less insular in their attitudes toward foreigners and more tolerant of minority lifestyles than small-town or rural dwellers, who may find security in homogeneity. The effects of geography are revealed by comparing the hometown populations with home county populations for the 122 legislative sponsors (table 8.2). Among the sponsors in the eleven southern and midwestern states, 15 percent lived in rural areas with fewer than 1,000 residents; 53 percent resided in towns with fewer than 10,000 residents. Exactly two-thirds of these sponsors came from cities and towns with fewer than 25,000 people. For the most part, their hometowns were not in highly urbanized counties (Table 8.2). Again a major difference exists between the statutory states and the referenda states. Whereas 66 percent of the legislative sponsors in the South and Midwest lived in towns with populations under 25,000, only 20 percent of those from Arizona, California, and Colorado did so. On the other hand, only 2 percent of the sponsors in statutory states, compared with 41 percent of those in the referenda states, lived in cities of 100,000 or more. Notably absent were sponsors from large cities. Indiana's sponsors did not represent districts in Indianapolis; no one from Charlotte or Raleigh led the move to enact the North Carolina law; and in Tennessee the sponsors were not residents of Memphis or Nashville.

In sum, small-town constituencies typify the legislators who sponsored official English laws in the South and Midwest, whereas the virtually all-Republican group from Arizona, California, and Colorado resided in larger communities, likely within the suburban ring of metropolitan areas. This is suggested by the population figures for home counties.

The home counties of the sponsors in the eleven southern and midwestern states are not populous. Forty-one percent were located in counties with fewer than 50,000 people, and the majority (54 percent) came from counties with populations under 100,000, implying the absence of any large central city. Only one legislator came from a county whose population exceeded 500,000. But in Arizona, California, and Colorado, 87 percent of the sponsors lived in counties where the population was greater than 100,000, and for 53 percent the home county population exceeded 500,000. Thus, southern and midwestern legislative sponsors lived in small towns in less populated counties; those from the southwestern and mountain states were essentially suburbanites.[2]

The socioeconomic status profile of home counties shows yet another distinction between the mainly Democratic sponsors in the eleven southern and midwestern states and the virtually all-Republican delegation from Arizona, California, and Colorado (table 8.3). On two class variables, median family income and percentage below poverty, there is little differentiation between the home counties of Republicans and Democrats. All 122 sponsors

Table 8.2 Populations of Hometowns and Home Counties of Legislative Sponsors of Official English Laws in Fourteen States

Population of Hometown

	Under 1,000	1,000–9,999	10,000–24,999	25,000–49,999	50,000–74,999	75,000–100,000	Over 100,000
Statutory States	9 (15%)	23 (38%)	8 (13%)	10 (16%)	8 (13%)	2 (3%)	1 (2%)
Referenda States	3 (5%)	5 (8%)	4 (7%)	13 (21%)	5 (8%)	6 (10%)	25 (41%)
Total	12 (10%)	28 (23%)	12 (10%)	23 (19%)	13 (11%)	8 (6%)	26 (21%)

Population of Home County

	Under 25,000	25,000–49,999	50,000–74,999	75,000–99,999	100,000–500,000	Over 500,000
Statutory States	14 (23%)	11 (18%)	3 (5%)	5 (8%)	27 (44%)	1 (2%)
Referenda States	—	5 (8%)	—	3 (5%)	21 (34%)	32 (53%)
Total	14 (11%)	16 (13%)	3 (2%)	8 (7%)	48 (39%)	33 (27%)

Note: Only the primary sponsors are considered here, since a large number of representatives signed on as co-sponsors in Alabama, Arkansas, and Georgia.

Table 8.3. **Socioeconomic Attributes of Home Counties of Legislative Sponsors of Official English Laws in Fourteen States**

	College Educated[a]		*Median Income*[b]		*Below Poverty*[c]	
	State Average		State Average		State Average	
	Over	Under	Over	Under	Over	Under
			Democrats			
Statutory						
States	15 (35%)	28 (65%)	43 (100%)	—	5 (12%)	38 (88%)
Referenda						
States	—	3 (100%)	3 (100%)	—	—	3 (100%)
Total	15 (33%)	31 (67%)	46 (100%)	—	5 (11%)	41 (89%)
			Republicans			
Statutory						
States	8 (44%)	10 (56%)	18 (100%)	—	4 (22%)	14 (78%)
Referenda						
States	34 (59%)	24 (41%)	58 (100%)	—	2 (3%)	56 (97%)
Total	42 (55%)	34 (45%)	76 (100%)	—	6 (8%)	70 (92%)
Grand						
Total	57 (47%)	65 (53%)	122 (100%)	—	11 (9%)	111 (91%)

[a]Statewide averages for college education are: Alabama 12%, Arizona 17%, Arkansas 11%, California 20%, Colorado 23%, Georgia 15%, Indiana 13%, Kentucky 11%, Mississippi 12%, North Carolina 13%, North Dakota 15%, South Carolina 13%, Tennessee 13%, Virginia 19%. Derived from the 1980 census.
[b]Statewide averages for median family income are: Alabama $8,649, Arizona $10,173, Arkansas $8,479, California $12,567, Colorado $12,302, Georgia $9,583, Indiana $10,021, Kentucky $8,934, Mississippi $7,778, North Carolina $9,044, North Dakota $10,872, South Carolina $8,502, Tennessee $8,906, Virginia $11,095. Derived from the 1980 census.
[c]Statewide averages for families below poverty are: Alabama 19%, Arizona 13%, Arkansas 19%, California 11%, Colorado 10%, Georgia 17%, Indiana 10%, Kentucky 18%, Mississippi 24%, North Carolina 15%, North Dakota 13%, South Carolina 17%, Tennessee 17%, Virginia 12%. Derived from the 1980 census.
Note: Only the primary sponsors are considered here, since a large number of representatives signed on as co-sponsors in Alabama, Arkansas, and Georgia.

lived in counties with median family incomes above the state averages. Eighty-nine percent of the Democratic legislators and 92 percent of the Republican legislators also lived in counties with poverty levels below state averages. So both variables indicate that the authors of official English laws come from relatively affluent areas of their states.

Whereas 65 percent of the Democratic sponsors from southern and midwestern states resided in counties with college-educated percentages below the state averages, among GOP sponsors the proportion falls to 56 percent in the statutory states and to 41 percent in the referenda states. Thus, for Republican legislators, income, poverty, and education are more consistent and indicate a generally conservative milieu for their political constituency. For Democrats, however, the existence of many fewer college-educated residents may allow them to promote official English as a reverse class strategy to tap resentment against foreigners. For that tactic to be effective, one would think there would have to be a sufficient number of the target population, Spanish speakers, to arouse Anglo fears.

To address this dimension, I have evaluated three more demographic attributes of hometown counties (table 8.4). According to the U.S. census, *urban* signifies any place with a population greater than 2,500 people; this is not a very good indicator of population density. Rather, this statistic is meaningful as a measure of how many people do not reside in a town of any size, that is, rural dwellers. So 79 percent of the Republicans from Arizona, California, and Colorado lived in home counties more urban than the statewide averages. Of the small group of Republicans from midwestern and southern states, half lived in home counties that were more urban than state averages. But among Democrats from the South and Midwest, 51 percent lived in home counties with urban populations below state averages. (In fact, people living in rural areas were the majority in these counties.) So Democrats were representing small-town and largely rural constituents removed from large central cities.

Since the Democratic sponsors represented outlying areas in their states, one would anticipate a larger minority of blacks but small numbers of Spanish speakers. Both assumptions, however, are contrary to the findings, though these contradictions may hold an answer to why official English was promoted by at least some southern Democrats. The data show that the black populations of home counties were below the state percentages for 72 percent of

Table 8.4. **Demographic Attributes of Home Counties of Legislative Sponsors of Official English Laws in Fourteen States**

	Percentage Urban[a] State Average		Percentage Black[b] State Average		Percentage Spanish[c] State Average	
	Over	Under	Over	Under	Over	Under
			Democrats			
Statutory States	21 (49%)	22 (51%)	13 (30%)	30 (70%)	39 (91%)	4 (9%)
Referenda States	1 (33%)	2 (67%)	—	3 (100%)	—	3 (100%)
Total	22 (48%)	24 (52%)	13 (28%)	33 (72%)	39 (85%)	7 (15%)
			Republicans			
Statutory States	9 (50%)	9 (50%)	4 (22%)	14 (78%)	13 (72%)	5 (28%)
Referenda States	46 (79%)	12 (21%)	29 (50%)	29 (50%	8 (14%)	50 (86%)
Total	55 (72%)	21 (28%)	33 (43%)	43 (57%)	21 (28%)	55 (72%)
Grand Total	77 (63%)	45 (37%)	46 (38%)	76 (62%)	60 (49%)	62 (51%)

[a]Statewide averages for percentage urban are: Alabama 60%, Arizona 84%, Arkansas 52%, California 91%, Colorado 81%, Georgia 62%, Indiana 64%, Kentucky 51%, Mississippi 47%, North Carolina 48%, North Dakota 48%, South Carolina 54%, Tennessee 60%, Virginia 66%. Derived from the 1980 census.

[b]Statewide averages for percentage black are: Alabama 26%, Arizona 3%, Arkansas 16%, California 7%, Colorado 4%, Georgia 27%, Indiana 8%, Kentucky 7%, Mississippi 35%, North Carolina 22%, North Dakota 0.4%, South Carolina 30%, Tennessee 16%, Virginia 19%. Derived from the 1980 census.

[c]Statewide averages for percentage Spanish are: Alabama 0.4%, Arizona 16%, Arkansas 0.5%, California 19%, Colorado 12%, Georgia 0.7%, Indiana 0.9%, Kentucky 0.4%, Mississippi 0.4%, North Carolina 0.5%, North Dakota 0.1%, South Carolina 0.5%, Tennessee 0.4%, Virginia 1%. Derived from the 1980 census.

Note: Only the primary sponsors are considered here, since a large number of representatives signed on as co-sponsors in Alabama, Arkansas, and Georgia.

the Democrats across all regions, which far exceeds the Republican proportion (57 percent). On the other hand, 85 percent of Democrats came from home counties with percentages of Spanish speakers above the state averages; 72 percent of Republicans came from counties with below-average numbers of Hispanics.

Therefore, the finding of disproportionately fewer blacks and Spanish speakers in the Republican home counties reinforces the upper socioeconomic status makeup of GOP constituencies. The relative absence of blacks in the home counties of Deep and Border South sponsors, however, would imply that official English legislation is being directed to white voters by white southern Democrats and is not a ploy to exploit ethnic resentments between blacks and Hispanics. Thus, while Hispanics are numerically a very tiny minority (less than 5 percent in every southern state and home county), the existence of any Spanish speakers in this socially homogeneous milieu may be a politically significant fact. To illustrate the potential symbolic impact of English Only appeals, consider what happened in Georgia.

THE CASE OF GEORGIA

Resolution 70, which established an official language for Georgia, began as House Resolution 717 with two senators and five representatives as original sponsors. By the time of its adop-tion (with votes of 100–0 in the lower chamber and 45–0 in the upper chamber), a total of 129 representatives had signed on as co-sponsors.[3] Two of the original Democratic sponsors, Representative Bill Cummings and Senator Nathan Dean, came from the same town in northwest Georgia. "This is just to recognize that English is the language we use, even if we're not always proficient at it," said Cummings. He added: "We've seen a decline in the communications skills of students, including the attention paid to English in public schools." Furthermore, Resolution 70 "would not require anything," and Cummings compared it with other designations of an official state bird, mammal, and flower.[4]

Cummings and Dean resided in Rockmart, a town of 3,645 people in Polk County, which had a population of 32,386 in 1980. Polk County has no cities of any size (it is only 37.9 percent urban) and has fewer blacks (15 percent) as compared with statewide averages. But the county boasts a median family income ($15,736) above the state average and a degree of poverty (13 percent) below that for the state. Only 6 percent of Polk residents completed college, and fewer than 1 percent of its population are Spanish speakers. So why did either of these Democratic legislators bother to raise the specter of foreigners in a rural constituency where so few are found? The *Atlanta Constitution* countered that a sinister motive was behind the bill:

> It is such an obvious slap at dozens of Mexicans who came to Cummings' northwest Georgia district to work in a local meat-packing plant, only to find themselves targets of intense hatred and violence by local yahoos, that one wonders at the short span of some lawmakers' memories.
>
> Two employees of the plant, accused by locals of "taking jobs away" from the natives, were slain in separate roadside incidents in the last five years. Construction workers were tried and acquitted, in courtrooms packed with Ku Klux Klansmen. Many other Mexicans have been beaten and harassed. And the Ku Klux Klan has greatly stepped up its activities in the area since the plant began hiring Mexicans in the late 1970s; the Klan has distributed leaflets and staging rallies that, among other things, sought to raise money for one accused gunman's defense.[5]

To liken the official English law to those designating an official state mammal or state flower, the editorial continued, "is insulting not only to non-English-speaking laborers who will feel its sting, but to the intelligence of any legislators who are persuaded to vote for it." Instead, the legislation "could only have one purpose, and that is to focus attention and hatred on newcomers who already have reason to fear for their safety and the safety of their families, and who deserve, and should be able to expect, the full support and protection of the law."[6]

Examination of characteristics of legislative sponsors in Arizona, California, and Colorado, where the legislatures failed to pass an official English law, thus leading to successful grass-roots initiatives for referenda, and in the eleven states where official English statutes were enacted indicates an important political difference. Legislative sponsors in the former states are virtually all Republicans; those in the latter are largely southern Democrats.

These political differences reflect differing socioeconomic cleavages in the referenda states, where controversy surrounded the question, and in the statutory states, where a consensus was reached over what was to all appearances a "nonissue." The data con-

sistently point to Republicans acting in accordance with the ideological preferences of their voter base, which is typically
upper-income, better-educated, suburban, and reliably Republican
in supporting Ronald Reagan; these districts have few black or
Spanish-speaking residents. At the grass-roots level, Republicans
are ignoring the advice of George Bush, who in 1987 rejected an official English law for Texas. In California and other western states
with sizable concentrations of Spanish speakers, apparently the Republicans have defined English Only as a partisan issue to solidify
the GOP base and to attract conservatives within the Democratic
Party, which has a tradition of support for bilingual education.

It seems unlikely that southern Democrats used official language legislation to garner black support. Clearly Spanish speakers
pose no threat to the power structure in their communities, so the
motivation must lie with a general nativist reaction or, more specifically, efforts to exploit a reverse class animosity against people
who are perceived as displacing American workers.

While the home counties of the southern Democrats are not
the poorest in their states, one can hypothesize that even a tiny
number of highly visible non-English speakers may be enough to
trigger demagogic appeals within a socially homogeneous and
rural area that lacks a highly educated population. The legislative
history of Georgia's enactment offers support for this supposition.

Predicting Legislative Behavior

Voting on the final enactment of the official English bills was unanimous or nearly unanimous in both chambers in Alabama, Arkansas, Georgia, Kentucky, Tennessee, and Virginia (table 8.5).
Four states had a sizable minority in opposition; that occurred in
both houses of the North Dakota and Indiana legislatures as well as
in the lower houses in Mississippi and North Carolina. The senates
were more unified behind these bills than were the lower houses; 8
percent of the senators voted no as compared with 12 percent of the
representatives.

Who were the opponents? This analysis is limited to the lower
chambers because they had more partisan and racial diversity than
the state senates, as well as more opposition to the official English

**Table 8.5. Votes on Official English Bills in Both House and Senate
and by Party and Race in House**

	House and Senate		House of Representatives			
	Senate	House	Democrats	Republicans	Whites	Blacks
AL	29–0	69–4	50–3	19–1	64–0	5–4
AR	30–2	94–0	85–0	9–0	90–0	4–0
GA[a]	45–0	100–0[b]	—	—	—	—
IN	36–13	65–30	15–28	50–2	65–24	0–6
KY	35–0	84–7	66–3	18–4	82–7	2–0
MS	48–3	93–27	88–27	5–0	92–10	1–17
NC	47–1	74–25	44–24	30–1	73–15	1–10
ND	38–15	78–24	24–2	54–3	78–24	None
SC[a]	—	—	—	—	—	—
TN	31–0	84–1	50–0	33–1[c]	78–1	6–0
VA	39–0[d]	96–0	70–0	25–0[c]	94–0	2–0
Total	378–34	837–118	492–106	243–12	716–81	21–37
	92–8%	88–12%	82–18%	95–5%	90–10%	36–64%

[a]No votes were published in the House or senate journals of South Carolina; for Georgia the
roll-call results were published, but a tally of how individuals voted was not.
[b]Following passage in the Georgia House, two representatives announced that they would
have voted against the bill had they been present on the floor.
[c]There was one independent in the Tennessee House and one in the Virginia House; each
voted in favor of the official English bill.
[d]In Virginia, the official English bill was approved en bloc with forty-nine other bills.

laws. These data indicate more a racial than a partisan cleavage
among the legislators. Overall, 95 percent of Republicans, 90 percent of whites, and 82 percent of Democrats voted for enactment,
whereas 64 percent of black legislators (who comprised nearly 7
percent of the total House memberships in the nine states for which
there is data) opposed these laws. Opposition by black legislators
was pronounced in Mississippi and North Carolina, but on the other
hand, in states that passed bills early in the decade—Virginia and
Kentucky—the small number of black representatives joined their
white colleagues to favor the measures. It also seems fair to conclude that Republicans were somewhat more unified than Democrats in supporting official English on the bills' final enactment.

For an analysis of legislative behavior, all 1,460 members of the lower houses in fourteen states were coded based on their political party, gender, and racial and ethnic background, as well as the political, economic, and demographic makeup of their home counties.[7] The lower houses were chosen because ten times as many representatives as senators (347:31) were formal sponsors of official English legislation, and in addition, there was more opposition on the final vote among state representatives than among state senators. Also, more often the legislative districts of the representatives encompassed only one county—the "home county"—or at most two counties, whereas senate districts almost always comprised many more counties.

Voting on final enactment in the House of Representatives was unanimous or nearly unanimous in Alabama, Arkansas, Georgia, Kentucky, Tennessee, and Virginia, but 145 legislators abstained in this group of states. In Indiana, Mississippi, North Carolina, and North Dakota, a sizable minority cast votes in opposition. In this analysis, no-voters and non-voters were coded "0" to signify nonsupport for the bills; only those voting yes were coded "1."

To determine which variables exerted the greatest effect on the decisions to sponsor or not to sponsor the official English bills and to vote for or against them, I undertook a logistical regression analysis. Given the small number of representatives who sponsored this legislation or who voted against it in particular states, this examination is limited to states where at least 10 percent of the membership did sponsor bills and where nonsupport for the legislation was expressed (by casting a no vote or abstaining) by at least 10 percent of the membership. By these criteria, legislative sponsorship is analyzed for Alabama, Arizona, Arkansas, California, Colorado, Georgia, and South Carolina, and voting outcomes are examined for Alabama, Indiana, Kentucky, Mississippi, North Carolina, North Dakota, and Tennessee.

Independent variables initially were regressed against each of two dependent variables.[8]

1. Party: Democrats coded 1, Republicans 0 (DEMOCRAT)
2. Race: blacks coded 1, Hispanics 2, whites 3 (BLACK, HISPANIC)

3. Gender: men coded 1, women 0 (MALE)
4. Percentage of votes for Reagan in 1984 in legislator's home county (REAGAN)
5. Percentage of Spanish-speaking residents in legislator's home county in 1980 (SPANISH)
6. Percentage of black residents in legislator's home county in 1980 (% BLACK)
7. Median family income in legislator's home county in 1979 (INCOME)
8. Percentage of population living in urban areas in legislator's home county in 1980 (URBAN)
9. Total population in legislator's home county in 1980 (POPU-LATION)
10. Percentage of college-educated residents in legislator's home county in 1980 (COLLEGE)
11. Percentage of residents living below the federal poverty line in legislator's home county in 1979 (POVERTY)

In the analysis of legislative sponsorship, no predictors were deemed statistically significant in the regression models generated for Arizona, Arkansas, Georgia, or Colorado, but some parallel findings emerged for other states (see Appendix C, table C.5). In Alabama, considering the large group of sixty-three co-sponsors, still the tendency was for Democrats and blacks not to sponsor this legislation, while those who sponsored official English were from home counties that gave more votes to Reagan than the statewide average in 1984. In California, again Democrats tended not to be the legislative sponsors.

A separate regression was performed on information from Arizona, California, and Colorado, since, unlike the situation in the South, the legislatures in these states refused to pass official English laws and thus the proponents turned to the referendum process. For this subset of three states, only DEMOCRAT, with a negative value, was a significant predictor, which suggests that the sponsors of those unsuccessful bills tended to be Republicans.

On the voting outcomes for Kentucky, no predictors were significant in the regression models, but the results for other states were quite consistent (Appendix C, table C.6). DEMOCRAT (with a negative sign) was a significant predictor of voting in North Dakota and Indiana, meaning that Democrats in those states tended to vote no or to abstain.

In Mississippi, North Carolina, Alabama, and Tennessee, blacks were more likely to be nonsupporters of official English on the final roll call. In Alabama BLACK was one of two variables to reach the level of significance, the other being REAGAN, which means that representatives from home counties that gave more votes to Reagan in 1984 tended to support enactment of the official English law. In North Carolina, COLLEGE also was negatively related to legislative voting, while in Tennessee SPANISH also was negatively related to voting for Official English.

The results from an analysis based on the entire sample of states show that the logistical models predicted the pattern of voting more accurately than the pattern of sponsorship (Appendix C, table C.7). For a model based on sponsorship in seven states—Alabama, Arizona, Arkansas, California, Colorado, Georgia, and South Carolina—five variables are statistically significant. Again black and Democratic legislators tended not to be sponsors. Home counties of those who did sponsor bills tended to have smaller concentrations of Spanish speakers and blacks and, as signified by the negative value of COLLEGE, populations with fewer college graduates.

The pattern based on a model of voting in a different group of seven states—Alabama, Indiana, Kentucky, Mississippi, North Carolina, North Dakota, and Tennessee—shows negative values for DEMOCRAT and BLACK, so both Democrats and black representatives tended not to support this legislation across that group of states, but men tended to vote for official English more than women legislators. Those voting for English Only also came from home counties with smaller Spanish-speaking populations but larger percentages of blacks, where fewer people had a college education and proportionately more votes were given to Reagan in 1984.

A model examining voting in five states—Alabama, Kentucky, Mississippi, North Carolina, and Tennessee—shows three significant variables. Across that group of southern states, men voted more heavily to enact official English legislation than did women, and black legislators cast a disproportionate number of opposition votes or abstained. Also, legislators whose home counties had smaller percentages of college-educated people than statewide averages also voted for the bills.

These analyses imply that the hypothesis based on racism cannot be validated, since the SPANISH variable had no positive effects. The evidence is more conclusive that the ethnic competition hypothesis ought to be rejected, at least at the elite level, because black legislators were consistently more opposed to codifying English. There is support for the class hypothesis given the negative values for COLLEGE. The cultural hypothesis cannot be evaluated, since URBAN and POPULATION were excluded from the final analysis because of problems with multicollinearity. Another result, which was unanticipated, was that male representatives tended to give more votes to official English than did female legislators.

The most important finding was that DEMOCRAT and BLACK (both negatives) were the most consistent predictors of legislative sponsorship and voting behavior. Since white and Republican legislators are generally more conservative than blacks or Democrats (virtually all black legislators are Democrats), these patterns hint that an ideological cleavage underlies the debate over official English. Conservatives favored but liberals opposed those laws. In the one-party-dominant South—Mississippi, Alabama, North Carolina, and Tennessee—that ideological debate was manifested in a racial cleavage within the Democratic Party, whereas in two-party North Dakota and Indiana it was reflected in competition between Republicans and Democrats. DEMOCRAT did not surface in the vote model based on five southern states but was a significant predictor in the seven-state vote model, which added Indiana and North Dakota to the group. This disparity suggests that, within the South, white Democrats were voting alongside white Republicans to pass official English laws.

Whenever REAGAN surfaced as a significant predictor, always with a positive value, it meant that legislators may have been encouraged to favor official English laws because voters in their home counties gave extraordinary support to Reagan in 1984 and thus were likely perceived to be more conservative and/or partisan in their policy preferences.

What is highly suggestive from these patterns is that the movement for official English is elite driven; it does not represent a groundswell from mass opinion. Attributes of the legislators (party, race, gender) were far more important in explaining sponsorship and voting behavior than the characteristics of their home counties. This implies that political dynamics within the legislatures, rather than a commonality of constituency pressures from outside, were the driving force behind action on official language laws.

The important lessons from this statistical analysis can now be related to the case studies and research on public attitudes to draw some conclusions about official English and its future prospects.

CONCLUSION

RATIONAL ARGUMENTS, IRRATIONAL FEARS: IS THE OFFICIAL ENGLISH CAMPAIGN BENIGN OR MALEVOLENT?

What conclusions about official English can be drawn from the case studies, comparative research, and statistical analyses? Is this movement based on economic grievances or political opportunism or racial and ethnic animosities? Is the backlash being manipulated by political leaders, or are they being forced to accommodate an angry electorate? The evidence points in two directions, which offer differing though complementary explanations for why fifteen states enacted official English laws between 1981 and 1990.

IDEOLOGY AND POLITICS, NOT ECONOMICS

The racial hypothesis is a difficult one to evaluate. Polls are generally consistent in finding that whites are much more supportive of official English than any other racial or ethnic group, and WHITE was the strongest predictor in my analysis of the 1992 National Election Study. All the key sponsors of the bills were white, and of the white representatives who answered the final roll call, 90 percent voted in favor of the legislation. The racial hypothesis as conceptualized, however, has a contextual variable as well.

Despite all the hyperbole and accusations by the opponents, the most obvious fact is that most states that enacted official English laws do not have a large Hispanic minority, let alone a growing population of Spanish speakers. SPANISH also carried a negative value, contrary to expectations, in the analyses of referenda voting in California, Colorado, and Florida, and SPANISH showed the same statistical relationship to legislative voting and sponsorship in the seven-state model and voting on Official English among Tennessee representatives. Yet there is sufficient anecdotal information in the case studies to show that the reaction was anti-Hispanic, targeted against Cubans in Florida, Hispanics in Arizona and Colorado, and mainly Spanish speakers in California. In California, though, the agitation originated as a reaction against non-English-speaking Chinese in San Francisco and later involved resentment against local enclaves of Koreans and other Asian groups.

The racial argument—Anglos opposed to Hispanics—may well be sustained by the experience of the referenda states, each of which has a large minority of Spanish speakers. The 1992 National Election Study showed that respondents in those four states were much more likely to endorse English Only legislation. And within California and Florida, the majority of officially bilingual counties voted for English Only referenda by margins higher than the statewide percentages, even though across all counties in both states the presence of Spanish speakers reduced the level of support.

The ethnic competition hypothesis can be rejected at the elite level, since African American representatives were more opposed to official English in Mississippi, North Carolina, Alabama, and Tennessee, though the very few black legislators who voted on the earlier laws of Virginia and Kentucky supported those measures. Polls indicate that a majority of blacks now favor official English. The National Election Study confirmed that finding, and in Alabama the black-majority counties voted for the official English proposition by huge margins.

There is some support for the class hypothesis based on the negative values for COLLEGE in the various analyses. The populations of states with official English laws tend to have fewer college graduates, and COLLEGE surfaced as a significant (and negative) predictor in the analysis of legislative sponsorship and voting for selected groups of states. In the National Election Study of 1992, lower education correlated with support for official English laws, but existing state surveys do not validate the existence of a reverse class cleavage. Income and poverty were not important correlates determining which states adopted English Only laws; educational level was a somewhat better predictor than poverty in the analysis of referenda voting. These results are somewhat tentative, but they do suggest that future research might focus on educational variables to assess whether nativist outbursts are related to a generalized intolerance of nonconformists rather than a fear of economic competition.

Attempts to evaluate the cultural hypothesis with the URBAN and POPULATION variables were unproductive, and both had to be dropped from the analysis of legislative behavior. The best evidence that the official English movement can be viewed as the latest manifestation of nativist forces was the longitudinal analysis of votes by state delegation against the Begg Amendment and state adoptions of official English laws. For the group of largely southern states—plus California, given its anti-Asian history—there is some linkage between supporting official English in the 1980s and ardent opposition to immigrants when the National Origins Act of 1924 was debated.

The findings give most credence to the political hypothesis, or a variant of it. REAGAN was a significant and positive predictor, signifying that voters in counties with larger vote totals in 1984 for Ronald Reagan also favored the official English referenda in all five states (including Alabama). And the representatives from such counties were more apt to sponsor bills (in Alabama) or to vote for them (in Alabama, as in the group of seven states). One would assume that voters in those counties were more partisan and/or more conservative in their policy preferences than the statewide electorates.

DEMOCRAT, always with a negative sign, was a consistent predictor of sponsorship (in Alabama, California, and the three western states) and legislative voting (in Indiana, North Dakota, the five southern states, and the seven states model). This pattern, when coupled with results from the variable BLACK, strongly implies that an ideological cleavage underlies the debate over official

English. Conservatives favored but liberals opposed the laws. In Mississippi, Alabama, North Carolina, and Tennessee, that ideological debate was manifested in a racial cleavage within the Democratic Party, whereas in North Dakota and Indiana it reflected competition between Republicans and Democrats.

These findings on political elites comport with the three studies by Jack Citrin and his associates that determined that party and ideology were important determinants of support for official English laws. Citrin further argues that "Americanism" as an ethos yields a generalized antipathy toward newcomers that is also related to party and ideology. Party affiliation also was a significant variable concerning support for official English in the 1992 NES analysis.

ELITES, NOT MASSES

In response to my second overarching research question, what seems evident from this study is that the movement for an official English language—in most states—was elite driven, not a result of grass-roots agitation. The demands for official language laws were made by political elites, not by any particular stratum of the electorate. Attributes of the legislators' home counties were not related to the patterns of sponsorship or voting behavior, except for the REAGAN variable. This finding casts doubt on the interpretation by Citrin, Reingold, Walters, and Green that "the initiative process is the device that has allowed populist sentiment in favor of 'official English' to prevail over elite opposition."[1] Their observation, based on the 1986 California referendum, has relevance to other states where popular initiatives were used but does not extend to the larger number of cases where English Only statutes passed state legislatures.

In his study of McCarthyism during the 1950s, Michael Rogin offered a counterthesis that the Red Scare was not so much a mass movement as an effort by local political elites to exploit that issue for electoral advantage. James Gibson would agree with the Rogin view. Gibson analyzed the pattern of anti-Communist laws during the 1950s and concluded: "It is difficult to imagine that the repression of the 1950s was inspired by demands for repressive public policy from a mobilized mass public. . . . There can be no doubt that the mass public was highly intolerant in its attitudes during the 1950s. Absent issue saliency, however, it is difficult to imagine that the U.S. people had mobilized sufficiently to have created the repression of the era."[2] Gibson's observation seems equally prophetic about the official English movement today. Though huge majorities favor codifying the English language according to various state polls, and referenda were approved by overwhelming margins in Alabama (89 percent), California (73 percent), Colorado (64 percent), and Florida (84 percent), there is scant evidence that official English is a high-salience issue for most Americans. It is plausible that this policy agenda is inspired by political elites because official language movements, wherever they emerge in the world, "have the potential for establishing a new agenda and a new 'way' to talk about political and socioeconomic issues. . . . The emerging elites who espouse the language movement hope to substitute language conflict and its terms of reference for the existing alignment of political (and social and economic) conflict."[3]

While Republicans could be exploiting anti-Spanish feelings to gain a political foothold among Anglos in western states, that strategy seems problematic in places like Indiana and North Dakota. It seems more likely that GOP legislators in the Midwest and in the South are supporting English Only in accordance with the basic ideological tenets of their party, coupled with the fact that historically the GOP has been the more homogeneous of the two major parties and thus less open to minority groups.

But Hispanic and African American elites may have their own political agenda as well. The strident opposition of Hispanic political and community leaders is not matched by rank-and-file opinion, since a sizable minority (the 39 percent who voted for Proposition 63 in California) favor official English. It is plausible that Hispanics, like earlier generations of immigrants, might rally behind the English language in order to display their Americanism, but leaders of their community allege that Spanish speakers underestimate the hidden agenda behind the activities of U.S. English just as Anglos view support of official English laws as patriotism without understanding the dire implications for bilingual education. Hispanic elites perceive, and correctly so, that official English is a threat to the legitimacy of multiculturalism, but this linkage may not be explicit in the minds of most Spanish speakers.

If Anglos come to view bilingualism as nothing more than multiculturalism, then there are dangers that English Plus will be discredited. The 1992 National Election Study asked questions about the "melting pot," and the responses prompted Citrin and his colleagues to conclude that "the absence of significant social and political cleavages on this issue suggests that the melting pot symbol is, indeed, an ambiguous one among the American public. More important, many Americans may not consider maintaining one's ethnic heritage and blending into the larger society as mutually exclusive." What is mutually exclusive is blending into mainstream American society and maintaining a commitment to multiculturalism that repudiates the national ethos, also more an elitist than a mass phenomenon. Multiculturalism had its roots in the "black power" movement of the late 1960s. At about the same time, "Hispanic activists articulated the concept of language rights as a constitutional entitlement. Many advocated bilingual education as a vehicle for resisting cultural assimilation."[4] Scholars will debate this point for some time, but what so far has been academically contentious has the potential of reaching out and mobilizing the grass roots if majority-minority voters are polarized along linguistic lines.

The misalignment in opinion between African American elites and the black citizenry is less a matter of speculation. The comments by black legislators and the attributions by their white colleagues indicate that the behavior of African Americans is guided by a concern about civil rights and liberties. Similar values can affect black voters, and they apparently did when blacks voted against the 1980 Dade County English Only ordinance. Now, however, something else is shaping the behavior and attitudes of blacks, possibly the same thing that bothers whites.

In sum, there seems to be an elite-mass divergence across racial lines. White politicians are promoting official English even though the issue is not salient among whites in most states. Hispanic community and political leaders are strident in their hostility, and quick to allege racist motives, despite the fact that views among their constituency are not monolithic. English Plus and English

Only may illustrate elite manipulation of masses within both the Hispanic and Anglo communities. Among African Americans, elites are simply misrepresenting the mass citizenry. How the contagion of conflict may evolve in the future is indicated by the experiences of the statutory states versus the referenda states. What happened in the South and Midwest I will call stage 1, and stage 2 occurred in Florida, California, Arizona, and Colorado and would have engulfed Texas in a similar way had a ballot proposition been allowed. Thus, there is no one answer to the questions that undergird this research; everything depends on the context of conflict. Stage 1 was elitist, and stage 2 was mass-activated. Stage 1 seemed to represent nativist impulses—cultural conservatism—and stage 2 was grounded in ideology—political conservatism and the exigencies of party competition.

STAGE 1

The dynamics of stage 1 are illustrated by the pattern of enactments in North Carolina, South Carolina, Georgia, Alabama, Mississippi, Arkansas, Kentucky, Tennessee, Indiana, North Dakota, and Virginia, except that Virginia's action was a direct reply to provocation by the federal government in the form of bilingual education regulations. Legislation to codify English as the state's official language had sponsors from both parties, and party did not emerge as a significant cleavage in voting by representatives in Alabama, Mississippi, or North Carolina; when Tennessee and Kentucky were added to this group, party affiliation became significant, but less so than race. The pronounced racial cleavage in Alabama, Mississippi, North Carolina, and Tennessee suggests that white Democrats and white Republicans viewed the issue very differently than did black Democrats. For the African American legislators, English Only represented discrimination or prejudice.

Evidence suggests that legislative sponsors were "trustees" during the agenda-setting stage, because they were following their own views on what the public interest demanded rather than acting as "delegates" who were instructed by their constituents to promote a specific policy agenda. In considering the final result, the polls seem conclusive that policy congruence existed between elite opinion and the attitudes of voters, although it clearly was not the consequence of elite-mass interaction.[5] It is inappropriate, therefore, to impugn the legitimacy of official English laws by suggesting that they were approved notwithstanding the opinions of constituents.

The issue was promoted by policy entrepreneurs and, as a result, the question barely got any newspaper coverage, though editorial opinion in Indianapolis, Columbia, and Montgomery voiced strong support for the law. Indeed, the laws were symbolic precisely because the legislators were not responding to an immediate policy problem (except in Virginia). In sum, the enactments in this group of states were consensus acts and caused no ill feelings, though, predictably, local affiliates of the ACLU cried foul.

STAGE 2

The dynamics of stage 2 are different and best illustrated by California and Florida, where the beginnings of English Only agitation date back many years before referenda were approved in those states, and also by Arizona and Colorado. Majority control by the Democratic Party of the legislatures in California and Florida guaranteed that no official English law would emerge. In Colorado the Democratic governor threatened to veto any bill, and proponents backed down. Proposed legislation in Arizona caused enough of an outcry from Hispanics that the key sponsor chose to withdraw his bill from further consideration. In these states 95 percent of the sponsors were Republican; well-known Democrats were among the opponents; and party affiliation emerged as a significant cleavage in the sponsorship of these measures in the three western states.

Florida was a special case, for two reasons. Its being a southern state may explain why the backbenchers who introduced the legislation to codify English were mainly Democrats. And Cubans tend to vote Republican, unlike Democratic-leaning Hispanics in Texas and California. So unique political dynamics gave the Republicans electoral reasons not to promote this policy (unlike the situation in the West and Southwest), although the Democratic majority in Florida, as in the West, blocked consideration of the bills. It is consistent with the southern scenario that the Democrats who sponsored English Only legislation lived nowhere near Dade County; on the other hand, the bills of 1981 and 1982 were not just symbolic (like those in most southern states) but easily as restrictive as the controversial Arizona referendum. Inaction by the legislatures forced the advocates to turn to the initiative process to lay the question directly before the voters in referenda. To decry those referenda as the result of manipulation by single-issue activists and U.S. English is to miss the point. The petition drives garnered record numbers of signatures, and the Hispanic opposition failed to get alternative language on the ballot in Arizona, as it lacked both financial resources and signatures. Victory by U.S. English and its state affiliates was the successful climax of a broad-based movement. Besides, the polls showed tremendous support among all population groups, liberals being the one reliable source of opposition. Though some statewide Republican politicians disavowed English Only, state GOP organizations endorsed the measures in Arizona and Texas and gave implicit backing in Colorado.

NATIVISM REBORN, NOT REVISITED

Is the English Only movement a rebirth of nativist sentiment? Some parallels exist between the 1920s and the 1980s. U.S. English would never have emerged as a political movement had growing numbers of Spanish speakers not immigrated to the United States. The nativism of the 1920s has not been revisited as a normative force, however, since the official English backlash is decidedly more restrained than what resulted seventy years ago. Even the objectives of U.S. English seem benign when compared with the agenda of the American Protective Association of the late 1800s and the 1924 National Origins Act, with its explicit racial connotations.

Paradoxically, as the referenda campaigns in California and Florida vividly showed, racist charges seem to be hurled as much today as during the height of nativist hysteria in the aftermath of World War I. The Nebraska debate, in retrospect, looks to be an archetype of civility, rational argument, and political restraint. In 1910 foreign-born residents represented 14.8 percent of the population of Nebraska; this figure ranked the state above the U.S. average (14.7 percent) and twenty-third among the forty-eight states. In comparison, for the ten southern states that have passed official English laws, the percentage ranged from 0.3 percent (North Carolina) to 5.4 percent (Florida).[6] So the Nebraska episode would seem to be analogous to the dynamics of stage 2 conflict. In truth, any similarity ends there.

In 1920 the debate in Nebraska focused on English usage in public communications, not in private contexts, and even the opposition agreed that English ought to be the language of government and public life. They demanded that the home and the church be safe sanctuaries for the use of other languages. Today, however, those opposed to an official language will not accept the mandated use of English, even though they may readily acknowledge the primacy of English usage.

In Nebraska both sides accepted a "symbolic" declaration of English as an official language as the compromise position, while today opponents want bilingualism to enjoy the same legitimacy as English. Nobody who spoke in the 1920 constitutional convention demanded a public subsidy for non-English speakers; the linguistic minority of that day simply was asking the state to leave them alone. And though German Americans were put on the defensive about their loyalty to the United States, there was little ethnic- or race-baiting in that heated debate. Today's advocates of official English are routinely called bigots. To equate support for official English with racism involves a leap of faith, however; this leap is a dangerous one politically, given that the arguments by U.S. English make sense to a large number of Americans. In sum, the debate over codifying English as the official language of the United States has taken a sharp and ugly turn to the Left.

STAGE 3

The English Only versus English Plus controversy will have moved through two stages before erupting fully on the national political scene. So far, official English advocates are getting nowhere in Congress owing to the entrenched opposition of the Democratic Party. Among various bills still pending is the Language of Government Act (House Resolution 123), authored by Representative Bill Emerson (R-Mo.), who in 1993 repeated a familiar argument: "More than 150 languages contribute to the rich fabric of the American culture. Yet unless we have one language with which we can all communicate, our coexistence could be chaotic. Communication is at the heart of democracy. A democratic form of government cannot exist if members of a community cannot talk to each other. The government must remain in touch with the people it governs in order to function efficiently and effectively. The Language of Government Act moves us another step in that direction."[7] House Resolution 123—and Senate Bill 426, by Senator Richard Shelby (D-Ala.)—would designate English as the official language of the U.S. government. By the fall of 1993 these measures had attracted ninety-three co-sponsors (ten being senators) from thirty states (table CN.1).

If the pattern of party affiliation among these legislators is indicative of future developments, then many more Republicans than Democrats will be promoting official English at the national level. As before, bipartisanship exists in the statutory states (and all were southern with the exception of Illinois, Indiana, and Nebraska), but in California and Florida 93 percent of these co-sponsors belong to the GOP. In other states—including, for example, such liberal states as New York and Connecticut—Republicans are even more likely to endorse this legislation. The statutory and referenda states account for 61 percent of the sponsors, so these legislators must

Table CN.1   Congressional Co-Sponsors of House Resolution 123 and Senate Bill 426

	Republican	Democrat
Referenda States (2)	13 (93%)	1 (7%)
Statutory States (12)	30 (70%)	13 (30%)
Other States (16)	34 (94%)	2 (6%)
Total (30)	77 (83%)	16 (17%)

Sources: "Federal Update," *U.S. English Update* 10, no. 2 (Summer 1993): 3; "Co-Sponsor Lists Continue to Grow," *U.S. English Update* 10, no. 3 (Fall 1993): 3.

believe that official English is an issue that resonates with the electorate and that they are representing the opinions of their constituents.

But 83 is a long way from the 218 votes needed to pass legislation in the House of Representatives, though the political scenario may change if more representatives and senators are confronted with the kinds of incidents that triggered the outburst by Senator Robert Byrd described in the opening pages of this book. For a shift in the politics of this issue to occur, English Only will have to generate much more issue salience for the average voter than it has to date.

The 1990 census reports that English is a foreign language for a large number of recent immigrants. Fourteen percent of the 230 million people in the United States over age five speak a language other than English, a jump of 38.1 percent since 1980. This increase was mainly caused by Hispanic immigration.[8] Of all the newcomers, Hispanic children also are less likely to state a preference for knowing English rather than their native tongue. Interviews with five thousand eighth and ninth graders determined that only 44 percent of Mexican Americans preferred English over their parents' native language, as compared with 94 percent among Cubans, 88 percent among Filipinos, 87 percent among Haitians, and 51 percent among Vietnamese.[9]

Polls taken during 1993 and 1994 indicate the potentially grave consequences that may follow in the wake of what, to date, has been a very mild dose of antiforeign sentiment. A mid-June 1993 *New York Times*/CBS News poll found that 61 percent of the people surveyed felt that immigration should be decreased, and responses reflected a change in perceptions about the identity of the newcomers. In 1986, 49 percent believed that "most of the people who have moved to the United States in the last few years are here illegally," while today that belief is shared by 68 percent of respondents.[10]

Negative feelings toward immigrants were also recorded in other surveys.[11] A Gallup Poll of July 1993 found that 65 percent favored a reduction in immigration; only 49 percent expressed that view in 1986. The figure was 42 percent in 1977 and 33 percent in 1965, a time when the nation was beginning to liberalize its immigration policies. Majorities indicated that immigrants "mostly *threaten* American culture" (55 percent) and "cost the taxpayers too much by using government services like public education and medical services" (56 percent). Those resentments were targeted at the "new" immigrants, not the old: 62 percent said that there are "too many" immigrants from Latin American and Asian countries, whereas 52 percent indicated that the number from Europe was "about right." Negative feelings about Latin American immigration were highest among those who disapproved of President Clinton (71 percent said there were "too many" here), conservatives (70 percent), Republicans and southerners (both at 66 percent), and whites (66 percent).[12]

Events seem to be moving the country toward stage 3 at a quickening pace, and the referenda states are leading the way. Florida filed a lawsuit against the federal government in April 1994, seeking $1.5 billion in reimbursement for social services provided to illegal immigrants. "The people of Florida are saying, 'Enough,' to paying an unfair share of providing services to illegal immigrants," stated Democratic governor Lawton Chiles. "We refuse to pick up Washington's tab any longer." Similar legal actions were announced by Arizona and California, both of which have Republican governors, and Texas joined the parade of lawsuits, although its Democratic governor, Ann W. Richards (who faced reelection in November 1994), couched the issue in budgetary terms.[13]

But California Republican governor Pete Wilson—who as a U.S. senator had endorsed the 1986 official English referendum—exploited the issue of illegals in his uphill reelection bid, declaring that "if you have the resources, you can in fact control the border" and that if congressional leaders had "one-tenth the guts of the illegal immigrants" who daily crossed into the United States, they would provide those resources.[14] Wilson's ploy may work: a petition drive by Save Our State gathered six hundred thousand signatures for a November 1994 referendum to deny public education and nonemergency medical services to illegal aliens and to require teachers, health care workers, and the police to report any "apparent illegal immigrants" to federal authorities. One author of the popular initiative—which 86 percent of respondents approved in an earlier *Los Angeles Times* poll—was Harold Ezell, a former regional chief with the Immigration and Naturalization Service, who argued that without social services the illegals would "go back to where they came from."[15]

Support for Proposition 187 did not cut across racial lines. A *Los Angeles Times* exit poll found that a majority of African Americans, Asian Americans, and Hispanics were opposed. As the election approached, mounting adverse commentary by the media and political leaders coupled with raucous street demonstrations caused the backing for 187 to erode, especially among Hispanics. The issue also took on partisan overtones. Democratic Senator Dianne Feinstein, who had expressed concerns about unregulated immigration but avoided this question, ultimately risked her political future by declaring her opposition. She narrowly beat her Republican opponent, Michael Huffington, who more firmly backed the initiative; strident advocacy by Governor Wilson resulted in his decisive victory over Democrat Kathleen Brown, who had opposed Proposition 187.

The issue caused a split among conservative Republicans. Former HUD Secretary Jack Kemp and former Secretary of Education William J. Bennett both publicly attacked its divisiveness, while editor William F. Buckley gave his blessing to the referendum. As expected, editorials in *The Los Angeles Times* were opposed, but, despite the projections that Proposition 187 was losing ground in the final pre-election polls, it was approved by a lopsided 3–2 margin, mainly by white voters. The opposition turned again to the courts, gaining a temporary injuction to prevent implementation pending a legal challenge.

There seems little doubt that the political landscape is ripe for action on the immigration front. The 1994 elections produced a Republican landslide of historic proportions; the GOP won both houses of Congress and the majority of governorships, and it gained hundreds of state legislative positions. In its "Contract with America," the House Republicans, led by Speaker Newt Gingrich (R-GA), embraced a cut-off of federal benefits to illegal immigrants. In the Senate, Alan K. Simpson (R-WY), co-author of the 1986 immigrations reforms, indicated that he was opposed to such a Draconian measure though he favored cutting legal immigration and instituting some kind of national identity system. Even some liberals, including former Congresswoman Barbara Jordan (D-TX), an African American, were jumping on the anti-immigrant bandwagon. As chair of a presidential commission on immigration reform, Jordan reportedly favored restrictive measures similar to Proposition 187.

The cost of social services is a tangible burden to the taxpayers of states with large numbers of illegal aliens, and the California problem is aggravated by serious economic recession. But those are isolated cases, since most states are not being overwhelmed by such expenses. If anti-immigrant grievances are based on economics, then the contagion of conflict might not extend to other states. But this issue is emotive symbolic, and the danger exists that popular passions will be inflamed by the accumulation of symbolic indignities to the nation-state.

The eighty to one hundred thousand people who chanted "Ingles No!" to express opposition to a law making both Spanish and English the official languages of Puerto Rico may be seen by the American public as a minor nuisance in a faraway place. For the issue to hit home, the public will have to be exposed to a situation akin to what provoked the Anglos in Dade County in 1980—frequent uses of non-English in public forums. That is unlikely to happen across the breadth of the United States, but official uses of other languages can be quickly publicized as evidence that separatism is on its way. During the summer of 1993 federal district judge Alfredo Marquez, a Hispanic, for the first time in the nation's history permitted the oath for naturalized citizenship to be given in Spanish.[16] Episodes like that fly in the face of values that most Americans cherish.

APPENDIXES

Appendix A

Official Endorsers of English Plus Information Clearinghouse

Groups marked with an asterisk were the twenty-seven original founding organizations.

Advocates for Language Learning
*American Civil Liberties Union (ACLU)
American Council on the Teaching of Foreign Languages
*American Jewish Committee
*American Jewish Congress
*Asociación Política de Hable Español / Spanish Speaking / Surnamed Political Association, Inc.
ASPIRA Association, Inc.
Californians United
*Caribbean Education and Legal Defense Fund
*Center for Applied Linguistics
*Chinese for Affirmative Action
*Christian Church (Disciples of Christ)
*Coloradans for Language Freedom
*Committee for a Multilingual New York
*El Concilio de El Paso
*Conference on College Composition and Communication
Greater Miami United
*Haitian American Anti-Defamation League
*Haitian Refugee Center

*Image de Denver
*IRATE (Coalition of Massachusetts Trade Unions for Immigration
    Rights, Advocacy, Training and Education)
Japanese American Citizens League
Joint National Committee for Languages (JNCL)
League of United Latin American Citizens (LULAC)
LULAC Foundation
*Mexican American Legal Defense and Education Fund (MALDEF)
*Michigan English Plus Coalition
*Multicultural Education Training (and Advocacy) Project (META)
National Association for Asian and Pacific American Education
*National Association for Bilingual Education (NABE)
National Association of Latino Elected Officials
*National Coalition of Advocates for Students
*National Council of La Raza (NCLR)
National Council of Teachers of English (NCTE)
National Education Association
National Immigration Project, National Lawyers Guild, Inc.
National Immigration, Refugee, and Citizenship Forum
National Lawyers Guild
*National Puerto Rican Coalition
*New York Association for New Americans (NYANA)
*Organization of Chinese Americans
Society for the Psychological Study of Social Issues
*"Stop English Only" Committee, Hostos Community College,
    Bronx, N.Y.
*Teachers of English to Speakers of Other Languages (TESOL)
United States Students Association

Source: English Plus Information Clearinghouse, enclosure with form letter
addressed to "Dear Friend" from Mary Carol Combs, Director, n.d.

APPENDIX B

STATE OFFICIAL ENGLISH LANGUAGE LAWS

ALABAMA (1990)

Amendment no. 509, Constitution of Alabama of 1901

English is the official language of the state of Alabama. The legislature shall enforce this amendment by appropriate legislation. The legislature and officials of the state of Alabama shall take all steps necessary to insure that the role of English as the common language of the state of Alabama is preserved and enhanced. The legislature shall make no law which diminishes or ignores the role of English as the common language of the state of Alabama.

Any person who is a resident of or doing business in the state of Alabama shall have standing to sue the state of Alabama to enforce this amendment, and the courts of record of the state of Alabama shall have jurisdiction to hear cases brought to enforce this provision. The legislature may provide reasonable and appropriate limitations on the time and manner of suits brought under this amendment.

ARIZONA (1988)

Article XXVIII, Section 1, Arizona Constitution

1. *English as the Official Language; Applicability*
    Section 1.(1) The English language is the official language of the State of Arizona.
    (2) As the official language of this State, the English language is the language of the ballot, the public schools and all government functions and actions.

(3)(a) This Article applies to:

(i) the legislative, executive and judicial branches of government,

(ii) all political subdivisions, departments, agencies, organizations, and instrumentalities of this State, including local governments and municipalities,

(iii) all statutes, ordinances, rules, orders, programs and policies,

(iv) all government officials and employees during the performance of government business.

(b) As used in this Article, the phrase "This State and all political subdivisions of this State" shall include every entity, person, action or item described in this Section, as appropriate to the circumstances.

2. *Requiring This State to Preserve, Protect and Enhance English.*

Section 2. This State and all political subdivisions of this State shall take all reasonable steps to preserve, protect and enhance the role of the English language as the official language of the State of Arizona.

3. *Prohibiting This State from Using or Requiring the Use of Languages Other Than English; Exceptions*

Section 3.(1) Except as provided in Subsection (2):

(a) This State and all political subdivisions of this State shall act in English and in no other language.

(b) No entity to which this Article applies shall make or enforce a law, order, decree or policy which requires the use of a language other than English.

(c) No governmental document shall be valid, effective or enforceable unless it is in the English language.

(2) This State and all political subdivisions of this State may act in a language other than English under any of the following circumstances:

(a) to assist students who are not proficient in the English language, to the extent necessary to comply with federal law, by giving educational instruction in a language other than English to provide as rapid as possible a transition to English.

(b) to comply with other federal laws.

(c) to teach a student a foreign language as part of a required or voluntary educational curriculum.

(d) to protect public health or safety.

(e) to protect the rights of criminal defendants or victims of crimes.

4. *Enforcement; Standing.*

Section 4. A person who resides in or does business in this State shall have standing to bring suit to enforce this Article in a court of record of the State. The Legislature may enact reasonable limitations on the time and manner of bringing suit under this subsection.

ARKANSAS (1987)

Arkansas Code, 1987, Annotated, Section 1-4-117 (1989 Supplement)

(a) The English language shall be the official language of the State of Arkansas.

(b) This section shall not prohibit the public schools from performing their duty to provide equal educational opportunities to all children.

CALIFORNIA (1986)

Article III, Section 6, California Constitution

Section 1. (a) Purpose: English is the common language of the people of the United States of America and the State of California. This section is intended to preserve, protect and strengthen the English language, and not to supersede any of the rights guaranteed to the people by this Constitution.

(b) English as the Official Language of California. English is the official language of the State of California.

(c) Enforcement. The Legislature shall enforce this section by appropriate legislation. The Legislature and officials of the State of California shall take all steps necessary to insure that the role of English as the common language of the State of California is preserved and enhanced. The Legislature shall make no law which diminishes or ignores the role of English as the common language of the State of California.

(d) Personal Right of Action and Jurisdiction of Courts. Any person who is a resident of or doing business in the State of California shall have standing to sue the State of California to enforce this section, and the Courts of record of the State of California shall have jurisdiction to hear cases brought to enforce this section. The Legislature may provide reasonable and appropriate limitations on the time and manner of suits brought under this section.

Section 2. Severability: If any provision of this section, or the application of any such provision to any person or circumstance, shall be held invalid, the remainder of this section to the extent it can be given effect shall not be affected thereby, and to this end the provisions of this section are severable.

COLORADO (1988)

Article II, Section 30, Colorado Constitution

The English language is the official language of the State of Colorado.

This section is self executing; however, the General Assembly may enact laws to implement this section.

FLORIDA (1988)

Article II, Section 9, Florida Constitution

(a) English is the official language of the state of Florida.

(b) The legislature shall have the power to enforce this section by appropriate legislation.

GEORGIA (1986)

No. 70 (House Resolution 717) Georgia General Assembly, General Acts and Resolutions, vol. 1, 1986, p. 529

WHEREAS, the United States of America has attained hope, strength, and preeminence in world affairs through the unified effort of its diversified peoples; and

WHEREAS, continued and lasting unification of those diversified peoples offers the greatest promise of success when it is accomplished with a cultural fabric of one language which is spoken, written, and understood by all; and

WHEREAS, the reliance of a society on a single language facilitates the exchange of ideas, feelings, beliefs, and information and facilitates the full integration of all its members; and

WHEREAS, the English language is the basic language of commerce, education, and official business in this state; and

WHEREAS, it is only fitting and proper that we recognize the continuing, unifying role that the English language plays in the stability and cohesion of the lives of the people of this state and nation.

NOW, THEREFORE, BE IT RESOLVED BY THE GENERAL ASSEMBLY OF GEORGIA that the English language is designated as the official language of the State of Georgia.

HAWAII (1978)

Section 4, Hawaii Constitution

English and Hawaiian shall be the official languages of Hawaii, except that Hawaiian shall be required for public acts and transactions only as provided by law.

ILLINOIS (1969)

Illinois Revised Statutes, chap. 127, para. 177 (1987)

The official language of the State of Illinois is English.

INDIANA (1984)

Indiana Code, Annotated, Section 1-2-10-1 (West 1989 Supplement)

The English language is adopted as the official language of the state of Indiana.

KENTUCKY (1984)

Kentucky Revised Statutes, Annotated, Section 2.013 (1985 Supplement)

English is designated as the official state language of Kentucky.

MISSISSIPPI (1987)

Mississippi Code, 1972, Annotated, Section 3-3-31 (1989 Supplement)

The English language is the official language of the State of Mississippi.

NEBRASKA (1920)

Article I, Section 27, Nebraska Constitution

The English language is hereby declared to be the official language of this state, and all official proceedings, records and publications shall be in such language, and the common school branches shall be taught in said language in public, private, denominational and parochial schools.

NORTH CAROLINA (1987)

North Carolina General Statutes, Annotated, Chapter 145-12 (1990 Supplement)

(a) Purpose. English is the common language of the people of the United States of America and the State of North Carolina. This section is intended to preserve, protect and strengthen the English language, and not to supersede any of the rights guaranteed to the people by the Constitution of the United States or the Constitution of North Carolina.

(b) English as the Official Language of North Carolina. English is the official language of the State of North Carolina.

NORTH DAKOTA (1987)

North Dakota Century Code, Section 54-02-13 (1989 Supplement)

Section 1. English as official language. The English language is the official language of the state of North Dakota.

SOUTH CAROLINA (1987)

South Carolina Code, 1976, Annotated, Sections 1-1-696, 1-1-697, and 1-1-698 (1989 Supplement)

1-1-696. The English language is the official language of the State of South Carolina.

1-1-697. Neither this State nor any political subdivision thereof shall require, by law, ordinance, regulation, order, decree, program, or policy, the use of any language other than English; provided, however, that nothing in Sections 1-1-696 through 1-1-698 shall prohibit a state agency or a political subdivision of the State from requiring an applicant to have certain degrees of knowledge of a foreign language as a condition of employment where appropriate.

1-1-698. Sections 1-1-696 through 1-1-698 do not prohibit any law, ordinance, regulation, order, decree, program, or policy requiring educational instruction in a language other than English for the purpose of making students who use a language other than English proficient in English or making students proficient in a language in addition to English.

TENNESSEE (1984)

Tennessee Code, Annotated, Section 4-1-404 (1985 Supplement)

English is hereby established as the official and legal language of Tennessee. All communications and publications, including ballots, produced by governmental entities in Tennessee shall be in English, and instruction in the public schools and colleges of Tennessee shall be conducted in English unless the nature of the course would require otherwise.

VIRGINIA (1981)

Virginia Code, 1950 Annotated, Section 22.1-212.1 (1989 Supplement)

English shall be designated as the official language of the Commonwealth of Virginia. School boards shall have no obligation to teach the standard curriculum, *except courses in foreign languages*, in a language other than English. *School boards shall endeavor to provide instruction in the English language which shall be designed to promote the education of students for whom English is a second language.* [1986 amendment in italics]

APPENDIX C

MULTIPLE AND LOGISTICAL REGRESSION MODELS

Table C.1   Results of Logistical Regression Analysis of State Adoption of Official English Laws

	Coefficient (B)	Standard Error
Eight-Variable Model		
SPANISH	.0699	.0811
BLACK	.0704	.0787
INCOME	-.0006	.0006
COLLEGE	-.3022*	.1421
POVERTY	-.0140	.2421
REAGAN	.1645	.1111
POPULATION	.0023	.0013
RURAL	.0577	.0609
Constant	17.7558	10.4515
Chi-Square (df)	21.232 (8)	
Correctly Predicted	80%	
Reduction of Error	39%	
Number of Cases	46	

Table C.1   (*cont.*)

Five-Variable Model

SPANISH	-.0139	.0540
BLACK	.0543	.0496
COLLEGE	.2767*	.1395
REAGAN	.0350	.0876
HR1924	.0223	.0133
Constant	2.6990	4.2571
Chi-Square (df)	18.381 (5)	
Correctly Predicted	80%	
Reduction of Error	39%	
Number of Cases	46	

Two-Variable Model

COLLEGE	-.3014*	.1355
HR1924	.0289*	.0123
Constant	1.8469	2.1529
Chi-Square (df)	17.054 (2)	
Correctly Predicted	80%	
Reduction of Error	39%	
Number of Cases	46	

*Statistically significant at the .05 level.

Note: The variables are defined as follows: SPANISH is the percentage of Spanish-speaking residents in 1980, BLACK is the percentage of black residents in 1980, INCOME is the median family income in 1979, COLLEGE is the percentage of residents aged twenty-five and over with a college education in 1980, POVERTY is the percentage of families below the federal poverty line in 1979, REAGAN is the percentage of the two-party vote for Reagan in 1984, POPULATION is the 1980 population in units of 10,000, RURAL is the percentage of residents in areas with population less than 2,500; and HR1924 is the percentage of the voting members of each state delegation in the 1924 House of Representatives who opposed the Begg Amendment.

Table C.2   Logistical Regression of 1992 National Election Study for Correlates of Support for Official English Law

	Coefficient (B)	Standard Error	Significance
IDEOLOGY	.0742	.0426	.081
POPULATION	.0151	.0623	.809
PARTY	.1533	.0508	.003
EDUCATION	-.2336	.0485	.000
INCOME	.0211	.0134	.115
BUSH	.1781	.2396	.457
CLINTON	-.0408	.2167	.851
WHITE	.6320	.1723	.000
Constant	.3814	.3498	.276

Chi-Square (df)	91.013 (8)
Correctly Predicted	68.8%
Reduction of Error	0%
Number of Cases	1,017
Missing Data	1,468

Notes: IDEOLOGY, PARTY, EDUCATION, and INCOME were coded according to the standard NES categories; POPULATION in units of ten-thousands of persons; PARTY as Democrats (1) and Republicans (0); BUSH as Bush (1) and Clinton or Perot (0); CLINTON as Clinton (1) and Bush or Perot (0); WHITE as non-Hispanic white (1) and non-Hispanic nonwhite or Hispanic (0).

Table C.3   Eight-Variable Regression Model of Referenda Voting by County in Support of Official English Laws in Five States

	Alabama	*Arizona*	*California*	*Colorado*	*Florida*
SPANISH	-.081	-.495**	-.379*	-.650*	-.306**
	-1.138	-.299	-.218	-.483	-.293
BLACK	.661**	.073	.046	.000	.110
	.187	.626	.075	-.003	.051
INCOME	-.264	-.376	.411*	-.074	.223
	-.006	-.016	.008	-.002	.004
COLLEGE	.017	-.335	-.451*	-.356*	-.522*
	.025	-.826	-.442	-.451	-.486
POVERTY	-.172	-.554	.156	-.236*	-.431**
	-.153	-.863	.383	-.473	-.396
REAGAN	.895*	.354	.611*	.234**	.179
	.433	.503	.490	.283	.121
POPULATION	-.010	-.355	-.024	.031	-.419**
	-.006	-.104	-.001	.036	-.076
RURAL	-.126	-.590	.333*	.058	-.201
	-.032	-.363	.064	.020	-.030
Constant	723.607	898.820	370.283	653.499	856.089
Number of Counties	67	14	58	63	67
Multiple R	.624	.972	.909	.929	.785
Adjusted R^2	.305	.857	.799	.844	.564

*Statistically significant at the .001 level.
**Statistically significant at the .05 level.
Notes: In statistics, top value is the Beta Weight; bottom value is the b. The variables are defined as follows: SPANISH is the percentage of Spanish-speaking residents in 1980, BLACK is the percentage of black residents in 1980, INCOME is the median family income in 1979, COLLEGE is the percentage of residents aged twenty-five and over with a college education in 1980, POVERTY is the percentage of families below the federal poverty line in 1979, REAGAN is the percentage of the two-party vote for Reagan in 1984, POPULATION is the 1980 population in units of 10,000, and RURAL is the percentage of residents in areas with population less than 2,500.

Table C.4   Four-Variable Regression Models of Referenda Voting by County in Support of Official English Laws in Five States

	Alabama	Arizona	California	Colorado	Florida
SPANISH	-.074	-.073	-.409*	-.783*	-.465*
	-1.043	-.044	-.235	-.581	-.446
BLACK	.657*	.112	-.056	.004	-.030
	.186	.965	-.092	.025	-.014
COLLEGE	-.002	-.300	-.322*	-.325*	-.141
	-.004	-.741	-.316	-.412	-.132
REAGAN	.889*	.840*	.594*	.231**	.407*
	.430	1.193	.476	.279	.275
Constant	585.004	-150.681	572.687	591.055	708.047
Number of					
Counties	67	14	58	63	67
Multiple R	.607	.860	.884	.923	.675
Adjusted R^2	.328	.623	.765	.842	.420

Table C.4 *(cont.)*

	Ala.	*Ariz.*	*Calif.*	*Colo.*	*Fla.*
SPANISH	-.068	-.172	-.383*	-.545*	-.508*
	-.956	-.104	-.220	-.405	-.487
BLACK	.671**	.014	-.055	-.014	.128
	.190	.122	-.089	-.091	.059
POVERTY	-.029	-.341	.126	.014	-.231**
	-.026	-.531	.309	.028	-.212
REAGAN	.881*	.586**	.747*	.419*	.418*
	.426	.832	.599	.508	.281
Constant	589.788	70.716	416.997	336.052	707.822
Number of Counties	67	14	58	63	67
Multiple R	.607	.850	.848	.884	.686
Adjusted R^2	.328	.599	.697	.766	.436

*Statistically significant at the .001 level.
**Statistically significant at the .05 level.
Notes: In statistics, top value is the Beta Weight; bottom value is the *b*. The variables are defined as follows: SPANISH is the percentage of Spanish-speaking residents in 1980, BLACK is the percentage of black residents in 1980, COLLEGE is the percentage of residents aged twenty-five and over with a college education in 1980, POVERTY is the percentage of families below the federal poverty line in 1979, and REAGAN is the percentage of the two-party vote for Reagan in 1984.

Table C.5   Logistical Regression to Predict Sponsors of Official English Bills

	Alabama	California	Arizona, California, Colorado
DEMOCRAT	-1.7006***	-5.0468*	-3.8918*
	(.7939)	(1.4518)	(1.0524)
BLACK	-3.1087**	-5.5128	-4.9588
	(1.1246)	(35.9790)	(34.8553)
HISPANIC	—	-6.9139	-5.4911
	—	(56.9979)	(27.1827)
MALE	7.8358	.7280	.7170
	(26.6123)	(1.3091)	(.4691)
REAGAN	.0700***	-.0444	.0372
	(.0354)	(.0700)	(.0307)
SPANISH	-.8898	-.1572	-.0455
	(1.3491)	(.1064)	(.0384)
%BLACK	.0014	.0093	.1225
	(.0212)	(.1749)	(.0703)
COLLEGE	-.0563	.0099	-.0006
	(.0680)	(.0931)	(.0370)
Constant	-8.5906	4.5700	-3.3734
	(26.7305)	(5.8926)	(2.6362)
Chi-Square	46.666*	45.480*	65.244*
(df)	(7)	(8)	(8)
Correctly Predicted	77%	83%	78%
Reduction of Error	43%	35%	0%
Number of Cases	105	80	204

*Statistically significant at .001 level.
**Statistically significant at .01 level.
***Statistically significant at .05 level.
Notes: Coefficient (B) value is shown along with Standard Error in parentheses. The variables are defined as follows: DEMOCRAT is Democratic legislator, BLACK is black legislator, HISPANIC is Hispanic legislator, MALE is male legislator, %REAGAN is the percentage of legislator's home county vote for Reagan in 1984, %SPANISH is the percentage of Spanish-speaking residents in legislator's home county in 1980, %BLACK is the percentage of black residents in legislator's home county in 1980, and %COLLEGE is the percentage of college-educated residents in legislator's home county in 1980.

Table C.6 Logistical Regression to Predict Legislative Votes on Official English Bills

	Indiana	North Dakota	Mississippi	North Carolina	Alabama	Tennessee
DEMOCRAT	-2.6439*	-2.0181*	-6.1160	-1.0121	-.1520	.7421
	(.71403)	(.6064)	(26.8108)	(.6058)	(.7347)	(.8257)
MALE	1.5494	-.0729	-6.2010	1.0422	2.4723	.9799
	(.8653)	(.6387)	(34.8172)	(.6204)	(1.4311)	(.9961)
BLACK	-6.6896	—	-4.8621*	-2.9542**	-2.0577***	-2.4137***
	(23.1306)	—	(1.2129)	(1.1397)	(.7181)	(1.0168)
HISPANIC	-6.1263	—	—	—	—	—
	(60.4479)	—	—	—	—	
REAGAN	.0804	.0639	.0124	.0413	.0872**	.0500
	(.0633)	(.0414)	(.0678)	(.0426)	(.0330)	(.0560)
SPANISH	.0442	1.5732	-1.9438	.4872	2.7916	-3.3597**
	(.3004)	(1.5330)	(1.0826)	(.4964)	(1.7654)	(1.3518)**
%BLACK	-.0356	-1.2431	.0080	.0093	.0083	.367
	(.0590)	(.7420)	(.0406)	(.0250)	(.0200)	(.0341)
COLLEGE	-.0483	-.0298	.0604	-.0824***	-.0495	.1603
	(.0651)	(.0584)	(.0824)	(.0409)	(.0768)	(.0988)
Constant	-3.2098	-1.8831	14.3383	-1.4004	-7.7490	-2.5209
	(4.3424)	(3.0591)	(44.2874)	(3.3584)	(3.1866)	(3.7985)
Chi-Square	52.853*	24.219*	57.217*	39.197*	29.585**	13.317

Table C.6 *(cont.)*

(df)	(8)	(6)	(7)	(7)	(7)	(7)
Correctly Predicted	84%	80%	69%	78%	73%	84%
Reduction of Error	54%	23%	54%	42%	21%	0%
N=Cases	100	106	122	120	105	99

*Statistically significant at .001 level.
**Statistically significant at .01 level.
***Statistically significant at .05 level.

Notes: Coefficient (B) value is shown along with Standard Error in parentheses. The variables are defined as follows: DEMOCRAT is Democratic legislator, BLACK is black legislator, HISPANIC is Hispanic legislator, MALE is male legislator, REAGAN is the percentage of legislator's home county vote for Reagan in 1984, SPANISH is the percentage of Spanish-speaking residents in legislator's home county in 1980, %BLACK is the percentage of black residents in legislator's home county in 1980, and COLLEGE is the percentage of college-educated residents in legislator's home county in 1980.

Table C.7 Logistical Regression to Predict Sponsors and Legislative Votes on Official English Bills in Groups of Selected States

	Vote *Group 1[a]*	Vote *Group 2[b]*	Sponsors *Group 3[c]*
DEMOCRAT	-.3694	-1.3680*	-.5660**
	(.4268)	(.3124)	(.2190)
BLACK	-2.7956*	-2.7782*	-.6491***
	(.4113)	(.4076)	(.3128)
HISPANIC	—	-8.0318	-7.6275
	—	(22.2414)	(10.1138)
MALE	1.0133***	.7149***	.2853
	(.5016)	(.3584)	(.2504)
REAGAN	-.0094	.0306***	-.0166
	(.0226)	(.0142)	(.0114)
SPANISH	.1339	-.3822**	-.1376*
	(.4411)	(.1561)	(.0225)
%BLACK	-.0178	.0279*	-.0197**
	(.0127)	(.0088)	(.0067)
COLLEGE	-.0767**	-.0565**	-.0320***
	(.0274)	(.0203)	(.0138)
Constant	3.7822***	-1.0207	2.4050**
	(1.7636)	(1.0685)	(.9484)
Chi-Square	100.494*	140.178*	103.730*
(df)	(7)	(8)	(8)
Correctly Predicted	90%	86%	64%
Reduction of Error	29%	22%	22%
Number of Cases	468	665	712

[a]Alabama, Kentucky, Mississippi, North Carolina, Tennessee
[b]Alabama, Indiana, Kentucky, Mississippi, North Carolina, North Dakota, Tennessee
[c]Alabama, Arizona, Arkansas, California, Colorado, Georgia, South Carolina
[*]Statistically significant at .001 level.
[**]Statistically significant at .01 level.
[***]Statistically significant at .05 level.
Notes: Coefficient (B) value is shown along with Standard Error in parentheses. The variables are defined as follows: DEMOCRAT is Democratic legislator, BLACK is black legislator, HISPANIC is Hispanic legislator, MALE is male legislator, REAGAN is the percentage of legislator's home county vote for Reagan in 1984, SPANISH is the percentage of Spanish-speaking residents in legislator's home county in 1980, %BLACK is the percentage of black residents in legislator's home county in 1980, and COLLEGE is the percentage of college-educated residents in legislator's home county in 1980.

NOTES

INTRODUCTION

1. "Remark on Immigrants Brings Byrd's Apology," *New York Times,* July 27, 1992, 8.

2. Theodore J. Lowi, "American Business, Public Policy, Case Studies, and Political Theory," *World Politics* 16 (July 1964): 677-715.

3. Theodore J. Lowi, "Four Systems of Policy, Politics, and Choice," *Public Administration Review* 32 (July-Aug. 1972): 298-310. There is debate about the efficacy of Lowi's policy categories as a guide for analysis. See Robert J. Spitzer, "Promoting Policy Theory: Revising the Arenas of Power," *Policy Studies Journal* 15 (June 1987): 675-89; Aynsley Kellow, "Promoting Elegance in Policy Theory: Simplifying Lowi's Arenas of Power," *Policy Studies Journal* 16 (Summer 1988): 713-24; Robert J. Spitzer, "From Complexity to Simplicity: More on Policy Theory and the Arenas of Power," *Policy Studies Journal* 17 (Spring 1989): 529-36; Aynsley Kellow, "Taking the Long Way Home? A Reply to Spitzer on the Arenas of Power," *Policy Studies Journal* 17 (Spring 1989): 537-46; Robert J. Spitzer, "Complexity and Induction: A Rejoinder to Kellow," *Policy Studies Journal* 17 (Spring 1989): 547-49.

4. See Randall B. Ripley and Grace A. Franklin, *Bureaucracy and Policy Implementation* (Homewood, Ill.: Dorsey Press, 1986); Randall B. Ripley and Grace A. Franklin, *Congress, the Bureaucracy, and Public Policy,* 5th ed. (Belmont, Calif.: Wadsworth, 1990); Robert J. Spitzer, *The Presidency and Public Policy: The Four Arenas of Presidential Power* (University: Univ. of Alabama Press, 1983); William Zimmerman, "Issue Areas and Foreign-Policy Process," *American Political Science Review* 67 (Dec. 1973): 1204-12.

5. T. Alexander Smith, *The Comparative Policy Process* (Santa Barbara, Calif.: CLIO Press, 1975), 90. See James B. Christoph, *Capital Punishment and British Politics* (London: Allen and Unwin, 1962).

6. Donley T. Studlar, "Elite Responsiveness or Elite Autonomy: British Immigration Policy Reconsidered," *Ethnic and Racial Studies* 3 (April 1980): 207-23; Keith Richmond, "Daylight Savings in New South Wales: A Case of Emotive Symbolic Politics," *Australian Journal of Public Administration* 37 (1978): 374-85; Raymond Tatalovich and Byron W. Daynes, *The Politics of Abortion: A Study of Community Conflict in Public Policymaking* (New York: Praeger, 1981); idem, "Moral Controversies and the Policymaking Process: Lowi's Framework Applied to the Abortion Issue," *Policy Studies Review* 3 (Feb. 1984): 207-22; Joni Lovenduski and Joyce Outshoorn, eds., *The New Politics of Abortion* (Beverly Hills, Calif.: Sage, 1986).

7. Smith, *Comparative Policy Process,* 113.

8. See David M. Reimers, *Still the Golden Door: The Third World Comes to America* (New York: Columbia Univ. Press, 1985).

9. Max Weber, *Economy and Society* (New York: Bedminister, 1968), 302-7, 901-40; Seymour Martin Lipset and E. Raab, *The Politics of Unreason: Right-Wing Extremism in America, 1790-1977* (Chicago: Univ. of Chicago Press, 1978).

10. See William Kornhauser, *The Politics of Mass Society* (Glencoe, Ill.: Free Press, 1959).

11. Richard Hofstadter, "The Pseudo-Conservative Revolt," in *The New American Right,* edited by Daniel Bell (New York: Criterion, 1955). See Daniel Bell, *The Radical Right* (New York: Doubleday, 1964); and Richard Hofstadter, *The Paranoid Style in American Politics* (New York: Vintage Books, 1967).

12. See Lipset and Raab, *Politics of Unreason.*

13. Joseph R. Gusfield, *Symbolic Crusade: Status Politics and the American Temperance Movement* (Urbana: Univ. of Illinois Press, 1963); Louis A. Zurcher Jr., R. George Kirkpatrick, Robert G. Cushing, and Charles K. Bowman, "The Anti-Pornography Campaign: A Symbolic Crusade," *Social Problems* 19 (Fall 1971): 236.

14. Ann L. Page and Donald A. Clelland, "The Kanawha County Textbook Controversy: A Study of the Politics of Life Style Concern," *Social Forces* 57 (Sept. 1978): 279; Matthew C. Moen, "School Prayer and the Politics of Life-Style Concern," *Social Science Quarterly* 65 (Dec. 1984): 1070; Wilbur J. Scott, "The Equal Rights Amendment as Status Politics," *Social Forces* 64 (Dec. 1985): 499-506.

15. Clarence Y.H. Lo, "Countermovements and Conservative Movements in the Contemporary U.S.," *Annual Review of Sociology* 8 (1982): 111-12.

16. Pamela Johnston Conover, "The Mobilization of the New Right: A Test of Various Explanations," *Western Political Quarterly* 36

(Dec. 1983): 632–49; David O. Sears, Richard R. Lau, Tom R. Tyler, and Harris M. Allen Jr., "Self-Interest and Symbolic Policy Attitudes and Presidential Voting," *American Political Science Review* 74 (Sept. 1980): 670–84; David O. Sears, Carl P. Hensler, and Leslie K. Speer, "Whites' Opposition to 'Busing': Self-Interest or Symbolic Politics," *American Political Science Review* 73 (June 1979): 369–84; Donald R. Kinder and David O. Sears, "Prejudice and Politics: Symbolic Racism versus Racial Threats to the Good Life," *Journal of Personality and Social Psychology* 40 (March 1981): 414-31.

17. John Higham, *Strangers in the Land: Patterns of American Nativism, 1860-1925* (New York: Atheneum, 1965).

18. John Higham, "Another Look at Nativism," *Catholic Historical Review* 44 (July 1958): 151-52.

19. Ibid., 152-53.

20. Neil J. Smelser, *Theory of Collective Behavior* (New York: Free Press, 1962), 109.

21. Ibid., 116.

22. Lo, "Countermovements and Conservative Movements" 108.

23. Michael P. Rogin, *The Intellectuals and McCarthy: The Radical Specter* (Cambridge, Mass.: MIT Press, 1967); James L. Gibson, "Political Intolerance and Political Repression during the McCarthy Red Scare," *American Political Science Review* 82 (June 1988): 511-29.

24. Smelser, *Theory of Collective Behavior* 287-89.

25. Raymond Tatalovich and Byron W. Daynes, eds., *Social Regulatory Policy: Moral Controversies in American Politics* (Boulder, Colo.: Westview Press, 1988), 210-11.

26. Mancur Olson Jr., *The Logic of Collective Action: Public Goods and the Theory of Groups* (Cambridge, Mass.: Harvard Univ. Press, 1965), 160-61.

27. See Raymond Tatalovich and Byron W. Daynes, "The Lowi Paradigm, Moral Conflict, and Coalition-Building: Pro-Choice versus Pro-Life," *Women and Politics* 13, no. 1 (1993): 39-66.

28. Jamie B. Draper and Martha Jimenez, "Language Debates in the United States: A Decade in Review," *EPIC Events* 2, no. 5 (1989): 4 (*EPIC Events* is the newsletter of the English Plus Information Clearinghouse); "Advocate Plans to Run for Office," *Houston Chronicle,* Nov. 12, 1988.

29. William Trombley, "California Elections: Prop. 63 Roots Traced to Small Michigan City; Measure to Make English Official Language of State Sprang from Concern over Immigration, Population," *Los Angeles Times,* Oct. 20, 1986, pt. 1, p. 3.

Celebrated Americans have endorsed the goals of U.S. English. A recent informational pamphlet listed these persons on the organization's advisory board: Hon. Walter Annenberg, Clarence L. Barnhart, Jacques Barzun, Ph.D., Saul Bellow, Alistair Cooke, Denton Cooley, M.D., Sen. Joseph Corcoran, Dinesh Desai, Hon. Angier B. Duke, Andre Emmerich, George Gilder, Nathan Glazer, Ph.D., Sen. Barry Goldwater, Charlton Heston, Sen. Frank Hill, Ralph Hylinski, M.D., Charles Luckman, Sen. Eugene J. McCarthy, Barbara Mujica, Ph.D., Mrs. Eugene Ormandy, Norman Podhoretz, Randolph Rowland, Arnold Schwarzenegger, Karl Shapiro, W. Clement Stone, and Rosalyn Yalow, Ph.D. See U.S. English, *U.S. English: Towards A Unified America* (Washington, D.C., n.d.). (A notation within the text of the pamphlet indicates that other data were current as of March 1991.)

Norman Cousins and Walter Cronkite were listed on the advisory board in earlier years. See U.S. English, "In Defense of Our Common Language . . .," in *Language Loyalties: A Source Book on the Official English Controversy,* edited by James Crawford (Chicago: Univ. of Chicago Press, 1992), 147. Cousins resigned to protest the California referendum in 1986, and Cronkite resigned after a controversial memo with racial overtones by John Tanton came to light during the Arizona referendum campaign in 1988. Apparently persons close to Saul Bellow deny his affiliation with U.S. English; see S.I. Hayakawa, "The Case for Official English," in *Language Loyalties,* ed. Crawford, 100n9.

30. U.S. English, *U.S. English: Towards A Unified America.*

31. Katherine Bishop, "S.I. Hayakawa Dies at 85; Scholar and Former Senator," *New York Times,* Feb. 28, 1992, A11. Hayakawa's text *Language in Action* was published by Harcourt, Brace and Company in 1941.

32. "Proposed Official English Amendments to the U.S. Constitution," in *Language Loyalties,* ed. Crawford, 112.

33. U.S. Senate, Committee on the Judiciary, Subcommittee on the Constitution, *The English Language Amendment: Hearings on S.J. Res. 167,* 98th Cong., 2d sess., June 12, 1984, serial no. J-98-126 (Washington, D.C.: United States Government Printing Office, 1985).

34. Remarks by Senator Walter Huddleston, *Congressional Record,* 98th Cong., 1st sess., Sept. 21, 1983, vol. 129, no. 122, pp. S12640-43.

35. Ibid., S 12640-S12642.

36. U.S. English, "Possible Language for Constitutional Initiatives," Sept. 21, 1987, memorandum. In author's files.

37. Ibid.

38. Ibid.

39. Ibid.

40. U.S. House of Representatives, Committee on the Judiciary, Subcommittee on Civil and Constitutional Rights, *English Language*

Constitutional Amendments: Hearings on H.J. Res. 13, H.J. Res. 33, H.J. Res. 60, and H.J. Res. 83, 100th Cong., 2d sess., May 11, 1988, serial no. 120 (Washinton, D.C.: Government Printing Office, 1989), pp. 36-37.

41. Hayakawa, "Case for Official English" 98-99.

42. "The English Language Amendment and Congress: A Chronology of the 1980s," *EPIC Events* 2, no. 5 (1989): 5; Julie E. Inman, "'Language for All Peoples': Adding to the Confusion," *EPIC Events* 5, no. 5 (Feb.-March 1993): 1, 6.

43. Julie E. Inman and Kelly R. Sutton, "America: Melting Pot or Patch Quilt?" *EPIC Events* 5, no. 5 (Feb.-March 1993): 2-3.

44. *EPIC Events* 4, no. 1 (March-April 1991): 3.

45. "Statement of Purpose," English Plus Information Clearinghouse, enclosure with form letter to "Dear Friend" from Mary Carol Combs, director, n.d.

46. Ibid.

47. William J. Bennett, "The Bilingual Education Act: A Failed Path," in *Language Loyalties,* ed. Crawford, 358-60.

48. Mary Carol Combs, "English Plus: Responding to English Only," in *Language Loyalties,* ed. Crawford, 217.

49. Ibid.

50. Ronald J. Schmidt, "Language Policy and the Politics of Identity: Understanding the Stakes" (paper presented at the annual meeting of the Western Political Science Association, Albuquerque, N.Mex., March 10-12, 1994), 25. His position is consistent with my conclusion that the policy debate between "pluralists" and "assimilationists" is grounded in the divergent values of equality versus national unity, but Schmidt goes further by employing "instrumentalist," "primordialist," and "constructivist" analytical categories to probe the deeper ethnolinguistic and communal conflicts over "identity" politics.

CHAPTER 1. SCOPE OF THE STUDY, METHODS, AND HYPOTHESES

1. Two provisions of the New Mexico state constitution also give legal status to Spanish. Article VII, section 3, declares: "The right of any citizen of the state to vote, hold office or sit upon juries shall never be restricted, abridged or impaired on account of . . . inability to speak, read or write the English or Spanish languages." Article XII, section 8, states: "The Legislature shall provide for the training of teachers in the normal schools or otherwise so that they may become proficient in both the English and Spanish languages, to qualify them to teach Spanish-speaking

pupils and students in the public schools and educational institutions of the state, and shall provide proper means and methods to facilitate the teaching of the English language and other branches of learning to such pupils and students."

2. "Rhode Island Becomes English Plus State," EPIC Events 5, no. 2 (May-June 1992): 1. The text of the bill appears on p. 4.

3. Advocatory scholarship by those opposed to English language laws includes James Crawford, Bilingual Education: History, Politics, Theory, and Practice (Trenton, N.J.: Crane, 1989); and idem, Hold Your Tongue: Bilingualism and the Politics of "English Only" (Reading, Mass.: Addison-Wesley, 1992). Crawford's edited volume Language Loyalties is a collection of primary documents. Dennis Baron, The English-Only Question: An Official Language for Americans? (New Haven, Conn.: Yale Univ. Press, 1990), is a historical account of language policy. In Only English?: Law and Language Policy in the United States (Albuquerque: Univ. of New Mexico Press, 1990), Bill Piatt reviews legal precedents. A collection of scholarly articles is found in Karen L. Adams and Daniel T. Brink, eds. Perspectives on Official English (New York: Mouten de Gruyter, 1990). California exit polls are examined in Jack Citrin, Beth Reingold, Evelyn Walters, and Donald P. Green, "The 'Official English' Movement and the Symbolic Politics of Language in the United States," Western Political Quarterly 43 (Sept. 1990): 535-60. Ronald J. Schmidt examines North American language politics in "The Politics of Language in Canada and the United States: Explaining the Differences" (paper presented at the annual meeting of the American Political Science Association, Washington, D.C., Aug. 29-Sept. 1, 1991). Finally, Jonathan Pool, in "The Official Language Problem," American Political Science Review 85 (June 1991): 495-514, offers a model for resolving the language problem.

4. Lydia Chavez, "Leaders Ready for Fight over English-Only Bills," New York Times, Dec. 12, 1986, 19.

5. U.S. Department of Commerce, Bureau of the Census, Population Estimates by Race and Hispanic Origin for States, Metropolitan Areas, and Selected Counties, 1980-1985, Current Population Reports Series P-25, no. 1040-RD-1 (Washington, D.C.: GPO, 1989), 69.

6. Max J. Castro, "The Politics of Language in Miami," in Miami Now!: Immigration, Ethnicity, and Social Change, edited by Guillermo J. Grenier and Alex Stepick III (Gainesville: Univ. Press of Florida, 1992), 112-13; Allen Bronson Brierly and David Moon, "Political Representation in Dade County, Florida: A Comparison of Actual and Perceived Representation by Ethnic Groups" (paper presented at the annual meeting

of the Southwestern Social Science Association, Austin, Tex., March 19-21, 1992).

7. Dario Moreno and Nicol Rae, "Ethnicity and Partnership: The Eighteen Congressional District in Miami," in Miami Now! ed. Grenier and Stepick, 197.

8. V.O. Key, Southern Politics in State and Nation (New York: Vintage Books, 1949), 5; Earl Black and Merle Black, "The Wallace Vote in Alabama: A Multiple Regression Analysis," Journal of Politics 35 (Aug. 1973): 730-36; Robert A. Schoenberger and David R. Segal, "The Ecology of Dissent: The Southern Wallace Vote in 1968," Midwest Journal of Political Science 15 (Aug. 1971): 583-86; Michael W. Giles and Melanie Buckner, "David Duke and Black Threat: An Old Hypothesis Revisited," Journal of Politics 55 (Aug. 1993): 702-13.

9. Piatt, Only English? 173.

10. See Donald R. Matthews and James W. Prothro, "Stateways versus Folkways: Critical Factors in Southern Reaction to Brown v. Board of Education," in Essays on the American Constitution, edited by Gottfried Dietze (Englewood Cliffs, N.J.: Prentice-Hall, 1964), 139-58. Under the amended Voting Rights Act of 1965 there are officially designated bilingual counties in Florida (seven), California (ten), Colorado (twelve), and Arizona (fifteen). The proportions of votes to establish English as the official language of those states were higher than the statewide proportions in five Florida and nine California bilingual counties, six in Arizona, but only one in Colorado. So twenty-one of these counties (or 48 percent) gave more support to the referenda despite the presence of high concentrations of Spanish speakers. There may be a threshold effect, where the Anglo reaction occurs after the Spanish-speaking population grows to a certain percentage of the total, but clearly these data do not indicate that, a priori, there is reason to accept the contrary hypothesis that counties with more Hispanics would generate less support for official English on the premise that Hispanics are highly mobilized and exhibit high voting turnouts. Indeed, if anything, it is more likely that Anglos outvote Hispanics even where Spanish speakers are a sizable minority, because turnout among Hispanic voters is well below the rate for white voters.

11. Nathan Glazer and Daniel Patrick Moynihan, Beyond the Melting Pot: The Negroes, Puerto Ricans, Jews, Italians, and Irish of New York City (Cambridge, Mass.: MIT Press, 1963); Michael Parenti, "Ethnic Politics and the Persistence of Ethnic Identification," American Political Science Review 61 (Sept. 1967): 717-26; Raymond E. Wolfinger, "The Development and Persistence of Ethnic Voting," American Political Science Review 59 (Dec. 1965): 896-908.

12. Smith quoted in Larry Rohter, "A Black-Cuban Contest to Succeed Janet Reno," New York Times, March 19, 1993, B9; Castro, "Politics of Language in Miami" 121.

13. Paula D. McClain, "The Changing Dynamics of Urban Politics: Black and Hispanic Municipal Employment—Is There Competition?" Journal of Politics 55 (May 1993): 411. Also see Paula D. McClain and Albert K. Karnig, "Black and Hispanic Socioeconomic and Political Competition," American Political Science Review 84 (June 1990): 535-45.

14. Castro, "Politics of Language in Miami" 121.

15. Higham, Strangers in the Land 45, 266-67.

16. Eric Fong and William T. Markham, "Immigration, Ethnicity, and Conflict: The California Chinese, 1849-1882," Sociological Inquiry 61 (Fall 1991): 486.

17. Seymour Martin Lipset, Political Man: The Social Bases of Politics (Garden City, N.Y.: Anchor Books, 1963), 87-126.

18. See Tatalovich and Daynes, Social Regulatory Policy 216-17.

19. Jack Citrin, "Language Politics and American Identity," Public Interest, no. 99 (Spring 1990): 104-5.

20. "English Yes, Xenophobia No," New York Times, Nov. 10, 1986, 20; Crawford, Bilingual Education 63-65.

21. U.S. Department of Commerce, Bureau of the Census, Population Estimates by Race and Hispanic Origin 69.

22. I am indebted to the insight by Professor Kenneth J. Meier of the University of Wisconsin-Milwaukee that the use of longitudinal analysis may give stronger clues about why so many states passed English Only laws in the 1980s. The approach that is employed in this work, cross-sectional analysis, is geared to differentiating between states that did and did not approve official English. It may be that the growing presence of non-English-speaking immigrants, particularly from Mexico and Latin America, over time as compared with a baseline period in the recent past would explain the clustering of fifteen laws being passed between 1981 and 1990. This explanation is commonly made in the popular press and by leaders of the Spanish-speaking community, but no one to date has statistically validated that proposition.

CHAPTER 2. WARTIME HYSTERIA

1. Laws, Resolutions and Memorials Passed by the Legislature of the State of Nebraska, 37th sess., Jan. 7-April 18, 1919 (Lincoln: Secretary of State), chaps. 6, 234, 249, pp. 67, 991, 1019.

2. See House Journal of the Legislature of the State of Nebraska, 37th sess., Jan. 7-April 18, 1919 (Lincoln: compiled under authority of the House), 406, 422, 1345, 1347, 1381-82; Senate Journal of the Legislature of the State of Nebraska, 37th sess., Jan. 7-April 18, 1919 (Lincoln: compiled under authority of the Senate), 1396, 1399-1400, 1485-86.

3. The Revised Statutes of the State of Nebraska, 1913 (Lincoln: State of Nebraska, printed by State Journal Co., 1914), chap. 15, art. VI, secs. 1099, 1100, 1101.

4. It read: "That hereafter all public meetings held within the State of Nebraska; meetings held in compliance with the provisions of the Nebraska statutes; political meetings or conventions whether delegates or otherwise; and all meetings or conventions, the purpose and object of which are the consideration and discussion of political or nonpolitical subjects or questions of general interest, or relating to the well being of any class or organization in the State of Nebraska, or for the endorsement or rejection of any candidate, law or measure to be voted upon at any election within said state, shall be conducted in the English language exclusively; providing the provisions of this Act shall not apply to meetings or conventions held for the purpose of religious teachings, instruction or worship, or lodge organizations." LAWS: Resolutions and Memorials, Passed by the Legislature of the State of Nebraska at the Thirty-Seventh Session, Which Convened at the City of Lincoln, Nebraska, January 7, and Adjourned April 18, 1919, Published by Darius M. Amsberry, Secretary of State, Lincoln, p. 991.

5. LAWS: Resolutions and Memorials, Passed by the Legislature of the State of Nebraska at the Thirty-Seventh Session, Which Convened at the City of Lincoln, Nebraska, January 7, and Adjourned April 18, 1919, Published by Darius M. Amsberry, Secretary of State, p. 1019.

6. See Constitutional Convention, 1919-20, Proposal no. 77, introduced by Walter L. Anderson, of Lancaster County, and referred to the Bill of Rights Committee, "Relating to Right of the People to a Common Language"; Constitutional Convention, 1919-20, Proposal no. 326, recommended by the convention for a second reading, "Relating to the Bill of Rights," both in Nebraska State Library, Lincoln.

7. All the quoted material to follow is drawn from Journal of the Nebraska Constitutional Convention, convened Dec. 2, 1919 (Lincoln: compiled under authority of the Convention), 1:951-63, 1293-1307; 2:1903, 2189, 2646-47.

8. Proposed Amendments to the Constitution of the State of Nebraska as Adopted by the Constitutional Convention, 1919-20, pamphlet, Nebraska State Library.

9. The discussion and all quoted materials in this section are drawn from House Journal of the Legislature of the State of Nebraska, 40th sess., Jan. 4-April 28, 1921 (Lincoln: compiled under authority of the House), 1347-48, 2023-24, 1411-12; and Senate Journal of the Legislature of the State of Nebraska, 40th sess., Jan. 4-April 28, 1921 (Lincoln: compiled under authority of the Senate), 171, 695-96, 894-95, 1894-95.

10. Compiled Statutes of the State of Nebraska, 1922 (Columbia, Mo.: E.W. Stephens Pub. Co., 1922), chap. 63, art. XV, secs. 6456-62.

11. Among those who voiced objections to chapter 61 (Henry Behrens, R.R. Vance, Ernest H. Gifford, S.J. Franklin, Peter Hakanson, F.L. Anderson, and Henry Bock), only Bock was a Democrat, indicating that no policy consensus existed among Republicans.

12. Information and quotations concerning Nebraska District of Evangelical Lutheran Synod of Missouri v. McKelvie come from Reports of Cases in the Supreme Court of Nebraska, Sept. Term, 1919-Jan. Term, 1920, vol. 104 (Columbia, Mo.: E.W. Stephens Pub. Co., 1921), 93-104.

13. Information and quotations concerning Meyer v. State come from Reports of Cases in the Supreme Court of Nebraska, Sept. Term, 1921-Jan. Term, 1922, vol. 107 (Lincoln, Nebr.: Kline Pub. Co., 1923), 659-69.

14. The following material concerning the U.S. Supreme Court decision appears in Meyer v. Nebraska, 262 U.S. 390 at 390-403 (1923).

15. United States Reports, vol. 262 (Washington, D.C.: GPO, 1923), pp. 404-12.

CHAPTER 3. ANTECEDENTS OF NATIVISM

1. Higham, Strangers in the Land 4.

2. Ray Allen Billington, The Protestant Crusade, 1800-1860: A Study of the Origins of American Nativism (New York: Macmillan, 1938), 322; Higham, Strangers in the Land 9.

3. Higham, Strangers in the Land 9.

4. Donald L. Kinzer, An Episode in Anti-Catholicism: The American Protective Association (Seattle: Univ. of Washington Press, 1964), 16.

5. Higham, Strangers in the Land 196, 198.

6. Ibid., 223, 263.

7. See Senate Debates, 53d General Assembly of Illinois, 1923, pp. 233-34, Illinois State Library, Springfield.

8. See Senate Bill no. 15, 53d General Assembly of Illinois, 1923, introduced by Mr. Ryan, Jan. 10, 1923.

9. Committee report is available as Amendment to Senate Bill no. 15, 53d General Assembly of Illinois, 1923, reported from Committee on Judiciary, March 8, 1923.

10. Quotations from the floor debate are taken from Senate Debates, 53d General Assembly of Illinois, 233-34.

11. See Journal of the House of Representatives of the Seventy-sixth General Assembly of the State of Illinois (Springfield, 1969), 1:839, 1864; Journal of the Senate of the Seventy-sixth General Assembly of the State of Illinois (Springfield, 1969), 2325-26.

12. Telephone interview with Key Decision Maker no. 2 (Illinois), Feb. 26, 1990.

13. "Language by Legislation," Nation 116 (April 11, 1923): 408.

14. Ibid.

15. Ibid.

16. "Language as by Law Established," New York Times, Feb. 7, 1923, 14.

17. Vernon M. Briggs Jr., Immigration Policy and the American Labor Force (Baltimore: John Hopkins Univ. Press, 1984), 42-45.

18. The Pearson correlation coefficient between the percentage of foreign-born residents in each state and the percentage of no votes of representatives voting from each state delegation was -.646 on the Begg Amendment, which was designed to allow aliens a measure of due process before deportation. On final enactment of the 1924 act, a coefficient of -.619 was derived between the percentage of foreign-born residents and the percentage of yes votes.

The Pearson correlation coefficient between Catholic Church members as a percentage of total state population and the percentage of no votes of those representatives voting from each state delegation was -.483 on the Begg Amendment. On final enactment of the act, a coefficient of -.690 was derived between the percentage of Catholic residents and the percentage of yes votes.

The Pearson correlation coefficient between the percentage of foreign-born residents in each state and Catholic Church members as a percentage of total population in each state was .695.

19. There was a vacancy in the Louisiana Second District when the votes were taken, and George Favrot (6th-Baton Rouge) did not vote. James O'Connor (1st-New Orleans) and Ladislas Lazaro (7th-Washington) were Catholics who voted against the Begg Amendment and for the 1924 act, along with Whitmell Martin (3d-Thibodaux), John Sandlin (4th-Minden), Riley Wilson (5th-Ruston), and James Aswell (8th-Natchitoches).

20. See Michael C. LeMay, From Open Door to Dutch Door: An Analysis of U.S. Immigration Policy since 1820 (New York: Praeger, 1987), 87. LeMay implies that the burden of proof requirement was a repressive aspect of the 1924 act.

21. Congressional Record, 68th Cong., 1st sess., April 12, 1924, 65, pt. 6:6256-57. All quotes from the House debate in this section are drawn from these pages.

22. LeMay, From Open Door to Dutch Door 56.

23. Chae Chan Ping v. United States, 130 U.S. 581 (1889).

24. LeMay, From Open Door to Dutch Door 57.

25. Again, all quotations from the House debate come from the Congressional Record, 68th Cong., 1st sess., April 12, 1924, 65, pt. 6:6256-57.

26. Kenneth J. Meier, The Politics of Sin (Armonk, N.Y.: M.E. Sharpe Publisher, 1995), pp. 20-65; Oscar Handlin, Race and Nationality in American Life (Garden City, N.Y.: Doubleday, 1957), 74-110.

27. The 41 representatives not voting on the Begg Amendment came from California (2), Florida (2), Illinois (2), Iowa (1), Kentucky (1), Louisiana (1), Maryland (2), Massachusetts (3), Minnesota (4), Mississippi (1), Missouri (1), Nebraska (1), New Hampshire (1), New York (7), Pennsylvania (6), South Carolina (2), South Dakota (1), Vermont (1), West Virginia (1), and Wisconsin (1). Of this group, seven states (Illinois, Maryland, Massachusetts, Minnesota, New York, Pennsylvania, and Wisconsin) accounted for 108 yes votes (of the 198, or 55 percent) and 25 of those not voting (of the 41, or 61 percent) on the Begg Amendment.

28. An eight-variable model may be overspecified given the number of cases (forty-six), although there does not seem to be a problem of multicollinearity. The Pearson intercorrelation matrix among the eight variables shows values ranging from .017 to .566, which is well below the .75 level that indicates a likely problem.

29. The three remaining variables were far less significant (SPANISH = .80, BLACK = .27, and REAGAN = .69) than was HR1924.

CHAPTER 4. REFERENDUM POLITICS

1. Castro, "Politics of Language in Miami" 110; Joanne Bretzer, "Language, Power, and Identity in Multiethnic Miami," in Language Loyalties, ed. Crawford, 212.

2. Castro, "Politics of Language in Miami" 112, 113-14.

3. Joan Didion, Miami (New York: Simon and Schuster, 1987), 63.

4. Metro-Dade County, Board of County Commissioners, agenda item no. 7(g)(3), Resolution no. R-502-73, Declaring Dade County a Bilingual and Bicultural County, Metro-Dade County, Fla., 1973.

5. Michael Browning, "Anti-Bilingual Backers Celebrate Early," Miami Herald, Nov. 5, 1980, 11A.

6. Ibid.

7. Max J. Castro, "On the Curious Question of Language in Miami," in Language Loyalties, ed. Crawford, 179.

8. Reprinted in "Dade County 'Antibilingual' Ordinance," in Language Loyalties, ed. Crawford, 131.

9. William Trombley, "California Elections: English-Only Proposition Kindles Minorities' Fears," Los Angeles Times, Oct. 12, 1986, pt. 1, p. 1.

10. Maya Bell, "Dade Official Will Fight to Say Adiós to English-Only Law," Orlando Sentinel, July 20, 1987.

11. Justin Gillis, "Push Begins to Repeal Anti-Bilingual Law," Miami Herald, July 3, 1987.

12. Ibid.

13. Ibid.

14. Florida Legislature, History of Legislation, 1981 regular session, special sessions A and B, pp. 75-76, 132, Legislative Information Division, Joint Legislative Management Committee, State Library of Florida, Tallahassee (hereinafter cited as LID, Florida). Also see Florida House of Representatives, 1981, House Bill 275; Florida Senate, 1981, Senate Bill 389, both in Florida State Archives, Florida Department of State, Tallahassee.

15. Ibid.

16. Ibid.

17. Florida Legislature, History of Legislation, 1982 regular session, special sessions C, D, E, F, G, pp. 107, 218, LID, Florida. Also see Florida House of Representatives, 1982, House Bill 347; Florida Senate, 1982, Senate Bill 675, both in Florida State Archives.

18. No copies of the original bills for 1985 were available at the State Library of Florida. My search included the bills in the governor's file.

19. Florida Legislature, History of Legislation, 1985 regular session, 1984 special session A, p. 26, LID, Florida.

20. Florida Legislature, History of Legislation, 1986 regular session, 1986 special session B, p. 239, LID, Florida. Also see Florida House of Representatives, House Joint Resolution 277, Florida State Archives.

21. Andres Viglucci, "Official-English Push Sparks Battle of Words," Miami Herald, March 8, 1987, sec. 1, p. 1; idem, "Supporters of English Target Polls," Miami Herald, March 6, 1988.

22. Viglucci, "Official-English Push Sparks Battle," sec. 1, p. 1.

23. Fulton quoted in Viglucci, "Official-English Push Sparks Battle," sec. 1, p. 1; Jennie Hess, "Floridians Think U.S. Immigration Policy Should Be Tougher, Poll Says," Tallahassee Democrat, Jan. 31, 1988, 8A.

24. Viglucci, "Official-English Push Sparks Battle," sec. 1, p. 1.

25. Richard Wallace, "State Poll: 86% Want English 'Official Language,'" Miami Herald, Sept. 13, 1987, sec. 2, p. 1.

26. Gallegos quoted in Diana Smith, "Lawmakers Asked to Rule on English Amendment," Tallahassee Democrat, Jan. 10, 1988, 5E; Siegel and Kaminsky quoted in Viglucci, "Supporters of English Target Polls."

27. Smith, "Lawmakers Asked to Rule" 5E; Viglucci, "Supporters of English Target Polls."

28. "Petition is Arrogant Effort," Tallahassee Democrat, Jan. 6, 1988, 8A.

29. Viglucci, "Supporters of English Target Polls."

30. Carlos Harrison, "English-Only Law Faces New Attack by Commissioner," Miami Herald, March 24, 1988.

31. Cited in Andres Viglucci, "Supporters of English Target Polls," Miami Herald (March 6, 1988).

32. Andrade and Weber quoted in Maya Bell, "Just Saying No to State Language," Orlando Sentinel, June 27, 1988; Max J. Castro, Margaret Haun, and Ana Roca, "The Official English Movement in Florida," in Perspectives on Official English, edited by Karen L. Adams and Daniel T. Brink (New York: Mouton de Gruyter, 1990), 155.

33. Andres Viglucci, "Studies: Hispanics Are Learning English—and Fast," Miami Herald, July 31, 1988.

34. Viola Gienger, "'English Only' Gains Support," Palm Beach Post, July 4, 1988.

35. Andres Viglucci, "Petition Mix-Up Discovered Only a Week before Deadline," Miami Herald, Aug. 3, 1988; Pedroso quoted in Christopher Marquis, "It's Official: English Issue on the Ballot," Miami Herald, Aug. 9, 1988.

36. Andres Viglucci, "They View Campaign as a 'Losing Battle,'" Miami Herald, Aug. 9, 1988.

37. Ibid.

38. Ibid.

39. Nick Madigan, "Foes of English-Only Rule Unite against Amendment," Palm Beach Post, Aug. 15, 1988.

40. Paul Anderson, "81% Support Official English, Amendment Backers' Poll Shows," Miami Herald, Sept. 24, 1988.

41. Anderson, "81% Support Official English"; Gary Kane, "Opponents: Amendment 11 Says, 'Welcome, If You Speak English,'" Palm Beach Post, Oct. 10, 1988.

42. Kane, "Opponents."

43. Castro, Haun, and Roca, "Official English Movement in Florida" 157-58.

44. Ibid., 159.

45. Ibid.

46. Daniel McLaughlin, "English Petition Disputed," Tampa Tribune, Oct. 11, 1988.

47. Smith quoted in Kim Stott, "English Proposal Good for Unity, Backers Say," (Jacksonville) Florida Times-Union, Oct. 30, 1988; Martinez quoted in Dave Von Drehle, "Suit Filed to Block Official English," Miami Herald, Oct. 12, 1988.

48. Dave Von Drehle and Stephen K. Doig, "S. Floridians Agree: English Must Be Primary Language," Miami Herald, Oct. 16, 1988.

49. Toural quoted in Cathy Shaw, "Educators Worried about Amendment's Message," Miami Herald, Oct. 31, 1988, sec. 2, p. 1; Smith quoted in Dave Von Drehle, "Official English Relies on Vague Agenda," Miami Herald, Oct. 31, 1988, sec. 2, p. 1.

50. Dave Von Drehle, "U.S. Fights Language Petitions," Miami Herald, Nov. 3, 1988.

51. "Official English Stays on Ballot in Florida, Appeals Panel Rules," Tallahassee Democrat, Nov. 5, 1988, 2A; "Florida Language Appeal Dies," New York Times, July 4, 1989, 12. The cases pending before the Supreme Court were Delgado v. Smith, 88-1327, and In re Delgado, 88-1329.

52. Gary Kane, "Florida Makes English Official," Palm Beach Post, Nov. 9, 1988.

53. Dave Von Drehle, "It's Official: After Long Debate, Language Initiative Wins Easily," Miami Herald, Nov. 9, 1988, sec. 1, p. 1.

54. Soto quoted in "Fla. English-Only Law Said to Prompt Bias," Boston Globe, Nov. 16, 1988, 3; Maya Bell, "English-Only Rule Raises Concern," Orlando Sentinel, Dec. 11, 1988.

55. Robbins and Workings quoted in Todd C. Smith, "Backers of Amendment 11 Put Together New Strategies," Tampa Tribune, Dec. 4, 1988; Bell, "English-Only Rule Raises Concern"; Castro, "Politics of Language in Miami," 129.

56. "Dade County Commission Repeals English-Only Law," New York Times, May 19, 1993, A8; Larry Rohter, "Repeal Is Likely for 'English Only' Policy in Miami," New York Times, May 14, 1993, A7.

57. Rohter, "Repeal Is Likely," A7.

58. Ibid.

59. Assembly Constitutional Amendment no. 5, Dec. 4, 1978, California Legislature, 1979-80 regular session, California State Library, Sacramento.

60. Senate Joint Resolution no. 21, June 24, 1981, amended in the Senate, Aug. 12 and Aug. 31, 1981, California Legislature, 1981-82 regular session, California State Library.

61. Guy Wright, "Bilingualism," San Francisco Examiner and Chronicle, July 17, 1983, B9; Kathryn A. Woolard, "Voting Rights, Liberal Voters, and the Official English Movement: An Analysis of Campaign Rhetoric in San Francisco's Proposition 'O,'" in Perspectives on Official English, ed. Adams and Brink, 127.

62. Guy Wright, "Bilingual Scaredy Cats," San Francisco Examiner and Chronicle, May 15, 1983, B9; Woolard, "Voting Rights, Liberal Voters," 128.

63. Evelyn Hsu, "Kopp Mounts Attack on Bilingual Ballots," San Francisco Chronicle, July 7, 1983, 4.

64. The debate over language rights involves Article VIII of the Treaty of Guadalupe Hidalgo of February 2, 1848 (9 U.S. Stat. 922), which reads:

"Mexicans now established in territories previously belonging to Mexico, and which remain for the future within the limits of the United States, as defined by the present treaty, shall be free to continue where they now reside, or to remove at any time to the Mexican republic, retaining the property which they possess in the said territories, or disposing thereof, and removing the proceeds wherever they please, without their being subjected, on this account, to any combination, tax, or charge whatever.

"Those who shall prefer to remain in the said territories, may either retain the title and rights of Mexican citizens, or acquire those of citizens of the United States. But they shall be under the obligation to make their election within one year from the date of the exchange of ratifications of this treaty; and those who shall remain in the said territories after the expiration of that year, without having declared their intention to retain the character of Mexicans, shall be considered to have elected to become citizens of the United States.

"In the said territories, property of every kind, now belonging to Mexicans not established there, shall be inviolably respected. The present owners, the heirs of these, and all Mexicans who may hereafter acquire said property by contract, shall enjoy with respect to it guaranties equally ample as if the same belonged to citizens of the United States."

While there was no explicit mention of language, it has been alleged that an implict understanding extended Mexicans the rights to speak their own tongue. As evidence, the debates over drafting the California constitution of 1879 are often mentioned, since that document recognized Spanish language rights. See "Spanish Language Rights in California: Constitutional Debates," in Language Loyalties, ed. Crawford, 51-58.

65. Guy Wright, "Spanish Myth," San Francisco Examiner and Chronicle, July 31, 1983, B9; idem, "Beyond Bilingualism," San Francisco Chronicle, Oct. 23, 1983, B9.

66. Woolard, "Voting Rights, Liberal Voters" 128; Avila quoted in Jackson Rannells, "Kopp Files English-Only Ballot Measure," San Francisco Chronicle, Aug. 11, 1983, 7.

67. Woolard, "Voting Rights, Liberal Voters" 128, 129.

68. Senate Joint Resolution no. 7, Feb. 2, 1983, California Legislature, 1983-84 regular session, California State Library; Petris quoted in "Anti-Bilingual Bill Dies in State Senate," San Francisco Chronicle, Feb. 16, 1984, 9.

69. Cited in California Ballot Pamphlet, 1984 General Election, November 6, comp. March Fong Eu, secretary of state, California State Library, Sacramento, 51.

70. Ibid., 52.

71. Chavez quoted in Francisco Garcia, "Chavez Begins Fight against 4 Propositions," San Francisco Chronicle, Sept. 27, 1984, 11; Sapunor quoted in Guy Wright, "Bilingual Showdown," San Francisco Chronicle, Oct. 14, 1984, 9.

72. Secretary of State, 1984 General Election, November 6, 52, 53.

73. Mervin Field, "Voter Awareness Rises on Propositions 40, 41," San Francisco Chronicle, Nov. 3, 1984, 14; idem, "Most Californians Want Ballots in English Only," San Francisco Chronicle, Sept. 26, 1984, 8.

74. Secretary of State, "Supplement to the Statement of Vote— Results of the November Sixth General Election, Statewide Summary by County," 1984, Government Publications, California State Library.

75. Harre W. Demoro, "Why Voters Backed State Lottery," San Francisco Chronicle, Nov. 7, 1984, 8.

76. "Big Vote against Non-English Ballots," San Francisco Chronicle, Nov. 9, 1984, 70.

77. "Bilingual Initiative—Governor Acts," San Francisco Chronicle, Nov. 22, 1984, 12.

78. "Making English the State Language," San Francisco Chronicle, Jan. 9, 1985, 9.

79. Assembly Constitutional Amendment no. 30, May 20, 1985, California Legislature, 1985-86 regular session, California State Library.

80. Assembly Bill no. 201, Jan. 8, 1985, California Legislature, 1985-86 regular session, California State Library.

81. "English Language Rule Splits California City," New York Times, Aug. 18, 1985, 21.

82. Lily Eng, "Monterey Park Voids Stand for English as Official Language," Los Angeles Times, Oct. 29, 1986, pt. 1, p. 35.

83. Trombley, "California Elections; English-Only Proposition," pt. 1, p. 1.

84. Rich Connell, "Wilson Backs Initiative for English-Only Law in State," Los Angeles Times, Aug. 21, 1986, pt. 1, p. 3.

85. Stanley Diamond, "English—The Official Language of California, 1983-1988," in Perspectives on Official English, ed. Adams and Brink, 114.

86. Karapetian quoted in Trombley, "California Elections; English-Only Proposition," pt. 1, p. 1; Deukmejian quoted in George Skelton, "Deukmejian Opposes 3 Controversial Propositions," Los Angeles Times, Sept. 3, 1986, pt. 1, p. 3.

87. Trombley, "California Elections: English-Only Proposition," pt. 1, p. 1.

88. "The Region," Los Angeles Times, Aug. 6, 1986, pt. 1, p. 2; "The State," Los Angeles Times, Sept. 18, 1986, pt. 1, p. 2.

89. Diamond, "English—The Official Language of California" 115.

90. Letter to the Editor, from Etta-Belle Kitchen, President, League of Women Voters of Los Angeles, Los Angeles Times, Sept. 13, 1986, pt. 2, p. 2; John Dart, "Bishops Oppose English-Only Measure," Los Angeles Times, Sept. 26, 1986, pt. 1, p. 29.

91. Dart, "Bishops Oppose," pt. 1, p. 29.

92. "Shocking Language Barrier," Los Angeles Times, Sept. 25, 1986, pt. 2, p. 4.

93. "Wrong in Any Language," Los Angeles Times, Oct. 3, 1986, pt. 2, p. 4.

94. Ibid.

95. Diamond, "English—The Official Language of California" 113.

96. George Skelton, "The Times Poll: Anti-Toxics Proposition Has Huge 52-Point Lead," Los Angeles Times, Sept. 13, 1986, pt. 1, p. 1.

97. William Trombley, "Prop. 63 Finance Infraction Alleged; English Measure Foes Fault Backers in Reporting of Loan," Los Angeles Times, Sept. 19, 1986, pt. 1, p. 25.

98. William Trombley, "Prop. 63 Backer Will Try to Defeat Opposing Candidates," Los Angeles Times, Oct. 1, 1986, pt. 1, p. 3.

99. Ibid.

100. Cousins quoted in William Trombley, "Norman Cousins Drops His Support of Prop. 63," Los Angeles Times, Oct. 16, 1986, pt. 1, p. 3; "Seeing the Light," Los Angeles Times, Oct. 24, 1986, pt. 2, p. 4.

101. Trombley, "Norman Cousins Drops His Support," pt. 1, p. 3.

102. William Trombley, "California Elections: Many Supporters Also Favor Bilingual Education, Ballots; Latino Backing of 'English-Only' a Puzzle," Los Angeles Times, Oct. 25, 1986, pt. 2, p. 1.

103. Ibid.

104. Richard Rodriguez, "Prop. 63 Would Betray State's Future," Los Angeles Times, Oct. 26, 1986, pt. 4, p. 1.

105. S.I. Hayakawa, "A Common Language, So All Can Pursue Common Goals," Los Angeles Times, Oct. 29, 1986, pt. 2, p. 5.

106. Ibid.

107. Ibid.

108. Cathleen Decker, "California Elections: AIDS, English-Only, and Limits on Pay Put California in the Limelight," Los Angeles Times, Nov. 2, 1986, pt. 1, p. 3.

109. Secretary of State, "Official Declaration of the Results of the General Election Held on Tuesday, November 4, 1984, throughout the State of California on Statewide Measures Submitted to Voters," Elections Division, 1230 J Street, Sacramento.

110. Francisco Delgado, "Signs of the Times," (Long Beach) Press Telegram, Feb. 22, 1987.

111. Ray Perez, "A City Is Divided by Its Languages," Los Angeles Times, April 10, 1987, pt. 2, p. 1.

112. Mike Ward, "Bolstered by Prop. 63 Vote, Foe of Non-English Signs Renews Attack," Los Angeles Times, Nov. 9, 1986, pt. 9, p. 1.

113. "Monterey Park Library Caught in Political Crossfire," Library Journal 113, no. 20 (Dec. 1988): 20.

114. Mary Nichols, "The English-Only Movement Legitimizes Attacks on Brotherhood and Tolerance," Los Angeles Times, Feb. 19,

1989, Op-Ed, pt. 5, p. 5; librarian quoted in "Monterey Park Library Caught" 20.

115. Gutierrez v. Municipal Court of the Southeast Judicial District, 838 F.2d 1031 (9th Cir., 1988). Also see Laura A. Cordero, "Constitutional Limitations on Official English Declarations," New Mexico Law Review 20 (Winter 1990): 50.

116. Gutierrez v. Municipal Court of the Southeast Judicial District, 861 F.2d 118 (1988).

117. William Trombley, "Assemblyman Vows to Carry the Ball for English-Only Action," Los Angeles Times, Nov. 6, 1986, pt. 1, p. 3.

118. California Legislature at Sacramento, 1987-88 regular session, Senate Final History (Sacramento), 655.

119. Assembly Bill no. 183, Jan. 6, 1987, California Legislature, 1987-88 regular session, California State Library.

120. California Legislature at Sacramento, 1987-88 regular session, Assembly Final History (Sacramento), 214.

121. Jerry Gillam, "Bill Making English-Only Suits Harder to File Dies in Assembly," Los Angeles Times, June 5, 1987, pt. 1, p. 32.

122. Assembly Bill no. 2090, March 10, 1989, California Legislature, 1989-90 regular session, California State Library.

123. Ibid.

124. "In Plain English," Los Angeles Times, Nov. 7, 1986, pt. 2, p. 4.

125. Huerta quoted in Marilyn Lewis, "Little Effect Seen from English-Only Vote," (San Jose) Mercury News, Nov. 4, 1988; Sarah Henry, "Fighting Words," Los Angeles Times, June 10, 1990.

126. Woolard, "Voting Rights, Liberal Voters" 129.

127. Ibid., 126.

CHAPTER 5. THE AGITATION SPREADS

1. Deborah Shanahan, "'Official' Language Is Touted," Arizona Republic, Feb. 2, 1987.

2. Jackie Rothenberg, "English-Only Called Unifying Force, Racism in New Clothing," (Tucson) Arizona Daily Star, Feb. 8, 1987.

3. State of Arizona, House Bill 2031, introduced January 15, 1987, 38th Legislature, 1st regular session; State of Arizona, Senate Concurrent Resolution 1005, introduced January 14, 1987, 38th Legislature, 1st regular session.

4. State of Arizona, House Concurrent Resolution 2002, introduced January 15, 1987, 38th Legislature, 1st regular session.

5. Deborah Shanahan, "Language Bill Stalls in Senate," Arizona Republic, Feb. 4, 1987.

6. Minutes of Committee on Judiciary, Feb. 3, 1987, Arizona State Senate, 38th Legislature, 1st regular session; West quoted in Shanahan, "Language Bill Stalls in Senate."

7. Shanahan, "'Official' Language Is Touted."

8. Rothenberg, "English-Only Called Unifying Force, Racism."

9. Mary Jo Pitzl, "Governor Calls Plan Insult to Hispanics," Arizona Republic, March 3, 1987.

10. Deborah Shanahan, "Senator Reviving Plan to Make English State's Official Language," Arizona Republic, March 5, 1987.

11. Ibid.; Steiner and West quoted in Deborah Shanahan, "Language Bill Sent on for Vote by Full Senate," Arizona Republic, March 11, 1987.

12. Deborah Shanahan, "Official-English Bill Dead," Arizona Republic, March 27, 1987.

13. Kimberly Mattingly, "'English Only' Drive Protested," Arizona Republic, April 12, 1987.

14. Vicky Harker, "Hispanics Plan Counterattack on English Bill," Arizona Republic, May 24, 1987.

15. Deborah Shanahan, "Goldwater Will Assist Bid in State to Make English Official Language," Arizona Republic, Aug. 6, 1987.

16. Ibid.

17. Charles Kelly, "Group Forms to Counter English-Language Push," Arizona Republic, Oct. 10, 1987.

18. Ted Johnson, "Ex-Reagan Aide, McNulty at Odds at Debate," Tucson Citizen, Jan. 29, 1988.

19. State of Arizona, House Concurrent Resolution 2012, introduced February 2, 1988, 38th Legislature, 2d regular session; State of Arizona, Senate Concurrent Resolution 1007, introduced February 9, 1988, 38th Legislature, 2d regular session.

20. Melissa Rigg, "Foes 'Back' English-Only in Legislature," (Tucson) Arizona Daily Star, May 10, 1988.

21. Susan R. Carson, "209,154 Signatures Are Filed for 'English Only' Initiative," (Tucson) Arizona Daily Star, July 8, 1988.

22. Statement of Contributions and Expenditures, Arizona English, Francisco X. Gutierrez, Chairman, period ending Aug. 24, 1988, Secretary of State, State of Arizona, Phoenix.

23. Ruben Hernandez, "'English-Only' Campaign Blamed," Tucson Citizen, Aug. 31, 1988.

24. Andy Hall, "'English' Advocate Assailed," Arizona Republic, Oct. 9, 1988.

25. Ibid.

26. Ibid.

27. Ibid.

28. Andy Hall, "'English' Drive Takes 2 Setbacks," Arizona Republic, Oct. 14, 1988.

29. Andy Hall, "2 in U.S. English Quit over Charges of Racism," Arizona Republic, Oct. 18, 1988.

30. Ibid.

31. Andy Hall, "'English' Challenges Foes to Debate, Stop Racism Tack," Arizona Republic, Oct. 21, 1988.

32. Rodriguez quoted in Johnson, "Ex-Reagan Aide, McNulty at Odds"; David Pittman, "Language Proposal Myths Abound," Tucson Citizen, Oct. 27, 1988.

33. Andy Hall, "Proposition 106 Vague, 'Troubling,' Corbin Says," Arizona Republic, Oct. 29, 1988.

34. Andy Hall, "Church Chiefs Assail 'Official English,'" Arizona Republic, Oct. 27, 1988.

35. Ibid.

36. Pittman, "Language Proposal Myths Abound."

37. Mark Shaffer, "State Tribes Fighting 'English,'" Arizona Republic, Nov. 6, 1988.

38. State of Arizona, Official Canvass—General Election—November 8, 1988, Jim Shumway, secretary of state.

39. Andy Hall, "'English' Squeaks into Law," Arizona Republic, Nov. 10, 1988; Statement of Contributions and Expenditures, Arizonans for Official English, Robert D. Park, Chairman, Aug. 24-Dec. 31, 1988, Secretary of State, State of Arizona, Phoenix.

40. Camacho and Mofford quoted in Steve Cheseborough, "Tongue-tied: Lottery Officials Bemoan Passage of Official English," Phoenix Gazette, Nov. 10, 1988; Yniguez quoted in Russ Hemphill, "Lawsuit Asks Federal Court to Halt Official-English Amendment," Phoenix Gazette, Nov. 11, 1988.

41. Houston quoted in Steffannie Fedunak, "District's Houston Issues Memo," (Tucson) Arizona Daily Star, Dec. 1, 1988; Melissa Rigg, "Council Gets Attorney's Opinion," (Tucson) Arizona Daily Star, Dec. 1, 1988.

42. Steve Yozwiak, "Task Force Will Study 'English,'" Arizona Republic, Dec. 1, 1988; Mofford quoted in Don Harris, "Subdued Mofford Signs 'Official English' into Law," Arizona Republic, Dec. 6, 1988.

43. Corbin quoted in Jonathan Bass, "English Is Official, but Somewhat Misunderstood," (Tucson) Arizona Daily Star, Dec. 6, 1988; Martin Van Der Werf, "Corbin Welcomes Request to Set Matter Straight," Arizona Republic, Dec. 7, 1988.

44. Advisory Opinions of the Attorney General, State of Arizona, I89-009, Jan. 24, 1989, Supreme Court Law Library, Phoenix.

45. David Pittman, "Lawmakers Vow to Repeal Prop. 106," Tucson Citizen, Dec. 9, 1988.

46. State of Arizona, Journal of the Senate, 39th Legislature, 1st regular session, 1989, pp. vi-vii, 1158; State of Arizona, Journal of the House of Representatives, 39th Legislature, 1st regular session, pp. iii-v, 1211.

47. Felicity Barringer, "Judge Nullifies Law Mandating Use of English," New York Times, Feb. 8, 1990, A1, A17.

48. Ibid.

49. Yniguez v. Mofford, 730 F. Supp. 309 (1990).

50. Ibid.

51. "Legislating Language," Denver Post, Jan. 6, 1987, 4B.

52. Janet Bingham, "'English-Only' Bill Raked over the Coals," Denver Post, Feb. 13, 1987, 4B.

53. Jeffrey A. Roberts, "'English-Only' Bill Axed in Favor of Ballot Drive," Denver Post, March 6, 1987, B9.

54. Ancel Martinez, "Bishop Declares Opposition to Official-Language Drive," Colorado Springs Gazette Telegraph, Oct. 3, 1987.

55. John Sanko, "Opponents Begin Mapping Strategy," Rocky Mountain News, Oct. 30, 1987.

56. Peña quoted in Jeffrey A. Roberts, "Vote Will Decide Official Language," Denver Post, Nov. 14, 1987; Braveman quoted in Diane Griego, "English-Only Law Divisive, Foes Say," Denver Post, Nov. 11, 1987.

57. "Hispanic Vets Oppose English Bill," Denver Post, Feb. 16, 1987, B3.

58. Denver Post, March 3, 1987, 5B, cited in Susan Kirkpatrick and Stephen P. Mumme, "Fallacies in Setting the Agenda on Official English: The Foundations of Colorado's 1988 English Only Amendment," Dec. 1, 1990, 12, unpublished manuscript.

59. Berny Morson, "Language Bill Sponsor Resists Compromise," Rocky Mountain News, Nov. 19, 1987.

60. Carl Miller, "63% Favor 'Official' English Proposal," Denver Post, Feb. 4, 1988; idem, "Coloradans Back English-Only Law," Denver Post, June 29, 1988.

61. Juan Espinosa, "Local Hispanic Group Studies Anglos' Fear of Brown Resurgence," Pueblo Chieftain, May 8, 1988.

62. Mark Obmascik, "Sen. Armstrong Opposed to English-Only Measure," Denver Post, June 3, 1988, B4.

63. Joel Millman, "Tempers Flare at Debate over 'Official English,'" Colorado Springs Gazette Telegraph, June 25, 1988.

64. John Sanko, "Racism Denied in English Drive," Rocky Mountain News, July 10, 1988.

65. Ibid.

66. John Diaz, "Official English Taps State Resources," Denver Post, Aug. 17, 1988.

67. Kirkpatrick and Mumme, "Fallacies in Setting the Agenda" 14, 15.

68. Tom McAvoy, "English-Only Proponent Labels Opposing Lawyer Group 'Soviet Front,'" Pueblo Chieftain, Aug. 24, 1988.

69. Peter G. Chronis and Jeffrey A. Roberts, "Measure's Opponents Heartened by Ruling," Denver Post, Sept. 17, 1988.

70. Philips quoted in Peter G. Chronis, "Judge Rejects Petitions for Not Being Bilingual," Denver Post, Sept. 17, 1988; Woodard quoted in Michelle P. Fulcher, "Bilingual Ruling Imperils Old Laws," Denver Post, Sept. 23, 1988.

71. Sue Lindsay, "Official-English Campaign Gets $100,000 Boost," Rocky Mountain News, Sept. 23, 1988.

72. Peter G. Chronis, "Court OKs Official-English Vote," Denver Post, Oct. 13, 1988.

73. Tony Pugh, "Drive for Official English Divides State, Nation," Rocky Mountain News, Oct. 23, 1988.

74. Ibid.

75. State of Colorado, county election statistics for Amendment no. 1, Archives and Public Records Division, Denver.

76. Judith Brimberg, "Official English Quick to Spark Friction," Denver Post, Nov. 19, 1988.

77. Jeffrey A. Roberts, "Judge Refuses to Void Official-English Amendment," Denver Post, Nov. 23, 1988, B4.

78. Brian Weber, "Official-English Leaders Form Political Committee," Colorado Springs Gazette Telegraph, Dec. 3, 1988.

79. Jennifer Gavin, "Peña Outlaws Bias Based on Language," Denver Post, Dec. 28, 1988; Romer's executive order and Philips quoted in Alan Gottlieb, "Romer: English Law No License to Discriminate," Denver Post, Dec. 31, 1988, B1.

80. Kirkpatrick and Mumme, "Fallacies in Setting the Agenda" 15.

81. Felton West, "Official Language? Where's Need?" Houston *Post*, Jan. 22, 1985, 2B.

82. House Concurrent Resolution no. 13, House of Representatives, State of Texas, 69th sess., 1985-86, Legislative Reference Library, Austin.

83. House Joint Resolution no. 55, House of Representatives, State of Texas, 70th sess., 1987-88, Legislative Reference Library.

84. T. Gregory Gillan, "Hispanic Lawmakers Skeptical of English-Only Proposal Filed in House," Houston Chronicle, March 3, 1987.

85. Felton West, "Parts B and C Are a Bit Bothersome," Houston *Post*, April 22, 1987, B2; Mark Sanders, "'English First' Measure Stalls," Houston *Post*, April 21, 1987, 7B.

86. Sanders, "'English First' Measure Stalls" 7B.

87. Public Hearing Record, House Joint Resolution no. 55, April 20, 1987, Committee on State Affairs, House of Representatives, State of Texas, Legislative Reference Library.

88. Sam Attlesey, "Bush Opposes English-Only Law for Texas," Dallas Morning News, May 18, 1987.

89. Ibid.

90. John C. Henry, "7 of 10 Texans Favor English Plan, Poll Shows," Austin American-Statesman, May 14, 1987.

91. Sam Attlesey, "English Only Movement Set Back but Not Defeated," Dallas Morning News, May 24, 1987.

92. Ibid.

93. Ibid.

94. Henry, "7 of 10 Texans Favor English Plan."

95. Sam Attlesey, "GOP to Vote on 'English Only' Issue," Dallas Morning News, Nov. 22, 1987.

96. Referendum, GOP resolution, and Clements quoted in Attlesey, "GOP to Vote"; Zaeske quoted in John Gravois, "Critics Say GOP Plan on English Is 'Racist,'" Houston Post, Nov. 21, 1987.

97. Gravois, "Critics Say"; Vellasquez quoted in Attlesey, "GOP to Vote."

98. Jim Sullivan, "Callers Support English as Texas' Official Tongue," Dallas Times Herald, Feb. 29, 1988.

99. Zaeske quoted in "Advocate Plans to Run for Office," Houston Chronicle, Nov. 12, 1988; Edwards quoted in James McCrory, "State Senators Say They Have Votes to Block Official English Measure," San Antonio Express News, Nov. 23, 1988.

100. House Bill no. 2467 and House Joint Resolution no. 48, House of Representatives, State of Texas, 71st sess., 1989-90, Legislative Reference Library.

101. Public Hearing Record, May 8, 1988, House Bill no. 2467 and House Joint Resolution no. 48, Committee on State Affairs, House of Representatives, State of Texas, Legislative Reference Library.

102. Ibid.

103. Dario Moreno and Christopher L. Warren, "The Conservative Enclave: Cubans in Florida," in From Rhetoric to Reality: Latino Politics in the 1988 Elections, edited by Rodolfo O. de la Garza and Louis DeSipio (Boulder, Colo.: Westview Press, 1992), 127-45.

104. Combs, "English Plus" 223.

CHAPTER 6. MAJORITY OPINION

1. Michele Jacklin, "Residents Would Make English Official Language," Hartford (Conn.) Courant, Feb. 12, 1987.

2. David F. Marshall, "The Question of an Official Language: Language Rights and the English Language Amendment," International Journal of the Sociology of Language 60 (1986): 7; Selma K. Sonntag, "Political Saliency of English as Official Language" (paper presented at the annual meeting of the Western Political Science Association, Newport Beach, Calif., March 22-24, 1990), 2.

3. Sonntag, "Political Saliency" 11.

4. Carol Schmid, "The English Only Movement: Social Bases of Support and Opposition among Anglos and Latinos," in Language Loyalties, ed. Crawford, 204, 207, 209.

5. Connie Dyste, "The Popularity of California's Proposition 63: An Analysis," in Perspectives on Official English, ed. Adams and Brink, 144, 147.

6. Ana Celia Zentella, "Who Supports Official English, and Why?: The Influence of Social Variables and Questionnaire Methodology," in Perspectives on Official English, ed. Adams and Brink, 161-77, 175.

7. Citrin, Reingold, Walters, and Green, "'Official English' Movement" 536, 544.

8. Ibid., 546; Jack Citrin, Beth Reingold, and Donald P. Green, "American Identity and the Politics of Ethnic Change," Journal of Politics 52 (Nov. 1990): 1141.

9. If the samples for 1990 and 1992 are combined based on the percentages in table 6.1, then for the entire sample of 2,663, the percentage favoring the law is 68.6 in the four referenda states as compared with

60.8 in the eleven statutory states and 61.4 in the other thirty-five states without official English laws.

10. Tests for Tolerance (1 - R2) were done for each variable to assess any problem of multicollinearity. All values exceeded .70 except for PARTY (.455), BUSH (.450), and CLINTON (.423), which does not signal a serious problem. As validation, the logistical model was respecified by omitting BUSH and CLINTON. The variables PARTY (.000), EDUCATION (.000), and WHITE (.000) remained statistically significant at high levels, though IDEOLOGY (.006) and INCOME (.020) were also deemed significant. The overall model, though, did slightly worse than the previous one, predicting only 67.7 percent of the cases. The coefficient (B) values were ranked in this order: WHITE (.7533), EDUCATION (1691), PARTY (.1274), IDEOLOGY (.0966), and INCOME (.0255).

11. Jack Citrin, Ernst B. Haas, Christopher Muste, and Beth Reingold, "Is American Nationalism Changing? Implications for Foreign Policy," International Studies Quarterly 38 (March 1994): 14, 20.

12. The classic statement of this problem is in W.S. Robinson, "Ecological Correlations and the Behavior of Individuals," American Sociological Review 18 (1950): 663-64.

13. "Alabama ELA Wins in Landslide," U.S. English Update 8, no. 3 (May-June 1990): 1. This newsletter is regularly published by U.S. English.

14. Brooks Boliek, "House OKs English Language Legislation," Montgomery Advertiser, April 27, 1989.

15. "Yes on Amendment 1," Montgomery Advertiser, May 15, 1990, 6A.

16. Ibid.

17. Ibid.

18. Doron and McCaffrey quoted in "English-Only Amendment Wins Support," Montgomery Advertiser, June 6, 1990, 7A; Schoen quoted in "Voters OK English Language Amendment," Montgomery Advertiser, June 7, 1990, 2A.

19. "Voters OK English Language Amendment."

20. Marian Green, "Senator Shelby Introduces First Official English Act," U.S. English Update 8, no. 6 (Nov.-Dec. 1990): 1.

21. The correlation coefficient between the percentage of blacks and the percentage of Spanish speakers was -.029 for Arizona, .236 for California, .010 for Colorado, and -.081 for Florida. For Alabama, the coefficient was .706.

22. Voter turnout was higher among whites than Hispanics in presidential and congressional elections for the period 1972-88. See Harold W. Stanley and Richard G. Niemi, Vital Statistics on American

Politics, 3d ed. (Washington, D.C.: CQ Press, 1992), 87; and Raymond E. Wolfinger and Steven J. Rosenstone, Who Votes? (New Haven, Conn.: Yale Univ. Press, 1980), 91-93.

23. At that time, the California state legislature had six black representatives (Speaker Willie Brown, Elihu M. Harris, Teresa Hughes, Gwen Moore, Curtis Tucker, and Maxine Waters) and two black senators (Bill Greene and Diane Watson). The year after the 1986 referendum, Harris introduced legislation to impose obstacles on the implementation of the law (see chapter 4). The legislative history indicates that he requested a temporary suspension of the rules to gain floor consideration, but he was defeated. On that key vote Harris was joined by Hughes, Moore, Tucker, and Waters (Speaker Brown did not vote). This result strongly indicates the opposition of black officials in California to the official English law.

CHAPTER 7. LEGISLATIVE INTENT

1. Journal of the House of Delegates of the Commonwealth of Virginia, 1981 Session (Richmond: Commonwealth of Virginia, 1981), vols. 1 and 2, pp. 156, 444, 512, 556, 585, 879, 1316, 1338; Journal of the Senate of Virginia, 1981 Regular Session and 1981 Reconvened Session (Richmond: Commonwealth of Virginia, 1981), vols. 1 and 2, pp. 459, 468-69, 512-13, 574-76, 580-82, 975.

2. Journal of the House of Delegates of the Commonwealth of Virginia, 1981 Session, vols. 1 and 2, pp. 74, 240, 265, 293, 968, 970, 1067, 1185; Journal of the Senate of Virginia, 1981 Regular Session and 1981 Reconvened Session, vols. 1 and 2, pp. 243-44, 557, 606-7, 662-64, 667, 859.

3. House Joint Resolution no. 236, in Acts of Assembly, 1981 (Richmond: Commonwealth of Virginia, 1981), 1365.

4. Journal of the House of Delegates of the Commonwealth of Virginia, 1986 Session, vols. 1 and 2, pp. 198, 606, 672, 713, 750, 805, 1269, 1274, 1337-38, 1387-88, 1462-63, 1467, 1469, 1605, 1618; Journal of the Senate of Virginia, 1986 Regular Session and 1986 Reconvened Session, vols. 1 and 2440, pp. 416, 419, 730-31, 783-86, 845, 878-79, 901, 905, 938-39, 946, 1064.

5. Summary of legislative action in State of Indiana, Index to House and Senate Journals, 103d General Assembly, 2d regular session, Nov. 22, 1983-March 1, 1984, 96. The votes are recorded in State of Indiana, Journal of the House of Representatives, 103d General Assembly, 2d regular session, Roll Call no. 344; State of Indiana, Journal of the Senate, 103d General Assembly, 2d regular session, Roll Call no. 149.

6. "English in Indiana," Indianapolis Star, Jan. 23, 1984, 10.

7. Ibid.

8. Dan Carpenter, "A Swipe at Bilingual 'Crutch,'" Indianapolis Star, March 3, 1984, 25.

9. Telephone interview with Key Decision Maker no. 7 (Indiana), March 6, 1990.

10. Telephone interview with Key Decision Maker no. 9 (Indiana), March 6, 1990.

11. Carpenter, "Swipe at Bilingual 'Crutch,'" 25.

12. Ibid.

13. Telephone interviews with Key Decision Maker no. 9 (Indiana), March 6, 1990; with Key Decision Maker no. 7 (Indiana), March 6, 1990; and with Key Decision Maker no. 8 (Indiana), March 6, 1990.

14. See State of Tennessee, House Journal of the Ninety-third General Assembly, 2d regular session, Feb. 23-May 24, 1984 (Nashville), 2:2852-53, 3083-84; State of Tennessee, Senate Journal of the Ninety-third General Assembly, 2d regular session, Feb. 23-May 24, 1984 (Nashville), 2452-53.

15. Tape recordings of floor debate in the House of Representatives, May 8, 1984, Tennessee General Assembly, State Library, State Capitol, Nashville.

16. "Senate Panel OKs English as State Language," Nashville Banner, May 8, 1984, C-2.

17. Tape recordings of floor debate in the Senate, May 14, 1984, Tennessee General Assembly, State Library.

18. Tennessee Blue Book, 1983-1984 (Nashville: Secretary of State, 1983), 23.

19. Telephone interview with Key Decision Maker no. 6 (Tennessee), March 6, 1990.

20. Telephone interview with Key Decision Maker no. 3 (Tennessee), March 5, 1990.

21. See Journal of the House of Representatives of the General Assembly of the Commonwealth of Kentucky, regular session, Jan. 3-April 13, 1984, 2:2672-73, 2771; Journal of the Senate of the General Assembly of the Commonwealth of Kentucky, regular session, Jan. 3-April 13, 1984, 1:187-88.

22. Telephone interview with Key Decision Maker no. 13 (Kentucky), March 12, 1990.

23. General Acts of the Seventy-sixth General Assembly of the State of Arkansas (Atlanta: Darby Printing Co.), vol. 1, bk. 1, pp. 76, 180; Journal of Proceedings of the House of Representatives, Seventy-sixth

Session, 1987; and Journal of Proceedings of the Senate, Seventh-sixth Session, 1987. Legislative histories are indexed by bill and date of action, not page numbers. Materials were consulted at the Elections Library, State Capitol, Little Rock.

24. Telephone interview with Key Decision Maker no. 11 (Arkansas), March 12, 1990.

25. Telephone interview with Key Decision Maker no. 13 (Arkansas), March 12, 1990.

26. Telephone interviews with Key Decision Maker no. 11 (Arkansas), March 12, 1990; and with Key Decision Maker no. 12 (Arkansas), March 12, 1990.

27. Telephone interview with Key Decision Maker no. 11 (Arkansas), March 12, 1990.

28. See Journal of the House of Representatives of the State of Mississippi, 102d regular session, Jan. 6-April 5, 1987 (Jackson), 632-35, 364-65; Journal of the Senate of the State of Mississippi, 102d regular session, Jan. 6-April 5, 1987 (Jackson), vols. 1 and 2, pp. 325, 1637-38. The original bills are archived in House Bills 115-208, 209-78, and 600-703, Mississippi Legislature, 1987 regular session, and are located at the Legislative Reference Bureau, Jackson.

29. Telephone interviews with Key Decision Maker no. 1 (Mississippi), Feb. 26. 1990; and with Key Decision Maker no. 4 (Mississippi), March 5, 1990.

30. Telephone interview with Key Decision Maker no. 1 (Mississippi), Feb. 26, 1990.

31. Telephone interview with Key Decision Maker no. 4 (Mississippi), March 5, 1990.

32. Telephone interviews with Key Decision Maker no. 1 (Mississippi), Feb. 26, 1990; and with Key Decision Maker no. 5 (Mississippi), March 5, 1990.

33. Journal of the House of Representatives of the General Assembly of the State of North Carolina, First Session, 1987, pp. 1059-60; Journal of the Senate of the General Assembly of the State of North Carolina, First Session, 1987, p. 182, both in Library, State Legislative Building, Raleigh. A legislative history of Senate Bill 115, including House and senate action, committee reports, and roll-call votes, was made available at the library at the State Legislative Building.

34. Senate Bill no. 115, March 5, 1987, General Assembly of North Carolina, 1987 session, Legislative Library.

35. Written testimony by Norman E. Jarrard, Professor of English, North Carolina Agricultural and Technical State University, dated April

1987, included in legislative history of S115, House Judiciary-I Committee hearings, June 2, 1987, Legislative Library.

36. Don Pride, "N.C. OKs English Language Bill," Charlotte Observer, June 25, 1987.

37. Ibid.

38. Ibid.

39. Bill Graves, "English as State Language Disturbs Some Educators," Raleigh News and Observer, June 27, 1987.

40. Ibid.

41. Digest, House and Senate Bills and Resolutions, 1st session of the 107th South Carolina General Assembly, Legislative Information Systems; Journal of the Senate of the First Session of the 107th General Assembly of the State of South Carolina, regular session, 1:457, 883, 1072-73, 1226; Journal of the House of Representatives of the First Session of the 107th General Assembly of the State of South Carolina, regular session, 1:243, 452-53, 479. No committee documents or votes were available in South Carolina, nor were there any recorded floor votes in either legislative chamber.

42. "Senate Says English Official Language," (Columbia, S.C.) State, March 26, 1987, 9C.

43. Skip Johnson, "English-Only Movement Rolls On," (Charleston, S.C.) News and Courier, July 7, 1987, 3B.

44. State of North Dakota, Journal of the House of the Fiftieth Session of the Legislative Assembly, regular session, 1987, pp. 450-51, 700, 1719, 1740-41, 1858-59; State of North Dakota, Journal of the Senate of the Fiftieth Session of the Legislative Assembly, regular session, 1987, pp. 97, 219, 238, 290, 1512, 1715.

45. See legislative history, Senate Bill 2096, North Dakota State Library, Bismarck. The committee hearings included prepared written statements and general summaries of the oral presentations. All direct quotes in this section are from the written statements on file.

46. "Bill Reinforces English Language," Bismarck Tribune, Jan. 21, 1987, 1B.

47. 1987 House Standing Committee Minutes, March 9, 1987, Education Committee, House of Representatives, Senate Bill 2096, North Dakota State Library. All quotations in this section come from these minutes.

48. "Tribes: Veto Language Bill," Bismarck Tribune, March 11, 1987, 4B.

49. Gwen Ifill, "The 1992 Campaign: Reporter's Notebook; Bush and Clinton Spar, but Out of Arm's Reach," New York Times, April 25, 1992, sec. 1, p. 10.

CHAPTER 8. STATE LEGISLATIVE PROCESSES

1. The group of sponsors studied here is limited to the key sponsors, whose names usually appear on the bill being introduced. Excluded from this examination are those who signed on as co-sponsors of official English legislation in Georgia (129), Arkansas (73), and Alabama (63). In the logistical regression analysis that follows, the entire group from Georgia, Arkansas, and Alabama is included.

2. Seven Colorado sponsors lived in Jefferson or Arapahoe Counties, which encompass Denver, but none resided in the city of Denver. Of fourteen Arizona sponsors who resided in Maricopa County, only two lived within the city of Phoenix. Of California Republicans, six were residents of independent cities (Whittier, Long Beach, Norwalk, Covina, Arcadia) within Los Angeles County, and six resided in communities of Orange County (Cypress, Newport Beach, Fountain Valley, Fullerton, Orange, Anaheim).

3. Following the vote in the House, two representatives announced for the record that, had they been present on the floor, they would have voted against the bill. But the official vote was 100-0.

4. "State Bird, State Flower—Now State Language?" Atlanta Constitution, Feb. 14, 1986, A12.

5. "Bill Pushes an Official State Prejudice," Atlanta Constitution, Feb. 18, 1986, 22A.

6. Ibid.

7. It was easy to include gender as a variable in this analysis, based on information in legislative records. Among Anglos, the male-female difference in exit polls from California (66 to 64 percent) and Texas (71 to 67 percent) show that men were barely more supportive of official English than women. See Schmid, "English Only Movement" 205. Taking as a group the representatives for the fourteen states only, women comprised 12 of the 122 primary sponsors—5 in Arizona, 4 in Colorado, and 1 each in California, North Dakota, and South Carolina. If the large number of co-sponsors in Alabama, Arkansas, and Georgia is added, of the total 347 legislators who formally endorsed official English legislation, 34 were women. In the nine states for which roll-call votes were taken, men voted 87 percent in favor compared with 77 percent of women. If those members who abstained are included in this calculation, then 37 percent of the women either voted nay or did not vote, compared with 21 percent of the men. In all fourteen lower houses, women represented 11.8 percent of the total memberships; in the nine houses for which recorded votes are available, women constituted 9.7 percent of the memberships. In the aggregate, women were underrepresented among

legislative sponsors of official English bills and were four times more likely to vote nay or to abstain where roll calls were taken.

8. Tests for Tolerance (1 - R2) were done for each variable in every equation based on the eleven variables. The values indicate a serious problem of multicollinearity from POPULATION, URBAN, and INCOME, and they were eliminated in the logistical models that are reported in Appendix C, tables C.5, C.6, and C.7. For twelve models in those three tables, all values exceeded .50 with the following exceptions (there are compelling theoretical reasons for not eliminating certain variables that most directly test the alternative hypotheses): In table C.5 there was one value below .50 for the three-state model (.32 for BLACK) and three for California (.16 for % BLACK, .33 for SPANISH, and .37 for REAGAN), but none for Alabama. In table C.6, there were three values below .50 for Indiana (.02 for % BLACK, .23 for SPANISH, and .28 for REAGAN), two for North Dakota (.42 for % BLACK and .44 for SPANISH), three for Mississippi (.20 for REAGAN, .21 for BLACK, and .41 for COLLEGE), three for North Carolina (.34 for REAGAN, .44 for COLLEGE, and .45 for % BLACK), and none for Alabama. In table C.7 none of the models had any values below the .50 level. Given the problem indicated by the value of .02 for % BLACK in the Indiana vote model (table C.6), the model was respecified without that variable, with the result that DEMOCRAT (-2.2952 was the B value, at .0002 significance), as before, was the most important predictor (Democrats tended to vote no or to abstain), but MALE (1.6799 was the B value, at .0396 significance) also reached significance, indicating that men were more likely to vote for the bill than women. Also, REAGAN (.1423 was the B value, at .0047 significance) signified that legislators tended to vote for the bill if their home counties gave more votes to President Reagan in 1984.

CONCLUSION

1. Citrin, Reingold, Walters, and Green, "'Official English' Movement" 535.

2. Rogin, Intellectuals and McCarthy 248-60; Gibson, "Political Intolerance and Political Repression" 519.

3. Selma K. Sonntag, "Elite Competition and Official Language Movements," in James W. Tollefson, ed., Power and Inequality in Language Education (New York: Cambridge Univ. Press, 1994), 91-111.

4. Citrin, Haas, Muste, and Reingold, "Is American Nationalism Changing?" 15-16, 9.

314 Notes to Pages 250–256

5. I am indebted to Professor Joseph Stewart Jr. of the University of Texas-Dallas for this important distinction between the trustee and delegate role orientations at the agenda-setting stage versus the enactment stage of the policymaking process.

6. U.S. Department of Commerce, Bureau of the Census, Abstract of the Fourteenth Census of the United States, 1920 (Washington, D.C.: GPO, 1923), 103.

7. "National Official English Bill Introduced," U.S. English Update 10, no. 1 (Spring 1993): 1.

8. Felicity Barringer, "Immigration in '80's Made English a Foreign Language for Millions," New York Times, April 28, 1993, A1, A10.

9. Deborah Sontag, "A Fervent 'No' to Assimilation in New America," New York Times, June 29, 1993, A6.

10. Seth Mydans, "A New Tide of Immigration Brings Hostility to the Surface, Poll Finds," New York Times, June 27, 1993, 1, 14.

11. See T. Morganthau, "America: Still a Melting Pot?" Newsweek, Aug. 9, 1993, 16-23.

12. David W. Moore, "Americans Feel Threatened by New Immigrants," Gallup Poll Monthly, no. 334 (July 1993): 3-5, 13.

13. Chiles quoted in "Florida Sues U.S. over Aid to Aliens," New York Times, April 12, 1994, A10; Sam Howe Verhovek, "Texas Plans to Sue U.S. over Illegal Alien Costs," New York Times, May 27, 1994, A7.

14. "Wilson: Border Blockade Works," USA Today, April 22, 1994, 3A.

15. Seth Mydans, "Californians Trying to Bar Service to Aliens," New York Times, May 22, 1994, 10.

16. "'Ingles, No!' Puerto Ricans Shout," New York Times, Jan. 25, 1993, A9; "New Citizens Take the Oath in Spanish," New York Times, July 3, 1993, 7 (photo). Apparently Marquez's action provoked representatives Bill Emerson (R-Mo.), Toby Roth (R-Wis.), and seventy-eight others to co-sponsor House Resolution 2859: "All public ceremonies in which the oath of allegiance is administered pursuant to this section shall be conducted solely in the English language." See "Action Taken to Stop Non-English Language Citizenship Ceremonies," U.S. English Update 10, no. 3 (Fall 1993): 1, 8.

INDEX

318   *Index*